Bernard Manning

Also by Jonathan Margolis

Cleese Encounters
The Big Yin
Lenny Henry

Bernard Manning

A BIOGRAPHY

Jonathan Margolis

ORION

First published in Great Britain in 1996 by
Orion
An imprint of Orion Books Ltd
Orion House, 5 Upper St Martin's Lane, London WC2H 9EA

A CIP catalogue record for this book is available from the British Library

ISBN 0 75280 505 3

Set by Selwood Systems, Midsomer Norton
Printed in Great Britain by Butler & Tanner Ltd
Frome and London

For Matthew and Gabrielle

Preface
A Man of His Time

It doesn't bother me one iota that they say I'm a fascist. It's money
in the bank.

Bernard Manning, August 1996, aged sixty-six

T he comedian, spruce and cheeky in his dinner jacket and
bow tie, eyes the audience and decides that they are ready
for something a bit daring, a bit *risqué*, even though this is a
prime-time, mid-evening ITV show, and it's only 1971. 'This mate
of mine,' he begins, in a heavy, e-ba'-gum northern accent, 'He's a
Jew boy. He went to the dentist. "I want them all out, the lot," he
says. So the dentist says, "That'll be expensive, that'll cost you
twelve guineas." "Twelve guineas!" he says. "Here's a dollar.
Slacken 'em." '

He is followed by another comic, also smart in evening dress and
with a naughty gleam in his eye. The delivery is deadpan, northern
again: 'I hear the corporation toilets in Birmingham are losing a
fortune,' he drones. 'All these Jamaicans are doing the limbo under
the door ... I knew a fella once who spent thirty years in darkest
Africa looking for the lost Masazuki tribe. He eventually found
them over a chip shop in Bradford.'

In response to neither comedian is there any recoil, any gasp of
horror, not at the use of the racially abusive term 'Jew boy', nor at
the crude, petty, little-England sentiment of the jokes about blacks.
The gags slide by with polite laughter, and the performers, a black
Yorkshireman, Charlie Williams, who told the Jew boy joke, and a
white comedian, Mike Coyne, who did the immigrant gags, continue with their acts. Both are comedically overshadowed a few
moments later, however, by an obese forty-one-year-old Mancunian,
who has never been on TV before, and is virtually unknown outside
of the Manchester club circuit.

The Manchester comic is in a different league from Williams and

Coyne from the first moment. Bernard Manning's material on this evening of the first of Granada TV's *The Comedians* series was harmless almost to the extent of being bland. His delivery was polished and technically faultless, the stream of gags seeming carelessly brilliant but, to the experienced eye, clearly the result of many years of practice.

As he puffed insouciantly on a cigar, Manning's jokes were barely even *risqué*; he left the racism, the sexual innuendo and the camp gags to others. One of Manning's jokes featured a man selling seagulls at Blackpool, taking money and saying to the punters as he indicates skywards, 'Take that one there.' A couple of his stories were affectionate Jewish jokes that would not be out of place at a synagogue social evening. There were one or two Irish jokes, but so innocent that they might easily be told in Dublin, as Kerryman gags.

Other stories Bernard Manning told on his TV debut were superior student-rag magazine material: 'A fella went to the doctors. He said, "I've examined you and I can't find anything wrong with you. You must have Alice." He said, "What's that?" The doctor said, "I don't know, but Christopher Robin went down with it." ... Two attendants on a boating lake. One shouts, "Come in, number 91, your time is up." The other said, "We've only got 90 boats." "Oh," he said, "Are you having trouble, number 16?" ' Manning, the newcomer to national exposure, was probably one of the two cleanest and least offensive performers on the show.

Nearly twenty-five years later, now a diabetic, a pensioner and a widower, the same Bernard Manning appears at his own Embassy Club, in north Manchester. A millionaire many times over, with a Rolls-Royce parked outside the club, he does not even need to be working, but does so all the same. It is partly habit, partly the fact that, since his nonagenarian mother, with whom he lived after his wife's death, has also died, Manning has little else to do.

But there is another reason for his continuing to perform as a stand-up comedian. It is that events – the advent of race-relations laws, the coming of 'political correctness', the growth of alternative, victim-free comedy – have coincided to make him the demon of every decent, liberally-inclined person in the country. His outrageous, socially blasphemous jokes about racial minorities, combined with a great deal of swearing – a 'fuck' count of around four per minute (plus several 'cunts') – have made Bernard Manning, as he enters old age, an all-purpose hate figure for the intelligentsia. Earnest articles in academic magazines try, with metaphorical clothes-pegs over their noses, to analyse his dinosaur humour from a sociological perspective. Intellectual journalists from broadsheet newspapers are attracted to him like moths to a light bulb; they come, one after the other, from London to relate to their astonished readers the shameful jokes Manning gets away with in Manchester, and have a crack at describing his florid taste in home furnishings on the way out. For middle-class readers in need of a fix of outrage, a bit of Bernard can be even better than Bosnia. Manning even rated a mention in *An Phoblacht*, Sinn Fein's newspaper, in its 1995 Christmas quiz: 'English "comedian" Bernard Manning said in April, "Isn't this better than swinging through the fucking trees? Having a night out with nice people?" Was the revolting rotund racist talking to: (a) Lenny Henry, (b) A hotel doorman, (c) A police officer?'

Being loathed by sociologists, liberal journalists and IRA sympathisers all at the same time sounds a little unpleasant, but not only does this mischievous, stubborn old goat enjoy every minute of his notoriety; his humour is so *outré*, it has perversely become sought after by middle-class professionals tired, or so it seems, of the low-fat, denatured fare of modern stand-up comedy. In spite of themselves, lawyers, doctors and company executives come to the Embassy Club, a barely disguised shack; and in spite of themselves they laugh. Forbidden fruit, for such is much of Manning's comedy, always becomes sought after, even if it is, in a moral sense, rotten.

The Embassy Club is as fantastic an anachronism as its clown-faced proprietor. It is a predominantly red room, shabby, but clean and tidy, with a red carpet, chandeliers, square tables, leatherette-topped bar stools, and on every wall framed pictures of Bernard smiling with almost every slightly dated celebrity it is possible to imagine. There is a stage with an organ and drum kit behind an amateurishly painted sign proclaiming the Dave Green Trio. Behind the band (in its thirty-seventh year of residence, on every night of which so far Bernard has made out in his act that he is sacking Mr Green, the organ player) is a browny-gold ruched curtain permanently in place; ahead of them is a seventies disco ball ('Gary Glitter was in here last week, he left one of his bollocks'). There are coloured spotlights, and an extremely efficient bar staff in white mid-length jackets, looking like one would imagine bar stewards on a Soviet cruise liner did about thirty years ago. One of the men in white jackets will sometimes be Manning's loyal driver, Tony Sharkey, a hard-looking man with a soft interior, who was once charged with grievous bodily harm while over-enthusiastically protecting Manning from a drunken and violent customer. Convicted of a lesser offence, he was supported by both Manning and Sir Cyril Smith, the Liberal Democrat MP for Rochdale, who defended his character stoutly in letters to the court.

The Embassy Club holds 380 people; each night they range from tattooed working men to old timers from professionals, in from the Cheshire suburbs in their suits, to pretty young secretaries who have come straight from work in their boyfriends' Escorts. When the girls dance around their handbags in front of the ancient organ after Bernard has done his nightly turn, it could be forty years ago.

The number of racist jokes Bernard Manning tells in the average evening seems to depend entirely on the extent to which he feels like being mischievous. When he does his more spiteful jokes, and starts on Pakis, niggers and Irishmen, there is a frisson of discomfort among the audience. They laugh nervously, wishing almost tangibly, it sometimes seems, that he would not do it. Customers will often shake their heads as they laugh. To many, he cuts a rather sad figure, an accomplished, brilliant comic, telling race gags nobody really wants to hear any more; but the slight revulsion seems to spur him on. He appears to be unaware that, in the mid-1990s, a good number of our national heroes are black, that large sections of several generations have now grown up very nearly colour blind and, even if they are a little prejudiced, believing quite deeply that it is wrong to make fun of other people's race.

Manning does not just tell jokes at the expense of blacks and Asians. The entire package of yesterday's prejudices is opened in his act. A fine singer in his day, he will launch into a stirring rendition of 'La Donna e Mobile' in the style of Luciano Pavarotti, then refer pointlessly to the man he has just taken off with aplomb as 'a fat, greasy Italian bastard'. Anyone in glasses will be picked on as a 'Jap sniper', and become the butt of a series of Japanese jokes, most of post-war vintage. Bernard Manning is in almost every sense a man of his time, and any effort spent criticising him is wasted if this is not borne in mind continually.

But he is cleverer than being merely the last relic of a forgotten era. If he wants to surprise an audience pleasantly – just to be awkward – he will turn in an immaculately clean performance. One such, in 1996 at Jongleurs, an alternative comedy venue in Camden Town, north London, was impeccable both in taste and delivery. It won him a standing ovation from the trendy crowd, including a few black people, and was shown on Sky TV. Manning's appearance at the venue was especially ironic since it was here, a few years previously when the club opened, that a burning effigy of Bernard Manning was tossed into the Regent's Canal in celebration of the supposed demise of his type of comedy, and its replacement by the newer, younger, more ideologically sound version of stand-up. Such has been the rediscovery of the old comics as they fade from memory – Les Dawson, Ken Dodd, Benny Hill, Tommy Cooper, Frankie Howerd, Eric Morecambe – that all have been reappraised and re-evaluated over recent years. Manning was consequently greeted almost as a hero at Jongleurs.

This was particularly surprising because his appearance there came less than a year after a *World in Action* researcher secretly taped and broadcast Manning doing a series of racist jokes for a police audience; the gags were so offensive and over-the-top that there was a national scandal, with even the Prime Minister waiting in line to savage Manning.

Why, then, do educated people laugh as heartily as Manning's bedrock white working-class audience at his dated and sometimes obnoxious comedy? Why do people as refined as Stephen Fry and John Fisher, the head of entertainment at Thames TV and a writer on comedy, respect Manning? Fisher believes Bernard Manning is the closest Britain has produced to Groucho Marx, for his adeptness with an insult and his ability to destroy pomposity. Why, for that matter, have I rocked with laughter at Manning's shows? On the most recent occasion, he went on stage after we had been discussing our shared Jewish roots – Manning claims to have Jewish ancestors. With a gleam in his eye, he was quickly telling a Jewish joke; then he changed tack. 'Anyway,' he rasped. 'We'll have no more Jewish stories tonight. I've just discovered that I lost my grandfather in Auschwitz . . . He fell out of the machine gun tower.'

Why have I written this biography? The reason is that I believe Bernard Manning is a neglected genius. Late in his career, he has chosen to marginalise himself, to the extent that – beyond a vague and entirely incorrect idea that he does mother-in-law jokes – few people know, or care to know, just what he can do, and how technically superb he is as a comedian. His popularity is underestimated; despite being clearly unsuitable for television ('When I'm on screen,' he says, 'I feel like a horse that is held back at the starting gate . . . It's a terrible feeling.') he is probably the wealthiest comedian in Britain, and certainly one of the richest and most famous men *not* listed in *Who's Who* – Max Bygraves, Ken Dodd, Ernie Wise, even Ben Elton, all are, or have been, but not Manning. He has refused to bend either to political correctness or to the luvvie traditions of show business – he was making himself unpopular long before the racist issue came alive, by being brutal in his assessment of his fellow comedians; he believes most of them to be lazy and untalented.

He is more than a mere jeer-leader. His material *is* sometimes shocking, and yet I have found it difficult throughout the research for this book to diverge from the belief that respectfulness has no part in comedy. Humour *must* be offensive and dangerous, must make light of that which we are accustomed to taking seriously. Comedians must also be merciless with their audience. One of Manning's cleverest routines involves him toying with the prejudices of his audience, then throwing them back quite humiliatingly. He will get them warmed up and happy, then announce, 'We've got a couple of lads in here tonight. They fought at Goose Green.' A raucous applause, cheering and whistling grows until, at precisely the correct moment, Manning adds, very downbeat and matter-of-fact, 'They're Argentinians,' and carries on with his act, having reminded people that more than one side fights a war. The joke could very easily be taken as anti-war, and anti-jingoism. It is never quite obvious where Bernard Manning is 'coming from'.

I am also intrigued, and have become increasingly so, by Bernard Manning as a man. He is actually quite lovable, yet reckless and abusive the second he sees a microphone. He has a compulsive daringness; on stage, he will happily suggest in front of hundreds of people that he waters the beer he sells in his club, that he has salted money away where the taxman will never find it, even that when the Embassy Club burned down in 1989 it was an insurance job and he pretended items were lost in the fire which were not. Tackle him on any of these points, and he is aghast at your naivety. 'It's a joke,' he says, eyes popping. 'I hope you don't take those racialist gags seriously. It's all a joke.' He repeats the last four words audibly underlining each. Manning thrives on being shocking, and it seems, in a reverse of the conventional ageing process, that he needs to be so more as he gets older, rather than less. After almost every performance today, he puts in a plug for his own videos, which are always on sale. He then says, tellingly: 'There's videos in there, they'll be collectors' items soon. People will say they don't believe what I get away with. They'll say, what the fucking hell was that?'

Is Manning as racist as his material suggests, then, or is it 'all a joke'? There is, of course, a strong argument that what he feels privately is of no consequence compared to what he says publicly, but, nevertheless, I think his personal feelings are of importance. He denies vehemently and consistently that he dislikes anyone on the basis of their race. He insists that he takes everyone as they come, that his act specialises in being vile about every group, but that it is not meant to be taken literally. I would suspect that, in reality, Bernard Manning *is* racially prejudiced, but no more so than the vast majority of people of his generation. He simply has no compunction or embarrassment about venting his prejudice, a trait he shares with the likes of Philip Larkin, Richard Wagner, Roald Dahl, Rudyard Kipling, Hilaire Belloc, and T.S. Eliot, among other artists who mysteriously do not attract the same opprobrium as Bernard Manning. (Neither, for that matter, do middle-class racists. When *Private Eye* ran a cover on the Japanese Emperor Hirohito visiting Britain under the headlines 'There's a Nasty Nip in the Air: Piss Off Bandy Legs' it was regarded as rather jolly.)

A small point, of course, is that Bernard Manning's racism (not to forget the sexism and homophobia) are never targeted at the victims in person, other than when he is on stage. In a year's research, I have yet to come across a reported example of him being personally abusive to anyone on racial grounds; it may be that this proves Manning to be a coward and hypocrite as well as a racist. But he is a polite, thoughtful and generous man, and extends those characteristics to everyone he meets. When *he* is abused, as he has been in public by blacks and gays, as well as disgusted white customers who have walked out of his shows, he leaves the situation rapidly rather than get involved in trouble.

Does Manning have any conception of the offence he causes in his act? He adopts a disingenuous stance when asked this. He insists that what he tells are jokes, and are not designed to be taken literally. His naivety is genuine up to a point; you do not become as rich as Bernard Manning by being *thoroughly* naive. The most shocking thing he has said on stage in the time I have been observing him concerned the black London teenager, Stephen Lawrence, who was killed by racists in 1995 while he was waiting at a bus stop. After the failure of a police prosecution, Stephen's parents pursued a private case against the alleged killers. On the day that case failed in court, Manning alighted on it in the evening at the Embassy Club. The case made him 'fucking cry' he said mockingly. It seemed clear, incredibly, that he was actually celebrating the failure of the attempt at prosecuting racist killers.

What was he playing at, I asked Manning the next morning at his home? If he was covering up for an excessively outrageous remark, he was certainly quick on his feet. 'It's these QCs,' he said without a second's thought or hesitation. 'They shouldn't take cases to court when they have got no chance of winning them. They were told there was no chance of winning before they went to court, and the lawyers caused that coloured family a lot of expense and a lot of grief. They should have been advised by a QC not to go into court in the first place. Court cases cost fortunes, and normal people shouldn't be lured into them.' He explained that his anger at the case related to when he was involved in an industrial tribunal in Derby. (Two black waitresses claimed in 1995 that they had felt forced to leave their job at a hotel after Bernard Manning performed there and allegedly abused them with jibes and racial comments. They lost their case, and Manning believes they were encouraged by lawyers to take it up to make some money.)

I have a personal, wholly subjective, benchmark for judging people's moral quality. It is to wonder what a particular character would be doing today had the Nazis successfully invaded Britain in 1940, and were still in power. While certain comedians, I believe, would be happily doing Gestapo socials and Führer's Command Performances, I am convinced, having known him for a year, that Bernard Manning would have been shot as a subversive on day one of the invasion. (I put this hypothetical question of Bernard's likely survival chances under the Nazis to the *Observer* journalist John Sweeney, who once wrote a magnificently coruscating piece on Manning. Sweeney believed I was exaggerating. He thought it would have been at least day three before the Nazis executed Bernard Manning.)

Although writers like Sweeney have made sterling points against Manning, a great deal of the comedian's appeal – beyond the question of his simply being an extremely funny man – is caused by the deep weaknesses of those who oppose him. It is fascinating, for example, to notice how much of the criticism of Bernard is based on the rather childish business of spluttering about how fat and ugly he is. This seems, if one may say so, a deeply prejudiced line to take, especially for people whose pride is their lack of prejudice. There is, however, a fashionable middle-class belief currently that fat people are of low intelligence, and even intelligent, educated people find it difficult not to be sucked along with that attitude. Being fat in Bernard Manning's day, of course, had some cachet – it meant you could afford food.

On the question of the effects of his racial material, another hole in liberal beliefs is uncovered. The people who say Bernard Manning incites racial hatred are, one suspects, the very same as those who would pour scorn on the notion that film violence incites real violence. If anything, the hypothetical link between Bernard and active racism is weaker than between movie violence and the real thing; while the films that liberals are loath to censor clearly glorify the brutality they portray, Bernard Manning does not for a moment condone beating black people up – he just tells jokes at their expense.

Bernard Manning's fault, I would contend, is to be unremittingly, irredeemably working class, but sadly not the kind of working class that the middle class imagines the working class to be. Manning's white, working-class definition of good taste, for example, dictates that he will (almost) always draw the line at jokes about handicapped people, and tries to avoid swearing in front of the ladies. He also, a little bizarrely perhaps, avoids certain terms of racial abuse. He never refers, for example, to 'Yids', and says he finds the term 'wogs' unacceptable.

Three years ago, in an article on TV comedy programmes, the magazine *New Statesman & Society* carried the following paragraph, which exemplifies the kind of dreamland the left can still inhabit when trying to envision working-class comedy: ' "TV is very lazy in terms of images," argues the homosexual Marxist stand-up Bob Boyton. "Its idea of a working-class comic is Jim Davidson or Bernard Manning. Producers reflect the move to the right since 1979. I reflect a class anger which they feel very uneasy with – my comedy comes out of my experience of real life." '

The idea of a Marxist homosexual being more in tune with working-class life and attitudes than Manning, or even the less delightful Davidson, is laughable. Despite his millions in the bank, Bernard Manning is entirely authentic, completely unreconstructed. He would never join a golf club, eat foreign food (curries excepted) – or convince Bob Boyton that it is he, not Boyton, that is the authentic (if dated) voice of the working class.

It is hard to know what really lies in a comedian's heart when he cracks racial jokes, let alone to assess what damage or otherwise dubious humour has on its audience. The truth is probably that the majority of Bernard Manning's audience find in his jokes no more than a cathartic belly laugh, while a few might gain sustenance in seeing their own nastier beliefs validated. Perhaps the wisest judgement on racist jokes comes from the American Jewish comedian, Jackie Mason, a former rabbi who is himself frequently accused of odious racism.

'If people have hate in their hearts,' Mason has said, 'then emphasising difference can be dangerous. But if people have love in their hearts, it can be a lot of fun. Academically, it's called the study of comparative cultures.'

Bernard Manning would not see himself as a very keen student of comparative cultures; yet I believe he could – just about – be on the side of the good guys. As the writer on film, Tom Hutchinson, noted in an article on Manning in the *Guardian* in September 1996: 'Like him or not, he is one with Frankie Howerd, Les Dawson, Eric Morecambe, Tommy Cooper, Marti Caine, Frank Randle, Sandy Powell'.

Hutchinson concluded: 'As the recently rerun Michael Parkinson interview with the late Les Dawson reminded us about great comedy, and BBC TV begins its autumn shows to reveal how dreary humour has become, I've decided that Manning is one of the few who can still gut-punch audiences into belly-laughs. It's technique I'm talking here, not the racist, sexist schtick that makes Manning infamous. For the best comedians are fascist in their totalitarian command: that's Manning; I have watched him work.'

Hutchinson is right: Bernard Manning deserves to be considered as one of the great comedians.

My thanks for making this book possible are due principally to Bernard Manning himself, to Young Bernard, and his wife Julie. But equally, I am indebted for their generous help to the following: Alma Cameron, Rene Stockford, Johnnie Hamp, Chris Graham, Barry Clark, Melville Davies, John Fisher, Gabrielle Morris, Matthew Norman, Bryony Coleman, Paul Horrocks of the *Manchester Evening News* (and that newspapers's excellent library staff), Andy Chapman, Len Astill, Len Smith, Tony Sharkey, Molly Moxon, Sammy Dardick, Daniel Harris, Jack Massirak, Alex Williams, John Sweeney, Marje Alleman and Graham McOwan of The Lighter Side Bookshop, Upper Richmond Road, London SW14.

Jonathan Margolis, September 1996

Fat Manning

My parents were great. When I was a lad I asked dad: 'Where's the Hebrides?' He said: 'Ask your mum, son. She puts everything away in this house.'

Bernard Manning

The birth was in an upstairs room, at 4.30 a.m. on a warm, muggy Wednesday in August. Outside, the horse-drawn milk floats were getting to the end of their rounds, and the first buses were starting to grind smokily out of Manchester to the mills and factories to the north of the city. A few hundred yards down the road – the family then lived almost in the centre of the city – at the *Daily Express*'s brand new, black glass-fronted northern offices, the final bundles of that day's newspapers were being loaded on to vans, and Lord Beaverbrook's giant presses were being shut down for another night. Downstairs at number 183 Great Ancoats Street, later demolished and renamed Ancoats Lane, John Manning was busy. Having admired his second child, a substantial nine-pound son, he was now arranging the few sacks of potatoes and carrots that comprised his greengrocer's shop, as well as making cups of tea for his wife, Nellie, and the midwife, and seeing to breakfast for Jack, his seven-year-old. The Mannings always made sure there was plenty of food on the table, even when times were hard, and in the summer of 1930, at the depth of the worldwide Great Depression, they were never harder.

Bernard John Manning was born into a Britain where unemployment and poverty had gone beyond the status of a mere nightmare for the urban working class. Just twelve years from the end of the Great War, millions of the surviving heroes of the trenches and their children were still awaiting some kind of material salvation from destitution. In the two years since 1928, unemployment had doubled to 25 per cent. Crimes with their roots in poverty – robberies and horrific domestic violence in particular – were rampant.

1

Not that any of this troubled historical background is evident from the Manchester *Evening News* on 13 August 1930, the day Bernard was born. The birth of a child who would become a comedian was celebrated, albeit unwittingly, with an unremitting feast of silly-season nonsense. Perhaps it was just a slow news day, but half the front page was taken up with cricket news. Another leading story concerned the town clerk of Salford, who had been playing golf when his shot hit a cyclist. When Mr Harry Tomson went to apologise, the man said admiringly, 'You'll never do that again, mister!' and withdrew the stray ball from the breast pocket of his jacket where it had landed. A third big story was about a new survey by office efficiency experts. It highlighted the fact that in 1930 sexual equality was still some way off being discovered. The report, in the great liberal newspaper of northern England, sister paper to the Manchester *Guardian* no less, began: 'Boys are too boisterous and girls, though less mentally capable, are better for offices.' Bernard Manning was born – something that should never be forgotten when trying to understand his subsequent career – into very different times, and a very different culture, from our own.

John Manning, the proud father of the newly-born Bernard, was an exceptionally handsome man of thirty-four, always immaculately dressed, with piercing blue eyes, that people now say were the image of Paul Newman's, and wavy, black hair. The family maintained that there was Jewish ancestry a few generations back, but as far as the renowned Jewish humour was concerned, even if Bernard would one day become a master of the perfectly told Jewish joke, John Manning was no George Burns. Perhaps it was the struggle of trying to run a business and keep a family in the great slump, the greengrocer could be a rather dour, authoritarian man – friendly and cheery to customers: 'a typical sort of shopkeeper', remembers one, and also a pleasant partner to play bowls with, but something of a martinet at home above the shop. 'He had a good sense of humour,' Bernard recalls. 'We used to listen to the radio together, to Tommy Handley and Max Miller, and he used to laugh at them a lot. But mostly, he was a bit serious. I never heard him tell a joke in his life.' John Manning rarely had to hit his children, they recall, because one stern look from him would be sufficient to silence them.

If John Manning was responsible for one thing in Jack, in little Bernard who had just been born and in the further three children Nellie was to bear him it was for instilling a ferocious work ethic in each of them along with a dogged northern attitude to borrowing in any form. 'Our Dad always said, "Never buy owt on tick and if you can't afford to pay for something you want on the spot, then do without it,"' Bernard was later to recall. It was a rule that Bernard stuck to. Despite never borrowing a penny in his life he later elaborated on his own homespun financial philosophy, a comic inversion of his father's belief: 'If you owe somebody a thousand pounds, don't worry about it – let the fellow you owe it to do the worrying.'

It would not have been difficult to predict even then that, despite being born in one of the poorest and roughest areas of Manchester, most of the Manning children would grow up to be millionaires. 'My father was one of those people who said to you, if you want to do it, go out and do it,' says Rene, the younger daughter, sixty-one. 'Me dad and mum worked really hard, and this is what we all did. Dad made us work for our spending money.'

Mary Ellen Manning, who was thirty when Bernard was born, was a very different character from her husband. She too was a provider, one of those women for whom the rigours of recession and the war, which began when Bernard was nine, were almost a challenge. 'I'll get it by hook or by crook,' was a favourite saying. Thanks to her scheming, the family always had luxuries like sugar, bacon and eggs when rationing began, and she would buy the neighbours' clothing coupons to ensure that, like her husband, she wore the best clothes going. She also had a sweet singing voice, but what marked out Nellie, as she was generally known, was that she was a funny woman. 'She came out with the strangest of sayings, and could be very dry and witty,' recalls Alma, the elder daughter.

Bernard's early days were spent kicking around the shop, playing in the street and, a particularly vivid memory, watching his father shave. His often-repeated joke, 'I was such an ugly child, my parents had to tie pork chops to my pram so the other kids would play with me,' is quite untrue – he was pretty and popular, too. When he was still a toddler, all curls and blue eyes, Bernard developed a liking for music, especially popular singers and big band music. He would often listen to music on the wireless and gramophone by pressing his ear up to the sitting-room keyhole when he should have been tucked up in bed. It was also evident from an early age that Bernard had inherited his mother's fine singing voice.

He was, by all accounts, a charming and considerate little boy, always his mother's favourite among Jack, the eldest, Alma the third, Cathrine (known as Rene from childhood) the fourth, and Frank, the baby. 'It's true, I was my mum's favourite,' Bernard admits. 'And she used to tell the rest of the kids, "You're not as thoughtful as him." Actually tell them. They'd say to her, "Your Bernard, oh, well we all know about your Bernard. He can do no wrong, can he?" But I did used to look after her. I *was* thoughtful.'

Just as in many families like the Mannings at the time, the father tended to be so busy scratching out a living that, despite the authority he paraded at home, the mother, in her quieter way, was really the boss of the house. The bond between comedians and their strong-willed mothers has become a cliché in comedy, yet in Bernard's case there seems to be something in it. He worshipped her. 'She's the greatest,' he would say before she died in her nineties. 'Bloody lovely.' Although he used to have a gag about her when he returned to live with her after the death of his wife ('She's wonderful my mum. Ninety-four years of age. Every morning, I carry her downstairs to make me breakfast.') it was a very tender relationship.

> It's just that you see your mother struggling (he explained to the writer John Hind while she was still alive), going to the washroom with a huge pile of washing and all that. My father went out for a drink, and mum stayed in of an evening and kept the house clean, kept us well fed. She hardly ever drank – only at party times. And that's what's missing today – the old-fashioned mums who let the father think he was boss when he wasn't at all. No doubt about that.

When Bernard was still young, much of the Great Ancoats Street area was demolished and, with it, the Mannings' home and business. Nearly a decade later, John would have another greengrocery shop but, for the time being, the family moved to a rented house in Aubrey Street, Moston, and later to the now-demolished Faulkner

Street, in the nearby area of Blackley – a cut above Ancoats, if only marginally – and it was here that the Manning children grew up. John got a temporary job as a bread man, with a horse and cart, while Nellie worked at the Post Office. Bernard's father also did spells of quite menial jobs, such as golf caddying, window cleaning, gardening and working on the roads. On one or two nights in those bad days, he was stopped from getting on buses and trams because he was so muddy and dirty from work. Bernard believes his father was on the dole at times. At one stage during this unsettling period for the family, he bought an ancient Ford van for £25 and started selling vegetables from door to door, amongst other areas, in Alkrington, the posh end of Harpurhey, where Bernard now lives.

With Jack virtually grown up, and both parents struggling to make ends meet, it fell to Bernard to look after his sisters and baby brother. He would have to get Alma, Rene and Frank up, washed, dressed, breakfasted, hair-brushed, shoe-shined and off to school, where they would be minutely inspected for cleanliness. Frank was especially difficult to get ready for school. Bernard was frequently late himself for classes as a result of this morning rush, for which the nuns at Mount Carmel, the Catholic school round the corner, would cane him. He was also caned for smoking in the lavatories.

Not that he has anything but happy, sentimental memories of Mount Carmel, where he was a pupil from the age of three until he was fourteen. 'I'll never forget my first morning at school. I went home at lunchtime raving about it. Then mum said it was time to go back. "What do you mean?" I said, "I've just been."' Mount Carmel was a no frills, no fuss Roman Catholic elementary school with separate sides for boys and girls, with no playground and no gym, but was positioned next to Harpurhey swimming baths. Bernard entered Standard One, alongside Bill Risby, who later became Lord Mayor of Manchester. One of Bernard's overriding memories of school is the morning in 1940 that Bill came to school after his father had been reported 'missing in action'. 'I can remember one morning Rizzer, as we used to call him, came into school breaking his heart because his father had been killed in a submarine. We all put our arms round him and hugged him.' Wilf McGuiness, who was later to manage Manchester United Football Club, also attended Mount Carmel. Even at that young age, Wilf and Bernard used to vie for position of being teacher's pet. Bernard recalls: 'Oh, aye, Wilf McGuiness had a flat head from people patting it and saying, "There there! Who's a good boy!"'

I can still remember my first teacher's name, Miss Matthews (Bernard continues). She wasn't a nun, of course, but she was marvellous. The nuns had beautiful angel faces and long flowing things, not like they are today. You really respected them and looked up to them in them days. Sister Mary Josephine or Sister Mary Agnes used to hit you with a ruler if you were naughty, not a big stick or anything, but it used to hurt all the same. A twelve-inch ruler, bang. Of course I was hit many times.

But even corporal punishment had its sunny side in Bernard's memory. Once, he recounts, he was being caned for being late as usual, when he pulled his hand away, and the administrator of the punishment, Mr Mulligan, whacked himself on the leg. For his own gaucheness, the teacher gave Bernard another six strikes. Mr Mulligan, better known as the former England soccer international, James 'Mick' Mulligan, was the sports master, who spotted Wilf McGuiness's promise and put him in the school team early on. Most of the lads at Mount Carmel played football, usually against the end wall of Wilf's house.

Because of the age difference between them and Jack, the four younger Mannings became a little unit almost separate from their elder brother. The little ones developed an adoration, which has never waned, for Bernard's kind disposition and generosity. 'He always looked after us, our Bernard. If anyone hit us he'd be out there. He would do everything for us,' recalls Alma, now sixty-three. Jack, meanwhile, went off to volunteer for the Army in 1939 at the outbreak of the Second World War, and was consequently something of a stranger, only coming home on leave, and then feeling a little left out. While the four of them went through a childhood, their brother was at Dunkirk, Arnhem and on the Normandy beaches. Jack and Bernard only become close in their twenties and thirties.

At the same time as shouldering these early sibling responsibilities, Bernard also managed to be as irritating an elder brother as he reasonably could be. 'I'd spit on my brother Frank's food when mum wasn't looking. He'd cry and tell her he couldn't eat his food, so I'd scoff the lot,' Bernard admits. Alma tells a similar story. 'I'd be sitting there having my breakfast, eating me bacon and eggs,' she recounts, 'and there would be a plate of bread in the middle of the table, and Bernard would come up and dip a bit of bread in my egg, tormenting me. I was always miserable in the morning and he was always happy. He used to say, "Go on, give me a dip butty our Alma," just to aggravate me. He loved food. Our Bernard used to sup milk for a pastime. He'd drink it all, and me mother would say, "Where's all the milk?" and he'd say the cat knocked it over. He always made excuses.'

He was also blessed with the mysterious ability some charismatic children have – a knack that has never left him – of gathering a tribe of acolytes around him prepared for no obvious reason to do his bidding.

> Our Bernard always had a gang (Alma says). He was the boss and they all had to do jobs for him. If he had any bottles to take back, they'd take them, and help him out with whatever he wanted. There was this lad who worked on a farm. Ginger, he was called. Bernard used to say to him, 'Get some eggs for me in the morning for me breakfast,' and Ginger would bring them. And this was in the war, when you couldn't get eggs.

Bernard himself saw his role as gang boss in a subtly different light. For him organising a mob of gofers was a necessary accompaniment to carrying out his domestic duties rather than an ego trip. If anything, he was the oppressed, not the oppressor: 'I was really goodie-goodie when I was young. I went in the school choir, I was an altar boy. I always looked after my mother. I used to run errands for everybody. I loved it.' Normally he would be rewarded with a penny or two for these services, although some calculating neighbours, coolly assessing the fat but willing boy, would sometimes offer payment in the form of jam butties.

The act of bringing money home and putting it on the table for his mother was a particularly gratifying routine for a loyal, if bossy, son with a slightly precocious sense of filial duty.

He started his paper round when he was about twelve (says sister Rene). They used to call him the Singing Paperboy. At Christmas he'd sing. 'Please remember the paperboy, brings your paper wet or dry, hail, rain, wet or snow and on my way I have to go.' He used to get loads more tips than anyone else, and then he'd come home and say to me mother, 'Here you are, mum, here's me tips.' Me mother used to give him about two bob back out of the five he made, but two bob in them days was a lot of money.

'As a child,' Bernard was to explain tellingly in later life, 'I'd already learned an important lesson that helped to put me ahead of the crowd – that it pays to be pleasant to people. I was delivering three hundred Manchester *Evening News*es every night, and I learned that golden rule. I got my tips purely because of my friendly smile. I was the envy of my non-smiling friends, who couldn't understand the secret of my success.'

Curiously, as in other working-class areas, the onset of war meant an increase in prosperity, which was felt in down-at-heel districts like Blackley and neighbouring Harpurhey. The rise in affluence gave John Manning the chance, towards the end of the war, to open another greengrocer's right on the main Rochdale Road. For some years now, he had been working in the greengrocery department of the Blackley Co-op in addition to doing his morning bread round. His long-term aim had always been to open his own shop again. John Manning and Son, as this shop was called, was nothing special, but kept the family going well into the 1950s. They were also able to move in above the shop, Bernard taking the garret bedroom at the very top of the building.

On one side of John Manning and Son was a grocer, W. Estall and Son. On the other stood Sidlows, an off-licence. Other shops in the row included Johnsons Cleaners and Dyers, Holroyds Pastry Goods and Confectioners. Money was short, as were apostrophes on shop signs. 'Ours was just an ordinary little greengrocer's, you know. I remember it being a bit dark and dismal, a few bags of potatoes and carrots and onions on the floor and a bit of a shelf. Nothing elaborate. Dad was a bit of a plodder.' Bernard says.

'Now my parents', says Sammy Dardick, a Jewish neighbour and friend of Bernard at the time, 'had the hardware shop on the corner of Rochdale Road and Moston Lane, right in the centre of Harpurhey. The Mannings had the small grocer's shop right on the next block. Just a little old grocery shop, with a few old sacks of stuff on the floor. I think we were a little more progressive. My dad called it the Harpurhey Bazaar.'

The proximity of plain, dusty old 'Mannings' to the smarter 'Harpurhey Bazaar', the Jewish shop, with its more modern retailing techniques and that worldly, clever allusion to the name of *Harper's Bazaar* (the fashion magazine of the day) could be seen as ominous, at least if one were looking for some explanation of how Bernard Manning would fifty years later be regarded as an arch racist. All over Europe since the 1930s, small, recession-hit shopkeepers were finding solace in the anti-semitism of the far right; the Jewish shopkeeper, with his frequently more adventurous and successful trading methods, was a particular focus of fascist hatred, both on the Continent and in Britain. Could it possibly be that Bernard's notoriety as a racist has its roots in the mediocrity of his father's little shop compared to its neighbour, run by recent immigrants, Benjamin and Dora Dardick? Were there ethnic tensions in 1940s Harpurhey that could have led Bernard, later in life, to become a racist?

Perhaps there were. Sir Oswald Mosley's Blackshirts had not so long ago been active in Manchester, and there was a large, visible Jewish community in the city. Had the Manning family displayed anything of the Blackshirt mentality, which focused, in the absence of any black people in the area at this time, exclusively on the Jews, Bernard might have developed the kind of hatred for Jews that his critics fifty years later would maintain he bears towards other ethnic minorities. The fact that he was, by ancestry, partly Jewish would have counted for little – so had been several leading Nazis. However, the strong evidence is that the Manning family, far from being even remotely touched by anti-Semitic sentiment, was then, and remains today, resolutely and doggedly friendly to Jewish culture. (Bernard, of course, maintains vehemently that he has no argument with black people either.) Yet Bernard's friendship toward the Jews, which is manifest, developed in spite of his being subjected to a certain amount of taunting as a boy *by* the Jews – in the person of Sammy Dardick, who was two years his senior.

As Dardick, now a Manchester taxi driver, as well as a professional crossword compiler, explains:

> I went to a Protestant school called Holy Trinity, which was about two hundred yards from Mount Carmel. Myself and my sister were the only Jewish people in the school and, very often, the Protestants would raid the Catholics – and I used to be the leader, the main instigator. We were all crazy in those days. The main thing was throwing stones, and of course you couldn't miss Bernard, because he was always well overweight and was known as Fat Manning by everybody. It was idiotic, but there were no riots or anything like that. It was just normal, a routine we went through almost every dinnertime. I think Bernard used to throw a few things back at us. I don't know how I became head stone-thrower. Maybe they appointed me. We'd just go out, throw stones, shout things, have some lunch and forget all about it. No one was ever injured or anything. The police were never called – it was just a bit of daft harmless fun.

Bernard, or 'Fat Manning', certainly seems to have borne no grudge against Dardick, whose family would ask him sometimes to light their fires on the Sabbath, when Jews are forbidden to do so. 'We were all friendly with each other, the Dardicks and the Mannings, and it carried on like that for a few years,' says Sammy Dardick.

> The religious divide didn't seem to make the slightest difference. Nobody ever bothered with it. What used to happen at school was forgotten or, if it was remembered, it was laughed off as a great joke. Bernard was always very jolly and making jokes. He seemed to have a natural flair for that sort of thing. Being rough and ready, he wasn't a disciplined sort of person. I think Bernard was the only one of the Manning family who was like that. All the others were a bit quieter.

The friendship continued well in the boys' teenage years.

> He would come into our house a lot. If he just happened to be passing he would call in for a cup of tea or a sandwich. It could be

any time, afternoon or evening. I played the piano, and he used to come in and entertain my parents, singing, and with me accompanying him as well as I could. I taught him the 'Song of Sorrento' – he had never heard of it. Yes, I got to know all his family very well. In fact, I fancied Bernard's younger sister, Alma.

Bernard too was a sometime participant in the innocent, pre-war business of teenage romance.

I had a crush on a girl called Winnie Whittaker (he recalls). We didn't have mixed classes, so she used to leave a note for me, 'BM I Love You', and I'd to leave one for her the same, 'WW I Love You'. I was only about twelve. I decided I wanted to take her out, so I took mineral bottles and milk bottles back for the money, and I saved fourpence up to take Winnie to the pictures, although it only cost tuppence to get in. I arranged to meet her outside, but she never turned up. Heart-breaking, that was. I can remember it as though it was yesterday. I had fourpence, never been so wealthy in all my life, and nowhere to go. I was taking her to see *Springtime in the Rockies*, with Harry James and Betty Grable.

The next day she said, 'Sorry, I couldn't make it, something came up with the family.' She became a nun years later. It could have been my influence, I could have put her off fellas. But, no, I was lovely in them days, I had lovely blue eyes and a nice physique and everything. But then no one taught me the facts of life. You just picked things up at school. I couldn't believe my mum and dad would do such things. I didn't even dare smoke in front of my father until I came home on leave, and even then I got a black look.

Bernard also hints at dalliances snatched with girls, when he went camping with his best school friend, Terry Alan, a steel erector, who later in life died in a fall. But even when he is talking about the beginnings of sexual stirrings, it is clearly the memories of childhood pranks conducted with Terry that have left a more vivid impression.

A couple of days after I started in Miss Matthews' class, they sat me and Terry next to one another and that was it. We used to share a desk. We used to play together and he'd come on my paper round and deliver a few papers for me when we were older. We'd go to the pictures and to the chippie together, and we used to go camping on a Sunday to Ashworth Valley in Heywood, go off to the country-side to rub a couple of Girl Guides together. He was a great guy. I thought he was funnier than me. We tried to get into the picture house one time with two dinner tickets. It was very dark where this fella stood and I thought we'll get in with these but he looked at them – a bloody torch, he had. We flew out and we never stopped running until we got miles away.

We were with a bunch of mates who used to pay our tuppences or threepences for front-row seats to see *Our Gang* at the cinema on Saturday afternoons, and we built up our own version of *Our Gang*. We became known as the Raggy Arsed Gang. We climbed trees, lit bonfires, knocked on doors and ran away, a raggy arsed little mob is exactly what we were. We pinched apples from trees, annoyed a few people. We walked to Blackpool once. Slept in a bus shelter, living on crab apples. Fifty-two miles, I walked. I tell you, I got me face cracked when I got home.

Unlikely as it sees, the youthful Bernard Manning was also some-thing of a sportsman.

My dad passed his love of football on to me (he says). He took me to my first Manchester City match when I was four. In those days there was no public-address system. Team changes were announced by a man walking around the pitch with the details chalked on a blackboard. And they'd let you in for nothing at half time. I played at centre-half in the first team at school, even though I was a big lad. The coach's advice before a match was always the same; 'Go and see how fast their centre-forward can limp,' he'd say. The trouble is I used to pant a lot. But I wasn't a bad player. I was reliable, always turned up, never took any prisoners. I think cricket, hockey and swimming should be made compulsory in schools. It was in my day and I loved every minute of it. I think kids are lazier nowadays.

If watching and playing sport ever palled, another aspect of the sporting life had become integral to Bernard's life by the time he was twelve. Despite his father's stern disapproval of the evils of such practices as buying goods on credit, Bernard was hooked on gambling, a love that was to become increasingly dear to him. He was laying – and frequently winning – twopenny bets with street-corner bookies long before off-course turf accountants were legalised.

Although the Mannings were not rich, thanks to John and Nellie's hard work and ingenuity, they always managed to avoid the kind of rock-bottom poverty other families were suffering. Nevertheless, what the young Bernard saw around him affected him deeply. Poverty was, and continues to be, perhaps, a bond between him and his audiences, even if, in Bernard Manning's case, it has become tinged with nostalgia of a sort. Harpurhey was never quite a bare-feet and hunger kind of area, but it was poor enough to stimulate Bernard as it did so many other comedians of his era. 'Most comics come from a poor background,' Bernard explains. 'Ancoats was very poor. The sort of district where you have to laugh just to keep going. It's the same sort of place as Liverpool, that other breeding ground for comics. There, if a lion escaped from a safari park, the kids would maul it to death.'

'Money was tight,' Bernard has said as part of his act. 'Dad once asked mum if she'd seen the new ten-shilling notes. She said she'd never seen an old one ... We were very poor. The soles of me shoes were that thin that in 1936 I could put me foot on a penny and tell you if it were heads or tails ... I always knew we must have been Jewish way back; when me father got his hand on a pound note, he nearly strangled the Queen.' He has another poverty gag about his first pair of football boots; these, he says, were a present from a neighbour, but because they were the only pair in the house, he had to share them with his brother. 'We had one each, so he played on one wing, me on the other.' The odd, unwary listener to this has been known to sympathise with the family's plight.

Despite these allusions to extreme poverty, the family in fact went on holiday to Blackpool every year for a fortnight. Albeit that the family would travel there on the back of their old greengrocery lorry, two weeks in Blackpool was a very lengthy stay indeed for the 1930s. 'When our mum and dad went out at night, we all used to hang out of the window of the boarding house, which was right on the front,' says Rene.

> I always remember our Bernard going in the bathroom, and he picked up this glass and said, 'Oooh, somebody's had their teeth in that.' That stuck in me mind. We used to think those two weeks were marvellous. We used to have a bucket and spade and we played all day on the beach, and we'd say, 'Dad, can we have such and such?' and he used to say, 'You're in Blackpool, aren't you?' Like, isn't that enough for you? We used to go in the Fun House for sixpence and stay there all day.

'I was skint,' says Bernard of those Blackpool holidays. 'I used to watch *Punch and Judy* on the beach and when the bloke with the bag came round I had nothing to put in so I just used to nod and say, "Thank you very much." '

Millions of city childhoods were disrupted by the war, which broke out when Bernard was nine. Soon after sitting listening to Neville Chamberlain's speech on the radio, he remembers receiving his gas mask. 'The first time I tried it on, I suddenly sneezed, and the window you were supposed to see through split.'

Harpurhey's preparations for German air raids were different from those in more spacious suburbs. There were few back gardens for air-raid shelters, and those that were tended to be too small, so a programme of building public surface shelters in the narrow streets began. 'They were put up in the middle of the cobbled cart-roads on twelve-inch-thick concrete rafts,' recounts a local historian, Joe Kay. The basement of the Victoria Avenue Cinema – Bernard's picture house – was converted into a public air-raid shelter, which, when the raids started, provided a social life for many people, and a chance for people who lived on their own to share the same fears and the dangers.

In 1940, along with most of the children of areas like Blackley and Harpurhey, the Manning children were evacuated. Bernard and Alma were sent together to Bacup, in Derbyshire.

> When they put us on the train at Manchester (recounts Alma) they gave us this carrier bag with food in it – biscuits, chocolate and

sweets – and me and Bernard sat on the train and ate all ours, ate the lot.

They took us in this school room, and people were coming in and picking you out like dogs – 'Ooh, that looks a nice one, I'll have that one.' At the end of the queue were me and him, two little fat kids that looked like we ate a lot, sitting there. Nobody picked us, so we finished up going to this woman's house. It must have been the worst house in Bacup. I wouldn't even go in the house in the first place. Bacup in those days was like going back a hundred years, big stone cottages and those toilets out the back with a bucket in. I had never seen anything like it. It was a mill town. They all wore clogs. All the women wore black with a white apron, and the woman who took us in had very black hair in a bob. I kept saying, 'I don't like that woman, she's Chinese.' When we got in, it was an old cottage, a two-up, two-down, and they had put up a plasterboard wall to divide one bedroom. They had a daughter and a son, and I had to sleep in the same room as the daughter, while Bernard was in with the son. It was horrible, I hated it, and we only stayed there about five weeks before we ran away.

Me mother gave us all our clothes neatly packed up but she never bothered about us. I don't know what she did with these clothes, but I never saw them. I used to come down and say, 'Where's me clean knickers?' and she'd say, 'Oh, you're too cheeky.' She didn't like us and we didn't like her. She wouldn't give us food, either. She used to give us dry toast, and we'd say, 'Is there no butter?' and she'd say, 'There's a war on.' We thought, it had only been on for about a day. Our Bernard said, 'Do we ever get, like, bacon and egg for breakfast here?' and she said, 'No, you don't.' On a Sunday morning at home, we always had bacon and egg. Even on weekdays we'd have had porridge or toast and jam.

Typically, Bernard's account of the evacuation to Bacup was altogether sunnier.

I was nine, and me sister Alma wouldn't go in the house. She didn't like the woman who was there, Mrs Butterworth. She was a lovely woman too, a big, fat jolly woman, who had a son and a daughter, but we didn't like it after a while. We got homesick. It was terrible, because we was home-loving kids. Alma kept crying, and I said, 'Come on, then, let's walk home.' So we started walking and we were about three miles outside Bacup, walking down the road on a good, lovely, sunny day, and this fella pulled up. He was the local butcher, who delivered meat for Mrs Butterworth. He said, 'What are you two doing here?' I'll never forget him a big, fat jolly fella, and I said, 'We're going home.'

'Get in the back of there,' he said. He took us back to Mrs Butterworth's. Mrs Butterworth didn't shout at us. She wasn't that kind of woman. She said we were bound to get homesick. But we got worse, so Mrs Butterworth phoned me mam, or got in touch with her by letter or whatever, and said your kids are not happy here, they are just talking about home all the time. So me mother came and got us and fetched us home. We'd been there for about four months. We stuck it out as long as we could.

Back in Manchester, where some air raids had already occurred, the Blitz proper was shortly to begin. It did so at 6.30 on Sunday evening, 22 December 1940.

Even while the sirens were wailing (wrote Joe Kay in a book on the history of Harpurhey), from this dark cloudless sky a cascade of flares appeared, floating down from on high. From tiny, distant, dots they drew into large bright flames as they glided down, illuminating the night sky. Then the sky was alive with activity and dangerous to be under. People who were walking in the street ran for cover. Anti-aircraft guns began to fire and searchlight beams moved swiftly in every direction. From the dark beyond, outside the range of anti-aircraft guns, came the droning of the bombers, their numbers making the sound distinctly louder than usual. They showered incendiary bombs over a wide area to cause fires and so light up target areas.

After a brief Christmas truce, which was extended into January by unusually cold weather in Europe that made bombing missions difficult, the raids became a constant feature of life after dark. They were mostly early in the evening, but sometimes came after midnight. The Blitz on Manchester and Salford provided the nine-year-old Bernard with his worst memories.

> I was coming home from the pictures that night the Blitz started, from the Adelphi. Me and my mate Norman Meadowcroft were in the shelter with a load of strangers. But in them days there were no lunatics and child abusers. People used to look after you. 'Come in, son,' and all that carry on, 'Get sat down there, don't worry. It'll soon be over.' I used to tell jokes in the air-raid shelters and sing songs like George Formby and Gracie Fields, tell stories like Max Miller and get them all at it.

Bernard's cheerful spirit and precocious performing ability had already become quite famous locally. His first known public performance was at a church hall, singing at an ARP wardens' Christmas party for children, just after he and Alma came home from Bacup.

> Bernard and I went, but because you had to be seven, Rene and Frank couldn't go. We had the jelly and the sandwiches and Father Christmas gave us all a little present. Then the woman came on and played the piano and said, 'Anyone who will come up and entertain can have another present off the tree.' So Bernard was the first up, and he danced and sang the 'Sailor's Hornpipe' to get a present for Rene. He came back, gave me the present and said, 'Right, now I'll go back and get one for our Frank.' But the woman said, 'No, Bernard, you've been on once.' He said, 'But I can do something different.' I said, 'He can recite,' but she wouldn't let him on. He wanted another present for Frank, and that to me sums up Bernard. He didn't get back up because, of course, everyone wanted a present. Can you imagine, a Christmas present in Harpurhey in 1939 – suddenly everybody could do something.

'I was a plump ten-year-old in patched trousers and a ragged jersey,' 'he remembers, 'and I had an audience captive in the air-raid shelter. There was no escape from me. If anyone left during my performance it was at the risk of getting their heads blown off. I learned how to handle audiences paying more attention to the

17

drone of bombers overhead than to my jokes and songs. It was a great training for some of the pubs and clubs.'

All great fun but, as Bernard says, 'I never thought about show business. I expected I would be a greengrocer all my life.' And when a clairvoyant in Blackpool once told Nellie that Bernard's name would be up in lights one day, she told her not to be so daft. There were much greater concerns of everyday survival on people's minds. 'They were very dark days for everyone. There was hardly anything to eat because of rationing and children were sent off to God-knows-where. It were truly awful,' Bernard explains. 'I can remember cowering with my mum under the stairs when bombs were raining down. There was hardly a building left standing in Manchester. Everything was in darkness except for the fires from the buildings. When you opened the front door the sky was red with burning shrapnel. The sound of bombers sent shivers through you. When I look back now, I wonder how we all got through it.'

Bernard's memories of widespread havoc and destruction ('I saw planes come that low that you could see the German pilots in the cockpits. And red hot shrapnel flying down.') are reminiscent of the film director John Boorman's recollections of the bombing, as portrayed in his film *Hope and Glory*. Yet in fact, just as Boorman's childhood memory of the destruction in his native Ruislip was exaggerated, there were, according to local histories, only three serious cases of damage in the Harpurhey district throughout the entire Blitz. A direct hit during the pre-Christmas bombing totally destroyed Harpurhey Library, a fine red-brick building which had been of great service to the community during the years of depression. Also destroyed was a row of houses, and the Victory Cinema, off Moston Lane, which was totally razed by fire from incendiary bombs.

With the children back early from evacuation, the Manning family continued by all accounts to develop as a close and loving unit. This is not only the ever-optimistic Bernard's reading of the past. The conscientious second child had early in life fostered a special bond with his father as well as his mother, whose long-established pet he already was. All the surviving children – Bernard, Alma and Rene – speak of the same near-idyllic harmony in the family.

The closeness between Bernard and his father might in another family have irritated his siblings, but there is no evidence of this having happened. 'I got on with me dad marvellously because I was with him all the time. I worked with him, you see. I was with me dad in the greengrocer's all the time. We were like brothers,' Bernard says. Rene confirms this, without hesitation or any apparent rancour. 'Bernard and me dad used to get on very well together because they worked together for years. Our Bernard has always worked for me mum and dad from being a young boy.'

Educationally, Frank, the youngest and skinniest Manning, was the undisputed star of the family. From having been the child that gave his elder brother the most grief when he tried to get him up and ready for school every morning, Frank went on to college, although nobody can quite remember what he studied there: 'He passed scholarships and goodness knows what,' Bernard recounts a little mistily.

Mrs Manning's funny remarks and sly humour continued to have a great influence on Bernard.

I remember once a friend, Mrs Macmillan, a lovely woman, came here (he says), and she said to me mother who had just got some new glasses, she said, 'Ooh, those glasses you've got, they're very thick, aren't they?' and my mother said, 'Yes, I can see all the lines in your face.' Stuff like that, she was always coming out with, not knowing she was funny, but making real cutting remarks, chopping your legs from right underneath you.

At school, I made them laugh with the little Irish stories, the Pat and Mick stories and Jewish stories. Little Catholic boy says to this Jewish lad, 'Our priest knows more than your rabbi.' Jewish lad says, 'I know, he should do, 'cos you tell him everything.' That was one of the first gags I told at school. I got into the Polish and Russian Jews and the funny way they used to talk.

I had a very happy childhood, me. It was real happy family life, we had a good family, a good father and good sisters and brothers. You know when you hear people saying that they got knocked about and abused as kids and didn't get enough food. My father and mother just provided. It wasn't a lot but it was there. You see, things were different in them days. There were no child molesters or people out to murder you. You could walk in the park and see the swans and the peacocks, smell the flowers, listen to the brass bands. And you were quite safe.'

Summa Cum Laude

I left school at fourteen. Everyone did unless you had some cash or a brain.

Bernard Manning

'My first job at fourteen,' Bernard Manning says of his graduation from Mount Carmel Roman Catholic School, 'reflected my academic abilities – throwing boxes of cigarettes on to a conveyor belt at the Senior Service factory in Manchester. It earned me £1 a week.'

There was never any question that the lad who would shortly become the 'and Son' part of John Manning and Son would have to go out to work away from the greengrocery shop. Although Bernard's father found the premises of the new shop in wartime, it did not open until just after the war. Another income in the family was essential, meanwhile. However, once he was on the job market, as Bernard readily admits, there were not many options open to him. 'I wasn't very good at anything really, honestly. I could spell and I could reckon a sum up, but I wasn't brilliant. I was average at everything, except for singing, being cheerful and fat and jolly, making people laugh.'

Bernard's father had found the job for Bernard and told him that he would be starting at the factory on Derby Road, Cheetham Hill, the following Monday. It had not been too difficult for John Manning to find Bernard a post. The factory was staffed mostly by women, practically all the men being away to war, and a willing lad too young for the forces was almost guaranteed work. And although the work was repetitive, the regime tough and, in some parts of the factory, conditions poor, the wages paid by the Pattreiouex company, which then made Senior Service, were reputedly the best in the area. Senior Service production line workers were pulling in up to £5 a week.

'Discipline was certainly very tight,' recalls Len Smith, one of his

Senior Service factory colleagues. 'A couple of the departments were also very unhealthy, and the people working in them reflected this in their appearance. You must remember that in many ways what was normal then would not be tolerated now. The foreman walked the floor pouncing on anybody for the slightest mis-demeanour. Everyone wore brown overalls, the girls' enlivened with a strip of green at the neck.'

The valuable and tradeable nature of the product Pattreiouex (locally pronounced Pattrio's) were making, as well as what might charitably be called an efficient management, ensured the plant in Cheetham Hill was a highly regimented place. Work started at eight and ended at six. The factory doors were locked at two minutes past eight. After that, staff had to ring for admission and would receive a penalty for lateness. These progressed from a simple quarter of an hour's suspension to a day, three days or a full week off work unpaid. The firm had some years earlier been located at Prestwich, and many workers had transferred with it and came to Cheetham Hill by train. If the train was late, people, sometimes entire families, were late through no fault of their own, but were suspended all the same, which could lead to real hardship.

The procedure for leaving the factory was equally stringent. The workers' overalls were deliberately designed with a single pocket at the back, so no cigarettes could 'fall in', and everybody had to sign an agreement that they could be bodysearched. Random searches at clocking-off time were routine. 'It was reasonably thorough,' says Mr Smith. 'I know that they found cigarettes, particularly amongst girls, in rather intimate places.' On Fridays, however, every worker would leave with legitimate contraband – a 200-cigarette allowance, which workers' families eagerly awaited.

During working hours, there were two daily breaks of seven minutes' duration. Workers were permitted to stop only when a light flashed on the wall and, in those seven minutes, scores of people had to be served tea from the trolley. Some would always fail to be quick enough to down their tea before a foreman went down the line switching on the machines and the light flashed to resume work. Lunch – called dinner, of course – was a similarly rushed affair, with half an hour allotted to queue up and eat. 'By the time you got your bleedin' spoon to your mouth you was back again,' says Bernard today.

The factory foremen were both feared and revered. 'They walked the floor in white coats,' says Mr Smith. 'One was called Mr Muendi. He was of Jewish extraction, small, squat, sallow-faced. His fellow SS man, Mr Wilkinson, was very tall and extremely thin. On the rare occasions that they stood together, they looked ridiculous. I hesitate to be crude, but everybody regarded them as bastards. It was the worst place that I have ever worked at. We could chat to each other, and there was a constant supply of piped music, programmes such as *Music While You Work*, but I was amazed, and still am, when I think about how the hundreds of mostly young girls stood to their tasks doing the same simple actions all day long.'

Not all the workers were quite as disenchanted as the older and wiser Len Smith. Molly MacDonald (then Molly Moxon) worked at Pattreiouex from the age of fourteen until she was seventeen – old enough to leave to join up.

> Our foreman was Mr Saul, a lovely Jewish gentleman. I can still think of him with affection. A group of us were once talking about the origin of the firm's name, and I was dared to ask Mr Wilkinson about it. He was a beanpole of a man. He would walk round the room, not speak to anybody, just looking superior. Well, I was sixteen years old and couldn't refuse a dare. True to form, he arrived and, quaking in my shoes, I asked him. He was very nice about it and told me he didn't know the origin, but it was the only name known with all the vowels. Of course he was there for three or four minutes talking to me, and the girls asked me afterwards, 'What was he saying?' and I said, 'Oh, he asked me for a date but I wasn't falling for it.' Of course they knew it wasn't true. It was a great place to work at then.

Bernard Manning's memories of Pattreiouex are every bit as sunny and unsullied by cynicism as Molly Moxon's.

> They gave me a pair of overalls the first thing on the Monday morning and I got my clock cards. Then I went to work as a grinder's mate. I sharpened the knives that cut the tobacco. I met a fellow

called Joe Dunn who died a couple of years ago. He was me pal. We used to go to dinners together. It was fabulous there. You could always hear me singing above the machines. I was always smiling and laughing, telling jokes and playing the goat.

Before he was fifteen, Bernard's larger-than-life character was becoming a big talking point. He had an advantage over other fourteen-year-olds in that he was used to adult, male banter from his occasional experience helping out his father on a fruit stall at Manchester's Smithfield market.

It was full of comedians there (he recollects), the stall owners and porters. There were always jokes flying around about summat in those days, about Hitler, Mussolini and all that fuckin' carry on. We heard that banter all day, and I joined in. So at the factory, I stood out with personality. I mean I hadn't been at the Senior Service tobacco factory for twelve months when I was in the very first post-war edition of their magazine, *Smoke Rings*, as Personality of the Year. I wish I still had a copy of that. It said Personality of the Year, and had a photo of me that I didn't like, and it said it is a pleasure to work with Bernard Manning who is always singing. You can hear him singing above all the noise of the place and he keeps us all going with gags.

Len Smith, despite being three years old than Bernard, was attracted to the young grinder's mate by his cheerfulness. They met in the canteen at lunchtime, when Bernard had been working at the cigarette factory for more than two years. 'We used to sit together. I liked the boy, we got on well together and eventually started to go out drinking together at the weekends. I remember him as short and very stocky and full-faced. It is easy from present-day photographs to see the boy he was. He also had a very good sense of humour and was easily amused. He didn't smile or chuckle – he laughed and when Bernard laughed, the whole world knew that he was laughing.'

The two would meet, along with another lad, Les Ball, at a pub on the Rockdale Road known as the Bottom Derby. Its name was actually the Derby Arms, but as there was another pub higher up the same road with the identical name, it was vital when arranging meetings to differentiate between the Top and the Bottom. Thus did 'Bottom' became an integral part of the name of the three lads' favourite pub – a venue which was to become the first half-way serious showcase for Bernard's growing talent. The jokes at this stage would be strictly for around the table, among mates. 'When I'm together with people, I'm always first in with a couple of gags,' Bernard says. 'I get on with everybody, me. It's just natural. You can't learn comedy – you're either funny or you're not.'

They didn't serve good ale at the Bottom Derby (Len Smith continues) but it did have a fairly big singing room with a small stage at one end, just big enough for a small band, and it also had a reasonably good microphone. Although the disparity in years was not great between Bernard and I, the gap in maturity and experience was. At this point, I had seen service in home waters and the Pacific, Les, a couple of years older than I, had served in the Army. So, to a great extent, the relationship between us and Bernard was akin to a younger brother. He was streetwise to a degree, but less so than many boys of the same age.

I always regarded Bernard as an extrovert, but at this time, it was struggling to assert itself. He was fairly naive, so we considered it our job to protect him from hassle or getting into trouble, which with the best will in the world was only too easy in a pub in those days. He did not want to call attention to himself, he was shy of doing so.

Mr Smith provides a description that is both acutely observed and not a little touching, of the embryonic performer Bernard Manning chafing at the bit to get up on to a real stage, whilst fighting to overcome the slight reticence that appeared to set in when the pressure was on. Some of this restraint may be explained by the fact that Bernard should not, at seventeen, have been in the pub, and he knew his father would have been furious had he found out about his son's new social life. Bernard maintains even now that he was 'goaded' into going on stage at the Bottom Derby by his mates, but Len Smith's version of events may be a little more credible.

The usual procedure (he relates) was for Bernard to resist our requests for him to get up and sing. Other people in the room would ask him and they all received the same answer – '*no*'. Eventually, after two or three pints, he would be looking more and more at the microphone, and it was inevitable that sooner or later he would get up.

On the stage, it was immediately a different Bernard. He was in his element. He gave a hundred per cent, and exuded vitality. I do wish I had the words to convey the exuberance that he displayed on that small stage. He had to be seen to be believed. Once up, he was there for the rest of the evening. Occasionally, the mike would be prised from his grasp by another amateur, but not often. He never crooned or sang romantic songs, as so many did, for Bernard it had to be a full-blooded song preferably with a rousing chorus. Around this time, there had been a re-release of *The Jazz Singer*, the Al Jolson story. Bernard took it to his heart. Every time he got up, he would run through the whole range of songs, 'Sonny Boy', 'Mammy' ... I can remember him singing them even now, and with Bernard you got the full range of impassioned actions as well. He worked very hard, never stopping, but I'm sure he enjoyed every moment of it.

Bernard never got the worse for drink. He never had the time. He would finish one song, a couple of gulps of his pint and he would throw himself into the next. He was very, very good, his audience loved him plus he was so jolly and affable with it. Another thing – in the time I knew him, Bernard never displayed bad temper, I never saw the slightest hint of aggression or violence in him, and that wasn't something that could be said of many of the young men in those days. There were no histrionics, no moods. With Bernard, what you saw was what you got.

'My recollections of Bernard on that stage some fifty years ago are sharp and vivid, which I think is an accolade for his performance,' Mr Smith concludes tellingly. Sadly, he says, he lost contact with Bernard, and has never been able to hear him in later years, since he has become totally deaf. 'I will always remember him with affection,' he adds. 'He was good to know and was part of my youth. I accidentally met him on Rochdale Road many years later, and we stopped for a chat. It was a different Bernard. He had matured and was more worldly wise, but I also remember that I went away thinking that he was suffering from a slightly inflated ego. Perhaps this wasn't a fair assessment. He was still very young.'

Because he was under age, the pub talent competitions Bernard had started to enter were causing trouble at home. When he first won such a contest, and brought home the prize – a spectacularly ugly pottery doll in a crinoline – his father, he says, belted him for having been in a pub. (His mother, however, kept the doll out on her sideboard into her old age.) Because of this awkward age problem, Bernard changed his strategy and started singing with bands in dance halls and clubs – which meant that, for the first time, instead of competing for tacky prizes, he was being paid a few shillings.

'When I say clubs, I mean places like the Eccles Conservative Club rather than nightspots,' says his sister Alma. 'He used to get these bookings, and be paid as much as two pounds, ten shillings, even though he was still only about seventeen. He'd say to us, "Right, girls, I've got a booking at such and such a place; you can come with me and have gin and oranges all night." So we'd say, "Oh, right," and off we'd go. It was magic.'

Despite being so young, serious professional show-business ambitions were starting to surface in Bernard. A week's holiday in Blackpool with a pal in 1947 – paid for with twenty-five shillings saved from his wages, and the only holiday, he claims, he has ever taken in his adult life – provided a vital stimulus for this process. 'We splashed out on a visit to the Opera House to watch Max Bygraves, and that confirmed it,' Bernard recounts. 'I can do better than that pudding, I thought. If he can make a living at it, so can I.'

In line with Bernard's increasing income and status, the job at the Senior Service factory clearly had to go. Three years after joining Pattreiouex, and now a fully fledged grinder rather than a mere mate, Bernard left to join his father full time in the business, getting up at 4 a.m. to pick up sacks of runner beans at the fruit and vegetable market, delivering greengroceries round the cobbled streets and the more well-to-do suburbs, and even knocking on doors to sell flowers.

Bernard was a fine-looking lad and, with his increasingly renowned performances in the pubs and clubs, had begun to appeal to young women, who in such places even in the 1940s could be quite pushy. Bernard's mates used to find it funny that he often failed to realise that he was being chatted up. When it did dawn on him, they noticed that he was visibly disconcerted, and had little idea of how to handle the admiration.

This slight awkwardness with girls was not the result of his being unused to the company of women, but the war had oddly distorted the start of his sexual career. When he started at the factory in 1944, it employed hundreds of young girls. It was a veritable cornucopia of females but, understandably, that delightful fact was not of great interest or use to a fourteen-year-old. In the early forties, all the men of military age had been called up. An older boy, perhaps of seventeen, who was fit and of reasonable appearance would have been in an enviable position. But by the time Bernard was seventeen and girls were openly chatting him up in pubs, his confidence with them had simultaneously taken a knock. At work, the older men had returned from the war, a lot of them, like Len Smith, having seen active service and having amazing, and eminently easy to embroider, stories to tell the girls. This development meant that a seventeen-year-old boy working in the Senior Service factory reverted to being very small beer indeed. Singing and joking with girls at the factory was one thing but, by doing this, he cast himself in the role of harmless male. And when, after he had spent a couple of years in the sexual backwaters, female attention was suddenly lavished on him he was less than sure of what to do with it. It encouraged his ambitions as an entertainer, sure enough, but he was curiously unable to use it beyond that. Bernard says his best chat-up line was 'Where do you live?' 'You had to ask that in the old days because nobody had cars and you could end up walking four or five miles just for a kiss goodnight, if you were lucky. Usually her dad was at the door and you might walk five miles home in the rain.'

When he was fifteen, Bernard met his first girlfriend at Pattreiouex, in spite of the competition from the influx at the factory of older, more experienced men released from the forces. Rose was a stripper, as he likes to say – a tobacco-leaf stripper, 'And that's all the stripping Rose Knight was prepared to do. It was a real love crush. I loved her from afar, but never took her out. She knew about it, but that was it. You see, in those days, you didn't go out with them right away, and you didn't try anything on right away. It just took you months and months to get to know them.' Nevertheless, Bernard succeeded in losing his virginity at seventeen. 'It was at a Christmas party with a girl I'd known for a month or two,' he says coyly, still too gentlemanly to name names. 'It was all over in a couple of minutes.'

Then, in the summer of 1948, just as he had overcome this obstacle to his young male pride, as well as begun to make a name for himself as Bernard Manning, the Choice Voice, the curtain came down on his life as a teenager. He was called up for National Service in the 1st Battalion of the Manchester Regiment.

Dicker Coming

Forget it, Manning. Just don't be so keen on obeying orders in future.

Sgt Sam Allport of the 1st Manchester Battalion, on his return from hospital after being accidentally stabbed with a bayonet by an over-enthusiastic Bernard Manning, 1948

Bernard's career in the Army and the military police followed the same rather contradictory pattern of much of his early life. Just as he had been a useless but conscientious scholar, a mummy's boy who remained popular with siblings and friends, and outgoing in the extreme yet simultaneously shy, he was, by any standards, a terrible soldier – a one-man disaster area – but oddly diligent with it. The Manning work ethic, that of striving to do as well as possible even in unpromising circumstances, was deeply imbued in the eighteen-year-old Bernard.

Brought up on his older mates' tales of all the fun there was to be had in the Army, he had insisted on not challenging his call-up. With his father getting older, not in the best of health, and with the business to run, he could probably have been exempted from National Service, but Bernard was determined to join up. His father, as ever the organiser-in-chief of his life, briefly explored the possibility of the boy doing his service closer to home, in the coal mines, as one of the famous Bevin Boys. Jack, the eldest Manning boy, had come safely through more than his share of active service after volunteering in 1939, and, even though there wasn't a war on in 1948, John and Nellie Manning were less than keen on risking their beloved Bernard's life too in the service of His Majesty. The mines were not a possibility, however, and in the autumn, Bernard, a £4-a-week private, was whisked off to Carlisle for twelve weeks' basic training. His father took on a local boy, Billy Taylor, to help him in the greengrocery business.

Three months of square-bashing, whitewashing coal, cutting grass with scissors, hurtling round assault courses and gasping through six-mile runs left Bernard, as with other boys of the time, fitter and healthier than he had ever been or subsequently would be. He even won a hundred-yard sprint race, and played football. 'I wasn't the best player in the world, but I always turned up,' he says. Stationed at a bleak camp near Hadrian's Wall, like many a miserable Roman legionary before him he was not a happy Bernard. 'He came on the phone one Saturday night, crying,' recalls sister Rene. 'He said it was the worst place he had ever seen in his life, and said, "Mum, I hate it, it's horrible, get me out." She said, "No, you've made your bed, now you're stopping there." ' There was a reason for Nellie's harshness: she had been bitterly opposed to her favourite son leaving her. It was Bernard who had insisted.

So Bernard did as he was told, and lay in the lumpy bed of his own making. It became increasingly comfortable. Before Christmas, he was sent to Germany, first to Wuppertal, later to Berlin, to begin a mixed career of blunder as a soldier – a military policeman, to be precise – and triumph as an entertainer. His main job in Berlin was to help guard three key Nazi prisoners in Berlin's Spandau jail – Hess, Doenitz and Speer. 'Funniest thing was watching them when they quarrelled among themselves,' he says. 'If only I could have understood what they were saying, it would have given me some great material.'

Bernard had not been in the Army long before he started to exploit his musical talent. Almost as soon as his singing voice became known, he was pressed into the Manchester Regiment's dance band. The colonel in charge of this outfit, which was quite separate from and altogether cooler, of course, than the regimental marching band, had been told of Private Manning's abilities, and summoned him to an audition as soon as his battalion arrived in Berlin.

The colonel immediately proclaimed Bernard 'fantastic' and assigned him to his first musical duty, the Christmas concert, at which he sang the very apt opener, 'Baby, It's Cold Outside' (the reference being to both the freezing, central European weather and the Cold War), with one of the officer's wives. It went down a storm in the camp, and assured Bernard an easy ride in the Army from then on. Engagements and tours kept him off guard duties and fatigues, and he built up a fan following of a hundred or so of the lads, who would come along in coaches to hear him sing a new repertoire of smoother, more American-sounding numbers than he had sung in the pubs and clubs of Manchester, 'the golden-voiced ballad stuff that was to be my style for several years', as he puts it.

Bernard's being put into the military police was a consequence of the discovery by the Army of his singing; the police was a common posting for recruits with a useful extracurricular role, such as boxing or playing an instrument. When the end of his National Service time was near, he was offered a sergeant rank and pay to stay on primarily as a singer. That was never an offer the homesick nineteen-year-old was likely to take up, but meanwhile, the band took him all over the British sector of Germany and into the American zone too. 'The NAAFI club in Berlin was a massive place and the Yanks were there as well as the British,' says Len Astill, Bernard's room mate in the military police block. 'He used to bring the roof down with the Yanks, he really did. He sounded like an American singer.'

Bernard Manning sharing the guard duty at post-war Spandau remains one of history's more curious footnotes. The idea of a fat northern amateur cabaret singer and comedian, who would one distant day get into trouble when he was discovered to be harbouring a bust of Hitler in his house (even if he had an innocent explanation for it) in his youth guarding some of the most notorious surviving Nazi criminals is the stuff of an Edinburgh Fringe play, at the very least. But it was a series of entirely parochial incidents, more worthy of a *Carry On* film, which in reality provided the more vivid memories of (and for) Bernard in this period of his life.

The stabbing of Sergeant Sam 'Rocky' Allport in particular was a corker, the definitive Bernard cock-up, which was to become the most legendary among his mates, although it was but one of many. Bernard had been *playing* the fat fool successfully for many years now, but was now, apparently, managing to be one, and doing so with some verve.

The unfortunate Sgt Allport was giving bayonet-drill instruction while Bernard's battalion was in Wuppertal. 'Now, Manning,' he said, 'come at me with your blade as if you really mean it.' Sgt Allport, a big man, had been adding a bit of reality to unarmed combat training by, strictly against the rules, allowing the boys to charge at him with the scabbard off the bayonet. The idea was to look fierce and run at the man as if you meant to kill him. He would then fall backwards and grab each rifle as its owner went over him. Bernard, however, took the exercise a little more seriously than the other recruits. 'I made such a horrible face and let out such a scream that it put him off,' he explains. It was partly Bernard's ferociousness, partly the fact that Allport was laughing, and partly his assailant's weight that left Sgt Allport lying screaming in a pool of blood in front of his entire platoon in the middle of a field in Germany. 'The bayonet went right into his chest and Bernard fell on the floor,' recounts Len Astill. 'The rifle was wavering about, and I had to run over and stop it from falling over, because they were heavy – at least nine pounds – and if it had fell over it would have ripped his chest out.'

A decent chap, Sgt Allport, who in civilian life became a tanker driver, bore no hard feelings against Bernard, and thirty years later, even accepted an invitation to appear on Bernard's *This Is Your Life* show.

Bernard was always getting into scrapes (Len Astill says). He let anybody in when he was on duty on the gates. The police used to have to search people going in, but he let three fellas in with a barrow, jut let them in. They had a pile of sand and buckets, and he never bothered to poke about in the barrow or anything like that. They showed him their passes, which were obvious forgeries, then went and blew up the adjutant's office. It turned out they were a specially trained squad of officers dressed as Germans and were testing everybody to keep us on our toes.

He also set fire to a three-ton truck. We were on an exercise to map the roads so the convoys could find the way. A lot of the roads in Germany hadn't even been named, let alone marked, so when you came to a crossroads or a left or a right turn you had paraffin lamps with arrows on them pointing either left or right or straight on. The sergeant and the driver were in the front, and as we got to each corner or diversion the sergeant would shout left or right or straight on and we used to have to find the lamp – there were hundreds of them in the back, all in big wooden boxes with sawdust on the bottom – and put it in place on the road. Manning picked one of these things up and went to light it with a match, couldn't light it, burnt his finger, and dropped the sodding match in this box of paraffin and sawdust. It went straight up. There were three of us in the back of there, and we nearly snuffed it. The truck was still moving, and so the flames and fumes were pushed back towards us. I had me Army knife, and I had to go straight down to the bottom end of the three-tonner, cut me way through and bang on the sergeant's window, because he didn't even know it was on fire. That's how we got out, but the truck burnt completely out.

Although Bernard was reprimanded for this near-fatal disaster, it merely seemed to enhance his growing reputation as a card and a joker. 'He was a bit of a joke among the rest of the police because of the things he did, but that's how he was,' Astill says. 'He was a born comic. He didn't tell many dirty jokes, or anything like that, though. It was the things he did, and that made him a very popular bloke amongst the NCOs. With it all, he was never cheeky or insolent, he was a good soldier for obeying orders. He wouldn't dare backchat to a sergeant or an officer or even a corporal.'

On another auspicious occasion, Bernard was on gate duty at the barracks in Berlin when a dog ran past him at the moment the regiment was trooping the colour on the parade ground. The General was on his charger, all the men (bar Manning, Pte B.) were turned out. The dog made straight for the horses, pursued by Bernard, who left his duty to chase it in and out of the rows of soldiers. The General's voice was heard bawling out over the parade ground, 'Shoot that bloody man' (rather than shoot the dog), when his horse reared up and he fell off. Bernard was reprimanded again.

I sneaked a bird into the barracks one night and the only place I could take her was in our room (Len Astill records). It was the early hours of the morning, well after the eleven p.m. lights out, and I thought from his breathing that Bernard was asleep. The beds were only about two feet away from each other. So after it, like, I went to sleep, and this young German girl woke me up and said, 'Dicker coming, Dicker coming.' Dicker meets fat in German, and she was trying to say fattie's awake and about. He put the lights on. He was stripped naked and had a boot in one hand and you can only guess what was in the other. He was going to give me a belt over the head with the boot. I screamed at him, 'For God's sake, put the lights out.' Then we heard this sound of boots coming down the passage, and I pushed this bird right up against the wall next to my bed and I put me shoulder across and buried her as the door burst open. The police block was quite big, but it had a lot of windows, and it was an orderly officer and an orderly sergeant who had spotted the light and come to investigate. So me and Manning cracked on to be asleep and they never spotted this bird at all so I got away with it. The trouble was that I'd sneaked her in but I couldn't get her out. During the day when I had to go on duty, I had to lock her in my bloody cupboard, a big wardrobe with massive swastikas someone had put all over it, and sneak food up to her. I kept her there for two days. I let her out now and again. I used to lock the door when we went down on duty. Bernard did his best to get in that wardrobe and try it on with her, but he never managed it.

Bernard's paucity of success with women was even now not really abating, according, at least, to his National Service colleagues. The strictly unavailable Rosie Knight back in Manchester continued to be the young man's all-purpose icon-cum-explanation-cum-excuse for his lack of action over in Germany. The sad reality in Germany at this time (sad for German womanhood, if not for the British boys placed by historical circumstance in their midst) was that almost any male with a pulse could have his pick of local girls. Such was the shortage and hunger for men locally that when recruits arrived in Germany they were not allowed out of barracks for six weeks. Much of this settling-in period was taken up with their being shown films about sexual diseases, in which German girls were portrayed unequivocally as being 'dirty'.

Every woman in Germany from the age of fourteen to sixty-five was issued by the Allied occupation forces with what was called a 'Housewife', a pass which they had to carry with them at all times. Every few months, they were required to attend a sexual health check, and the pass was stamped. All but the most cavalier soldiers would ask to see a girl's pass before sleeping with her. 'You used to sit down and have a drink with them and during the conversation it was just a matter of form. They expected it, and used to get in trouble if they weren't checked,' Len Astill confirms. Meeting women after the six-week curfew was no problem, either. Soldiers received plastic NAAFI money to spend on Crown premises, but no German currency, as a disincentive to spending time drinking in local bars and cafés. However, with the female-to-male ratio of five-to-one in some areas, if even the spottiest boy walked into a café, he did not need money, as there would be plenty of women happy to buy him drinks. Most were young, but many were older, respectable and frequently wealthy women who had lost their husbands in the war.

The official VD warnings served to intrigue almost as many squaddies as they frightened; for boys to whom the very idea of willing and able women was a complete novelty, the news of their abundance locally was like a starting gun. Bernard, however, was resolutely with the frightened contingent, who heeded the statistic that was being bandied about that claimed twenty men a week in the Manchester Regiment alone were going down with gonorrhoea and syphilis. Bernard talked endlessly about his girl at home, Rosie, giving mates the impression that he and his love were on the point of getting engaged. By this method, he cautiously exempted himself from trips into town. He did not go out with any women in Germany and, indeed, rarely went out of the barracks at night.

The truth was that Bernard was homesick, and in a big, embarrassing way. His father was sending him gifts continually, large cakes fresh from his mother's oven being a favourite. 'He was a mummy's boy all right,' Astill insists. 'He used to cry at night for his mum. I went into the room a couple of times, and he had been in tears because he missed his mum. Definitely. I did call him a big soft sod one night. I can't remember what he said, but it wouldn't have been very much at all, because by the time I got in at night, it was lights out any rate.'

Rose Knight turned out, inevitably, to be a disappointment to Bernard. He had heard that she had been seeing another man, and got the Dear John letter from her at almost the same time as he heard from one of his comrades, on his return from leave in

Manchester, that she had got married. He was shocked and, unusually for Bernard, went out and got drunk.

A shock of a different kind came to Bernard courtesy of a equally lovelorn sergeant.

Bernard always used to sleep naked (Astill says). I don't know why. He just used to like it. He wasn't funny or owt like that, but he always had a big fat bum, and it was always rosy red. There was one sergeant who was not a nice person, a swine actually. He was called Sergeant Lynch, and he come from Liverpool and looked like Lee Marvin – the same build and attitude. He was a tough fellow, and very clever with it as far as police matters were concerned, but he was having a bit of trouble with his wife at home, and he used to get canned up in the sergeants' mess. We would all be in bed fast asleep, and all of a sudden, the door would barge open and Lynch used to come in and he used to start on Manning. He knew that Manning slept with nothing on, and would try and get his hands under his bedclothes, until Bernard jumped up out of bed and started running round the police block with Lynch after him. I dread to think what would have happened if he'd have ever caught him. I have an idea that Sergeant Lynch was only joking, but I wouldn't put money on it. It happened a few times, and I was in fits of laughter, because of this rosy red arse he'd got. Bernard didn't laugh at all, though. He was frightened to death, terrified.

Fat Manning left the Army at the age of twenty-one, after over two years. He was wiser, more worldly and weighed just eleven and a half stone. Outside his closely knit family, only his Army pals had seen Bernard at quite such close quarters, and the telling insight they gained into his soul while all were living in one another's pockets on National Service did not enthuse him with any notion of keeping closely in touch with his comrades, once they had all returned to civilian life. It was as if they had been through a lot together, but he now urgently wanted to get home and get on. Bernard and Len would see each other very rarely over the decades that followed – 'Perhaps just to toot horns at one another if we passed on the road,' as Astill puts it – and he remained equally at arm's length from his other two main friends from the Army, also lads who had met on the same day at the camp in Carlisle, Eric Dewett and Jim Blain.

I liked him then, but I am not too keen at the moment because he's a bit too crude for me (Astill comments). I'm disappointed in the way his act has gone, but the thing I am more disappointed in, really, was that me and my wife went to the club one night, and she didn't like it. She wouldn't have a dirty joke, my wife, or swearing or anything like that. We were sat at a table, and Manning came on, spotted me in the audience right away, and told them exactly what went on when I slipped that young German bird in, and they were all laughing. I didn't like that one bit, and Nell didn't like it, not at all. I told her to take no notice, but he was still stirring it. The other thing was his voice. It was absolutely superb when I first knew him but the way he sings now, it doesn't have the same sincerity in it. He used to stand there with his eyes closed and his voice was wonderful. You could have heard a pin drop when he was singing – that's how good he was. It's different now.

I lost my wife ten years ago with breast cancer, and that was the last time I spoke to him. Somebody must have told him that Nell wasn't right, and he rang me up to say how sorry he was. She was in bed at the time, and all I can say is that I am glad I answered the phone and not my wife. The language on the phone was absolutely atrocious. I said to him, 'Bernard, for God's sake.' I believe that's how he is all the time, even in his club. If my wife had heard him like that she would have been really upset. He just laughed. He said, 'Are you bothering with women now?' and I said, 'No, I haven't been unfaithful to Nell in all me married life.' Then he said, 'Well, if you don't get any more, you've had your share,' and that's how he went off the phone.

The Fat Man Sings

There are only three things in life: to be born, have your own show,
and die.

Bernard Manning

Bernard re-entered civilian life determined to be a professional singer. However, having no contacts in show business, he began his journey to stardom by the more prudent
route of joining his father once again in the greengrocery business
and singing in local clubs at night. Now that Bernard was twenty,
there was nothing his father could do any longer to stop him from
entering licensed premises.

Picking up bookings after his time away was not a problem. His
singing had improved immeasurably in the Army. Now, in post-war
Manchester, he had another stimulus to help improve it still further.
Previously, Bernard's self-taught skill as a smooth, Sinatra-style
singer – not so much the crooning as the visual stuff, moving in the
right way, looking the part even if he was a greengrocer's boy from
Harpurhey – had learnt only by watching Sinatra and Bing Crosby
in films. Now, the big acts were coming to Manchester and, in 1950,
Bernard saw Sinatra, Nat King Cole and many others at the city's
Palace Theatre.

One of the Singing Greengrocer's first professional engagements
in 1950, the year of his return to Manchester, was at the annual
dance of St Clare's, a Catholic school like his own. It paid £2.
Another, slightly nearer the mark he wanted to hit, was a proper
cabaret club at the Leigh Road Social Club. The evening that
changed his life – was probably the most significant turning point
for Bernard, in fact – did not sound an overly auspicious one. It
was an impromptu, unpaid turn at the Barnes Green Catholic Club,
a social club off the Rochdale Road, round the corner from the
shop.

At the club that evening, however, were four men who might not normally have been at such a humdrum venue, except that there was a charity snooker match on, which all had been either keen or at least induced to attend. One of the guests was Jimmy James, the great comedian, who performed with Roy Castle. Another was Johnny Foy, a bigshot bookmaker in Manchester, who was also an ardent Catholic, a renowned charity fundraiser and general mover and shaker. The third unlikely visitor was his close friend Melville Davies, a thirty-year-old Jewish bookie, who had harboured show-business ambitions since childhood, and become a minor performer himself in the RAF. Lastly, there was Davies's boyhood friend from North Manchester Grammar School, Leslie Josephson, who used the stage name of Larry Jason, but was known to his friends only as 'Josser'. Josser was a big band singer and a sometime compère at the Whitehall Theatre in London, but was not working at that moment.

During the interval of the snooker match, as the audience members were having a drink, Foy turned to Davies, and, indicating a chubby young lad in a suit whom Davies had never seen before, said, 'You see that boy over there. He's a greengrocer on the Rochdale Road just near here. Name of Bernard Manning. Works for his father in his shop. He's got a lovely voice.' There happened to be a trio playing during the interval, and Foy asked Davies and Josser if they would like to hear the boy sing. 'Sure, let him sing a couple of songs,' said Josser. Bernard belted out two numbers. Then Foy brought him over to meet Josser. 'You know, I'd love to get him a chance on the stage,' Foy told Davies as Bernard shook hands with Josser. 'He so badly wants to get out of the greengrocery business.'

Jimmy James was close by, and Foy asked him as he had asked the others, if he thought the singer stood a chance in show business. James pronounced: 'I'd say he has a good future.' Davies meanwhile had been thinking about what he had seen. 'I know one or two people in the theatres,' Davies told Foy. 'That boy of yours has got a terrific voice, terrific, but he's very raw. To put him in a variety theatre ... I don't know. I'll see what I can do.' Before the end of the snooker evening, Davies, despite his reservations, had convinced Josser to have a stab at managing Bernard Manning.

Davies also took an active interest himself in encouraging

Bernard. It was little more than an enchantment with the theatre that persuaded Melville Davies to do so. Davies had gone as a boy to acting classes held by Joan Littlewood and, as an adult, never missed his schoolfriend Josser when he did a show at the Palace Theatre in Manchester. Whenever he could, Melville liked to meet people in the theatre, and appeared in air-force shows doing the odd sketches and monologue. Even after the RAF, he put on little charity shows. He knew Max Bygraves well, and would sometimes rope him in to do benefits.

Melville, now seventy-five, recounts: 'I decided to help out by going to see Dave Forrester, the owner of the Oldham Empire, which was a major theatre then, because I'd noticed that at the top of the bill there was a pal of mine, a comic called Len Young, who is married to one of the three Kay Sisters, Carol, and was known then as "The Singing Fool". (A few years later, Forrester became the manager of Ken Dodd and booker for the London Palladium. As Dodd's manager, he was legendary in show business because the two never had a contract between them. When Melville once asked Dodd why he had teamed up with Forrester on such a curious business basis, Dodd thought about it and explained, 'He looks just like my father.')

Melville told Forrester about the Singing Greengrocer, how tremendously he sang, and added sensibly the additional attraction that Bernard would not charge very much.

I said, 'I want him to be seen to give him a chance to start on the stage.' Forrester agreed to put him in the week after next, the show where my friend Len Young was on. That was handy, because it would give him time to iron out the wrinkles of how to walk on and walk off, how to take a bow, to learn things he didn't know. You must remember he was the complete raw article. He had to get his act together because he had no act. So I told Bernard he was in at the Oldham Empire, but I said, 'You can't just walk on and sing a song. You have to speak to the audience, and you've got to know what to say and when to do so.' Then I wrote him out what he should say after each number. Bernard once told me that he has kept that bit of paper to this day.

When Len Young arrived in Manchester, Melville was still working away to smooth the showbiz path for Bernard's discovery.

> I said, 'Listen Len, I want you to do me a favour. There's a boy making his first appearance ever at the Oldham Empire. Show him how to walk on and stuff,' and he said OK and Len became very firm friends with Bernard. Len is now an old man and lives in Brighton, but he laughs to this day about Bernard. He used to come to Len's dressing room each night armed with bunches of grapes from the shop to thank him for showing him how to walk on.

Years later, performing at a show in a Brighton theatre, Bernard spotted Len Young, then eighty-six, in the audience. After Bernard took a standing ovation, he held up his hand to hush the crowd and announced: 'I am particularly pleased to be appearing in Brighton because here in the audience is a very old friend, who gave me my first idea of how to work on the stage. He was a great comic in his day, a wonderful man, I love him, I'll never forget him. Stand up, Len.' Young took a bow from the stalls. Delighted, he later phoned Melville: 'Bernard never forgets,' he said. 'All the things on his mind, and he singled me out from the audience.'

Back in 1950, when his first big night at the Oldham Empire came around, Bernard was billed as 'Britain's Newest Singing Thrill', and was on the second half alongside performers such as Dr Crock and his Crackpots. Bernard's pay was an enormous £14. Josser, his new manager, was there with him, standing in the wings hissing, 'Move you bastard, move,' because, despite his last minute coaching, Bernard was still wooden and had little idea of how to move on stage. To Dave Forrester's delight, half of Rochdale Road turned out on the opening night to see the local hero. 'It was terrifying, nerve racking,' recalls Bernard's sister Rene. 'But I couldn't stop laughing. They'd done him up on the stage with these great big thick eyebrows. You felt for him, sitting there, thinking, "Oh God, don't do something wrong." But he did really well.' By the end of that week, Bernard was beginning to be at ease on the stage as well as singing as if his life depended on it.'

The Oldham Empire was his vital professional breakthrough, but Bernard's personal life had hit a great turning point in recent months too. At a dance just before Christmas 1949 at the Small and Parks brake lining factory social club – Bernard was actually home on his last Christmas leave from the Army, a few days before the end of his National Service – he met Veronica Finnerann, a pretty blonde secretary who worked in the office at a cotton mill. She had approached him as a fan. He had been in the audience, but by popular demand had just got up and sung the song 'Autumn Leaves', which happened to be her favourite. She went up to him and said, 'I think you're a fabulous singer, you.' Thanking the singer for a well-sung number sounds a little bold, but was common practice, almost a courtesy, in those days. Bernard had never seen Vera, as she introduced herself, before, but was immediately struck by how pretty she was. He danced with her, and then asked if he could see her home. He most certainly could, she replied. He has always said since then that this was the happiest moment of his life.

Being Bernard, meeting Vera wasn't quite love at first night. Impulsive and sentimental in most matters, he is still one to take stock of a situation before committing himself, one of life's tyre-kickers. Nevertheless, he was pretty sure from their first kiss, under the mistletoe at the social club, that she was the one. 'She was absolutely gorgeous, I'm telling you,' he says today. 'She was wearing a pale two-piece suit, long, blonde hair tucked under – I can see her now – big blue eyes, big eyelashes, absolutely wonderful skin with not a blemish on it. Good teeth, nails, everything. I weighed all this up. I can tell you what a woman's like by her nails.'

Bernard walked Vera home, but there was no goodnight kiss. Mistletoe was mistletoe, but snogging in the street with a nice girl you had just met would have been out of the question in 1949.

I asked to see her again, and arranged to meet her the next night under the clock, where all the couples used to wait for one another, at Higgins Piano Shop on the corner of Queens Road. She was there, looking ravishing, and we went to the Odeon picture house to see *Gone With The Wind*. I know we were there for a long time. I sat and held her hand for the whole four hours – nothing more, just holding hands. I kissed her that night.

After a couple of dates, Bernard had decided, however, that he could live very happily with this person. They like the same type of music; she was very feminine, was not pushy, and let Bernard do what he wanted. Everyone remembers her from this time as a sweet, charming girl with a smile for everyone. Most important of all to a man brought up in a well-run household, her family house was clean and orderly. Bernard's sister liked Vera too. At home, he and Alma would sing songs to one another in a jokey way about one another's beloveds. He would sing rudely about Jimmy Cameron, Alma's boyfriend (whom she married) and Alma would croon in return a popular melody of the day that involved the phrase 'sparrow legs', an affectionate reference to Vera's skinny legs.

Vera was Catholic, which was another advantage. She was a Leo, like him ('I don't believe in all these things, but we got on well together. You're not supposed to, but we did.') Vera's mother, May, was Welsh, an Evans, and her father Irish, but not from Ireland. 'Her father worked in a fish market, a very hard-working man called Leo. May was just a housewife. She looked after the house and the family. Lovely woman, thought the world of me, and we got on well together. Her dad liked me. She also had a brother called Leo and we got on, too.'

Despite all these positive augurs, it would still be four years before Bernard and Vera became engaged, and another three before they married. The couple's seven years of courting were spent relentlessly working and saving money.

It went on from those first dates to taking her to clubs where I was booked at, all over the show. I'd get about £2 a night. I'd bought a little car, a 1933 Standard Vanguard. Like a greenhouse it was. All the neighbours used to complain about the noise, bang bang bang. We went all over the country in that little car, earning money. We were saving up. You did in them days. You didn't go barmy, going mad and getting married. Every penny I earned outside me wages at the greengrocery, I put in the bank. She put her money away too, and we lived very, very stringently.

Not surprisingly, the young couple used to sleep together – although not in bed – during their marathon courting and engagement. 'Oh, aye, we did it,' Bernard says. 'It was always in funny, awkward places, because we couldn't go to our house and we couldn't go to theirs. So it was generally in a little Ford Popular. I was thinner then. And the backs of other cars. And in a bandstand once, in the Queens Park. But we never actually spent the night together until we were married.'

A couple of weeks after Bernard's Oldham Empire triumph, Josser heard that Oscar Rabin, leader of the Oscar Rabin Orchestra, one of the most popular big bands in London, was booked to come up to Manchester for a concert. Rabin's band was regularly appearing on BBC Radio's Light Programme, was the permanent band-in-residence at the Hammersmith Palais in west London and was also a regular attraction at the Lyceum Ballroom. Rabin employed a renowned female singer, Beryl Davis (who later went to America, teamed up with Jane Russell and toured the world as a double act), but the bandleader was known to be on the hunt for an extra male singer. Josser, as a big band singer of some note himself, knew Rabin very well, and told Bernard he was going to try to get him an audition. At the same time, according to Bernard, Jimmy James, who had been impressed with him that recent night at the Barnes Green Catholic Club, had put in a good word for the local boy with Oscar Rabin.

Josser saw Rabin at his suite at the Midland Hotel, the smartest in Manchester. 'Bring the boy up,' the musician said. 'I'll play the piano, I'll listen to him and see if he's any good.' Bernard was soon in Rabin's room. To his dismay, he found he was not the only local talent Rabin was auditioning. 'I stood trembling in a corner of the hotel, as the other lads sang their hearts out up in his suite,' Bernard says. 'Then it was my turn. I opened with "Just One More Chance", then went on to "Baby, It's Cold Outside". Oscar lit a cigar, took a couple of puffs and then said: "Bernard, you're in." ' As if confirmation were necessary, he was on the phone to Josser within minutes to organise a twelve-month contract at an unimaginable £100 a week, out of which Bernard would have to pay all his own hotel and subsistence expenses, but would still be left with almost half intact. Bernard Manning, big band singer, was expected in London for rehearsals two days later.

In great haste, he had to buy a wardrobe of suits, several pairs of shoes and even a set of dressing gowns, an item of apparel considered distinctly *outré* in Harpurhey, and one that consequently he has never worn in his life. He said his goodbyes to Vera and to the family – his father barely had time to find a new boy to help him in the shop – and departed with Josser for London and a room at the Mount Royal Hotel. 'That's when I met all the boys and got really into show business,' he explains.

Everything was new and daring for Bernard in London: the people, the gossip, the money, even the food he ate. Rabin introduced him to rich Jewish foods – chicken soup with kreplach, salt beef, wurst, salami – that he has retained a taste for. 'That was what started ballooning out my body to the size it is today,' he says. It was actually Len Young, the Singing Fool, who had helped him out at the Oldham Empire, who had first acquainted him with Jewish food. 'When I used to take him those grapes up, he really loved them. Jews are very fond of good food you know, grapes, smoked salmon, all that. They love their food. Not like the crap we eat.'

Before the invention of teenagers the big bands were the pop groups of the day, with a lifestyle and earning potential for their stars almost to match the rock and roll industry a decade later. The bands had probably already had their heyday, which was between the wars, but, much as the basic layout and sound of sixties-style pop groups has not changed in over thirty years, the music and ethos of the big band was by 1950 appealing to its third successive generation. The significance of being signed up by Oscar Rabin cannot, therefore, be underestimated. British bands were, of course, a pale imitation of those in America (Duke Ellington, Glenn Miller and the rest). The Oscar Rabin Orchestra was one of the top three bands in the UK; if Ken McIntosh and the Ted Heath Orchestra were the Blur and Oasis of the day, Oscar Rabin was Pulp, and Bernard Manning, a complete unknown to this moment, was being offered on a plate the chance to be Jarvis Cocker.

Friday and Saturday nights were big band nights. The scene was very similar to a disco today. People would go primarily to meet young people of the opposite sex, the audible, mood-enhancing soundtrack being supplied by a big band, playing loudly. Each band had to have two singers, a male and a female, and between fourteen and sixteen players, all good sightreaders who could play music they were handed at a moment's notice. To warm things up, they would be expected to play some strict tempo stuff, so that people could dance; there would be a waltz, a foxtrot and a quickstep. The girls were always more likely to know these steps than the boys, so the male role was to hold his girl close, and look competent. The better big bands, which had jazz musicians, would try and imitate the big swing bands of the US. They might get arrangements that they had poached from musicians who had gone over to New York on the liners – all the boats like the *Queen Mary* had big bands too. When the liner musicians got to New York, they would go round the music shops to buy up arrangements, which, after passing through several hands, would end up being played at places like the Hammersmith Palais, with Bernard Manning, all Brylcreem, shiny bow tie and quiff, as star.

America was still the lodestone, the Beatles still being more than ten years away, and Bernard, like all singers, affected an American accent. It was also a time when the Musicians Union was friendly towards Americans, and they were welcome to live and work in London, which meant a hard-working greengrocer from Harpurhey had some stiff competition in his attempt to pass for a Stateside crooner. A few yards from the hotel where Bernard was put up, great jazz musicians like Fats Waller would be living in the Savoy and playing at the Palladium for a month at a time. Smart fans would hang around the Savoy lobby in top hats and white silk scarves with their girlfriends waiting for the great man. They would buy him a bottle of gin when he appeared and persuade him to sit down and sing and play for hours, sometimes until dawn.

For the British bands, broadcasting was the measure of success. The Oscar Rabin Orchestra were doing two or three evening radio shows a month. They were also frequently on variety shows, where a comedian like Frankie Howerd would be top of the bill, and the band might play with a singer of the moment, such as Alma Cogan. The tradition of having a big band as the accompaniment to comedy was still current when the Goons appeared on radio in the late 1950s.

Bernard's first broadcast on the Light Programme turned out to be a huge disappointment. 'I should have broadcast the day the King died. *Mrs Dale's Diary* was on, then the announcement that he was dead, and they said there'd be no more broadcasts for the rest of that day. I'll never forgive him for that. Lousy bastard!' Joking aside, however, Bernard was unhappy with his new life almost from the beginning. He was quite capable of doing what he was required to do, and could not disagree with his influential new friends like Melville Davies and Josser that he was far too good for pub singing. But he missed home dreadfully. He felt he was becoming distant from Vera, from the day-to-day running of the shop, whose familiarity he missed as soon as he was away from it. News of Frank at school (he left with enough O levels to become a Ryvita salesman), of Jack, who was a director of a paint firm in Liverpool, Rene, who had gone into hairdressing as a junior, and Alma, who had joined Marks and Spencer (eventually to be a supervisor), all began to sound as if it came from another planet. 'Bernard didn't like it,' says Rene. 'He stayed for three months or so, then he used to come home for weekends when he had finished on a Saturday night. He'd get the train home and go back on Monday. But he used to say, "I don't want to go back. I don't like it." You have to remember he was courting Vera at the time.'

Melville Davies confirms this. 'One day, Josser went to call for him at the hotel and Bernard wasn't there. He had left a note to say he had gone back to Manchester. He was homesick. Bernard is basically a real Lancashire lad. The big city life didn't appeal to him, he missed his girl and he wanted to get married, so he left the band.' And although they remained very close friends to the day he died, some ten years ago, his managerial association with Josser ended.

Of course, all of Harpurhey knew about and shared the disappointment of the local boy who appeared to have abandoned his shot at stardom after just six months. There was, perhaps, a hint of *schadenfreude* from local friends, and many dark stories about the amount John Manning had needed to come up with to buy Bernard out of his contract with Rabin. (In fact, there had been no such buy out – Rabin liked Bernard and was perfectly sympathetic with his reasons for wanting to return. As generations of war service veterans and National Servicemen could testify, homesickness was far more of a problem than it is today for young people away from home, with our easy, cheap long-distance phone calls and faster travel.)

'Bernard went down there but he didn't last all that long,'

recounts Sammy Dardick, son of the owner of the hardware store close to John Manning's greengrocery.

> I met him a few months after all this and I said to him. 'So what's it all about?' He told me that when he got down to London they started to groom him and give him singing lessons, diction lessons, English lessons and all that, and he had to be up at a certain time and back in bed at a certain time, be at rehearsals on time. He said he had packed it all in because he couldn't stand the discipline, the grooming, the hair cuts, face massages and all this sort of thing. It was compulsory; it was part of the contract. Bernard is a rough and ready sort of character – nobody knows it better than himself – and rough and ready characters don't take very well to discipline, even if it is going to be to their advantage.

'He would have been far more famous if he had stuck with Oscar Rabin, I'm sure,' believes Bernard's Army mate, Len Astill. 'Although you can't really say he was wrong in not carrying on and, maybe, going on to TV with Oscar Rabin, because he is a millionaire now anyway. But that was Bernard, really. He just didn't want to be tied down. I thought it would have been quite a while before they knocked Bernard into any kind of gentleman.'

Cauliflowers to Comedy

When I walk down the street around here it's Hello, Bernard. Hello,
Bernard. You'd think I was the Duke of Edinburgh. I love it.

Bernard Manning, safely back in Harpurhey

The homesickness had been real and acute, but there were
also hard-headed professional reasons for Bernard to return
to Manchester in 1952. One of these was that he was convinced musical tastes were changing, and that the day of the ballad
singer, on the national scene, at least, was close to being over. That
was, perhaps, a matter of opinion – he was probably a bit premature
in his judgement – but more important to him was that his ability
to make people laugh was beginning to surface. Towards the end
of his career with Oscar Rabin, he started, almost surreptitiously,
adding a few gags to his stage act. He was not discouraged from
doing this – it was tame stuff, just compèring, but it was inevitable
that, eventually, Rabin might have to rein him in a little.

When he thought about his future, alone in the alien surroundings of his London hotel room, added to the gnawing homesickness were three thoughts: firstly, that back in the provinces, his
crooning might continue to have appeal and bring in money further
into the future than it would in London. The second nagging
thought was that concentrating on his talents as a compère and
comic, coming on between acts with a joke and a song, sharpening
his patter and learning how to handle audiences, was the future;
he was, in today's phrase, 'more comfortable' in that role. A third
significant consideration was that an astonishing cabaret club scene
was developing rapidly in Manchester. (He was not to know this in
1952, but by the end of the following decade there were some 700
cabaret clubs in Manchester.) Notwithstanding that, Bernard even
had the nous, at just twenty-three, to realise that throwing himself
into the maul of being a straight comic would be as much an error
of judgement for a young man as trying to rise on a retreating big

band tide down in London. In the north, he had seen too many younger lads crucified by audiences and giving up. The working-men's club culture demanded comics of a certain age and experience.

He soon got a job that suited him perfectly, and still left him free to keep in his hand at the not (quite) forgotten greengrocery trade. He was hired as the compère at the Northern Sporting Club on the Rochdale Road, a boxing and wrestling venue which was following a contemporary trend for fleapit-type places to upmarket themselves into a relatively plush cabaret clubs, with swanky lighting and big stars on the bill – besides the sweaty grunt and groan stuff. At the Northern Sporting Club, Bernard found himself introducing acts such as Ronnie Hilton and Roger Moore's first wife, Dorothy Squires, who was a singer. Time and again, visitors to the club would say to him, 'I don't know why you're wasting your time compèring here – you should be going out for big money.'

But (he explains) I wasn't wasting my time, because it was the greatest grounding in the world, compèring at a place where there are people coming in, and you are bouncing lines off them, and it did me the world of good. It was no use just being a singer there, you see. You've got to greet or abuse people as they come in, you've got to sing their requests, tell a few stories, a few ad-libs. And that's how it began. A couple of ad-libs lead to a dozen, you bounce lines, you grow. And it's bloody marvellous when everybody falls about. I used to write jokes on the back of my arm. Sing a couple of songs, then glance down. They used to be silly, clean, childish jokes, corny. A fella with glasses comes in, and you bounce a line off him, 'You must have good eyesight to see through them glasses.' A big fat women comes in, 'We're having a sponsored walk round you later on.' A guide dog slashed up this blind guy's leg. A fella dashed up and said, 'What a lovely thing you've just done. That dog pissed up your leg, and you've given it a dog biscuit.' Then the blind fella says, 'I'm just finding out where its mouth is. Then it's going to get a kick in the bollocks.' Funny (he reflects), You could get away with bollocks back then. I even heard it used on television.

But you see how it all builds up, and in the end you have got an act there, and you're never stuck for a word. People think you have just thought of it, but you haven't. It's all there, catalogued. Being a singer was my crutch. Do a song, whip in a couple of quips and gags, have a go at a few folk. One thing led to another and I could do two hours, no problem. It's infectious. So I got an agent, started doing the clubs and the crowds started coming. The word got around: he's a good comic that Bernard Manning; he's different, he's outrageous, he has a go at everybody, nobody is sacred. But he doesn't tell sick gags, cripples and all that carry on. (The blind man and the dog joke, Bernard would argue, shows the blind man being clever and canny.)

It may have been the influence of the sporting surroundings he spent his evening in at the club, but Bernard began to see his joking cut and thrust as a form of boxing. He needed to train to be quick, adaptable, able to ad-lib his way out of any tight spot. It was, almost literally, a matter of hitting the audience with gags to keep their attention in a busy, noisy club. He started to look on every encounter with an audience as a battle, and one that he was used to winning. Their form of submission (OK, sometimes it was more like wrestling than boxing) was to laugh. Hecklers were an obstacle from the moment Bernard began to be a *de facto* comedian. It seemed that they all wanted to be comics themselves. Some nights, even the boxing–wrestling analogy was something of an understatement. He would need to be more like a lion-tamer, but without the whip and the chair.

Although Bernard regarded his act in the early to mid-1950s as *risqué*, it was fairly tame by the standards of twenty years later. When he talks of 'swearing like mad', he means that the odd 'hell' or, occasionally, even a 'bloody' would slip into his patter. The accusation of being 'too blue', which was the precursor of the more modern complaint that his material was too racist, was not yet being made. The Bernard Manning of this era was a working-class comedian, but never quite what would then have been called 'barrack room'. 'He never, ever swore, and he was a brilliant comic,' affirms Rene. 'I really liked him. He was really, really funny. He played the tin whistle and people would scream with laughter. He'd fool with a guitar. He has always made us laugh. He comes out with the funniest quips. He would never swear at home, either.'

During the long, easy ride through his mid-twenties, through the endless, peaceful midsummers of the 1950s, it seemed that Bernard's life was settled for good. He was a big fish in his area of Manchester, but was there by choice, having turned down the chance of national fame. He was surrounded by his family, secure in the focused business of saving up with Vera to get married. He was making a fat living in the familiar streets of his childhood. His rise to national fame was still twenty years away, his elevation to notoriety still forty years in the future. World without end and, if possible, without change, Bernard had pretty well 'made it'. It was his first golden age, and it was in these stable, happy circumstances that he and Vera got engaged in 1953. He did not ask Leo Finnerann's permission – the inevitability of Bernard and Vera doing the decent thing was one of life's assumptions – but he followed the whole ring-buying and proposal routine impeccably.

The ring cost me fifty pounds. I bought it from a friend of mine who was a jeweller at Whites in Market Street. A diamond solitaire, not a big one, but a decent size. Later, we were out with some friends in a pub called The Three Arrows in Heywood, and I had the ring, all twitching I was with it in this box. She didn't know anything about it, but she knew I loved her. I pulled the ring out, and I said in front of everybody, because there was a table, a nice table full of friends, I said, 'I think it's about time me and Vera got married.' Then I said, 'Will you marry me, love?' and she said 'Certainly', and I said 'Well put that on, love.' And there we are. The Three Arrows in Heywood, still there, still get a nice meal there and everything. Nothing changes with pubs.

It was still three years before the wedding, however, and the couple had their share of minor tiffs. 'We should have kept the engagement ring on a rubber band, because we were always splitting up,' he says. Part of the tension was Bernard's lifestyle. His workaholic trait was now in full swing. Work meant that there was never to be a holiday, the cycle of working and saving overrode all thought of idle pleasure. Apart from going with his father to watch Manchester City play, Bernard had no form of relaxation. On the other hand, Vera realised this was his vocation and had to be done. There was no question but that Bernard would be a provider and, despite the louche nightspots where he did his work, and his good looks, he was the least likely man in the world to be attracted by other women. He never objected to Vera coming to see him perform, and consequently she was often there. But he did not need to have an eye kept on him.

'I'll never forget the year we got married, 1956,' Bernard says, 'because Manchester City won the FA Cup.' In the build-up to the wedding, the young couple had managed to buy their dream home – an end terrace, number 34, Lewis Avenue, Blackley, that Bernard, typically, had had his eye on since he used to deliver newspapers to it as a boy.

The house cost £1400 – three times as much as smaller, newly built homes in the same area, but worth it, the couple felt, because it was the best in the street, and they had no intention of ever moving from it. The repayments on the mortgage – the first and last loan Bernard ever took out – were £9 15s 8d a month, which was hardly going to break the bank.

> We made it nice (he recalls with delight forty years later). It was a dream, an absolute dream. It's a love story really. I was over the moon. I realised then that I had my life ahead. We did it like you should do. First, we made one room nice. We had a little TV, fitted carpet, Baxi fireplace, Georgian windows and everything like that. We spent every bit of pennies and halfpennies on the house. Then we had a nice bedroom, then each room, one by one. Lovely curtains, we had, a bathroom second to none, a shower put in and all the glass thing pulled round. All the business. If you look at that house, you can see the wall round it that I had built a few years later. It cost me two thousand pounds in those days, just for a wall round the house, but in beautiful brick, absolutely. I used to say to the fellas, 'I reckon you've only built two walls – this one and Hadrian's,' because it took them bleeding donkey's years to finish it.

The wedding was on 26 June 1956 at Mount Carmel Catholic Church, where Bernard had been an altar boy, and where his son, Young Bernard, would within a few years be an altar boy too.

It was a gorgeous, sunny day. I wasn't nervous. I didn't have no time off. I got married on Wednesday afternoon, when the shop shut, and I was back at work on Thursday morning. There was no honeymoon. I remember the ceremony, and signing the book and everything. Her hands were nervous, all shaky. I said, 'Calm yourself down, you're all right, don't worry.' Vera wore white with a beautiful veil and everything, and a lovely bouquet. My brother Jack was best man. We walked down the aisle, 'Here Comes the Bride', and all that.

The reception was at the Northern Sporting Club. The Moscow State Circus was appearing there that week, so some of the performers did the cabaret for the club's compère. They invited Bernard on to the trapeze, but he declined and had a brief wrestle with the Soviet tame bear instead. There was a bottle of champagne, the cork of which shot into Vera's headdress, which everyone said was a lucky omen.

So we had a lovely cabaret, and we went home, and the door had the Union Jack on, and there were bells tied on under the bed, and all the nonsense they used to do in those days to drive you crackers on your wedding night. All the blankets were sewn up, and the pillows sewn to the blankets. We had an hour's work, half pissed, trying to get the job straight.

Those first few weeks together were fabulous (Bernard says). Getting up, having a nice breakfast cooked for you, because she wasn't lazy, Vera, got the old bacon and egg on, or whatever we were having, then plenty of tea, than a good session in bed before we went to work. Happy days.

Professionally, life before and after the wedding was indistinguishable. There were another three years of this cosy routine before Bernard had the idea of buying an old Temperance Billiard Hall, by then being used as a leather-goods factory, and turning it into his own club. The Temperance Billiard Halls had flourished in the north-west before the war, but few like this branch had survived post-war demolition and development. The owner of the leather workshop was a customer at the shop, and had told Bernard over the cabbages one day in early 1959 that he was thinking of getting out. Having his own club was a logical progression, even if it had taken Bernard several years to realise, as he puts it, that 'what I could do for a gaffer, I could do for myself'. Apart from the freedom and independence, the profits to be made from selling the beer to his own audience were awesome.

The only thing that had prevented Bernard, in all probability, from opening his own club previously was the crucial factor for him that no local premises had come up – that is, as local as Bernard, a man who before he was forty chose the cemetery where he wanted to be buried, likes things to be. The billiard hall was across the road from his father's shop, and a hundred yards from the Northern Sporting Club. The problem now was financial; how was Bernard to raise the money to rent the hall and do it up? The answer, he had no doubt, was boldly to persuade his father to back him to the tune of £30,000. To do so would mean more than dipping into savings; converting the tatty old billiard hall into a state-of-the-art Manchester cabaret club would necessitate Manning Senior giving up the shop, and making his second son's club the family business. John Manning at sixty-three had to be enticed to move from cauli-flowers to cabaret, and risk everything he had.

Bernard tried the finance idea out on his mother first. 'That old place would make a smashing club,' Bernard mentioned casually to her one day when he was at his parents' house. 'Oh, I don't know if your dad would want to do that,' Nellie said. She was right. They could have bought the premises outright for £2000, but the old man immediately said that was too risky. He knew nothing about show business, so committing himself to Bernard's plan was a brave step. But Bernard had already planted the seed of the idea of his father retiring. The shop was looking increasingly old-fashioned, but could still be sold with plenty of 'goodwill' – established custom – the intangible element of a shop's price that can be worth more than the fabric of the building. Why leave it to go downhill and lose value?

Bernard succeeded in talking his father into the club plan, and his dynamism rubbed off on the rest of the family. They knew he was the most valuable family asset. He was famous in Manchester now – his wedding had been quite prominently reported in the

Manchester *Evening News* with a big picture and under the headline 'Now There Will Be 2 In Harmony' – and the decision was taken rapidly. The club would be called Bernard Manning's Embassy Club, named after the first venue Bernard had worked at in London, an Embassy Club on Bond Street, where Bernard Delfont was in the audience with his mother the night the young singer from Manchester appeared. The greengrocer's was sold, and Bernard's father went on a course to learn how to pull beers and look after cellars. Bernard learned what he could about stage work, booking artists and getting musicians together, and the family ranks were drawn up, 'Everything clicked into place. Me sisters and me brother were going to go behind the bar. John, my brother-in-law, went on the door. Mum would work the cash till, dad do the cellar and Vera keep an eye on the rest of the club. It was a real family concern, a right team, with few outsiders – and no fiddlers.'

But Bernard's last stand in the fruit and vegetable business had yet to come. During the nine weeks the workmen were converting the billiard hall into a club, Bernard, never one to miss a chance to make a few bob, took the rather eccentric step of accepting a job with the Manchester and Salford Co-op, running its greengrocery shop on the main street in posh Altrincham, Cheshire, well away from Harpurhey, and the Harpurhey gossip which might have given away his mildly devious intent. The local manager, a Mr Fellows, knew that Bernard was famous as a club singer and compère, and Bernard felt guilty at having to lie to him about the time he expected to be a Co-operative employee, which was two months at the outside. As soon as the builders had finished, and such matters as the drinks licence organised, his plan was to tell Mr Fellows that his dad had secretly bought a club, apologise for having led him up the garden path, and leave.

The Altrincham shop was a rundown affair but, knowing that his last exit from greengrocery was at hand, he took pride in turning it into a thriving business.

I made the place a marvellous greengrocer's shop (he still says with remarkable pride). I made the window lovely, got that green grass and some lovely baskets, sprayed the baskets, put big bows on and pears in. They'd never seen anything like it before. I made it like

Dingles – that was the firm in Manchester that had all the fruit shops. I made it very classy, because Altrincham was a high-class place. They used to come in in jodhpurs and the old riding bree-ches, 'Good morning', and all that. I really got it going. Introduced fish and rabbits, which they had never sold before, turkeys and chickens and all that. All in nine weeks. I was employed by the Co-op. I used to get there at seven o'clock in the morning in a little old Ford Popular – eh, happy memories this – get there, sort the job out and then the staff would start arriving about quarter to eight. There was an old girl there called Mrs Horwich, a lovely lady, and she said, 'You've made a right go of this place. I've never seen it so busy – and the staff are happy, because we all have a laugh.' Muriel, an Irish girl, she worked there, and a girl called Freda. They were sad to see me go after that nine weeks.

Bernard Manning's Embassy Club opened on the night of Friday, 11 December 1959. (It was later restyled Bernard Manning's WORLD FAMOUS Embassy Club, a name that seems a touch ironical, seeing as it is strictly a Manchester institution. The ironic tag was borrowed in the 1990s by Jack Dee, whose Channel 4 show was set in a mythical 'World Famous Bohemia Club'. Bernard, however, does not see world famous as anything other than a statement of fact, and has numerous examples of foreign visitors, especially from Australia, who have sought out the Embassy Club on trips to Britain.)

Not as yet world famous, John and Bernard Manning were a somewhat worried father and son team when they opened the doors on the first night, but their anxiety soon evaporated. Customers from the Northern Sporting Club (which could not withstand the competition and closed twelve months later) joined scores of the local Bernard fans who had packed out the Oldham Empire six years earlier for his first big professional gig. The opening act was a singer called Sheila Buxton, who was a great draw at the time. She was a Lancashire girl, and a big recording star with the North-ern Dance Orchestra. The first song Bernard, the twenty-nine-year-old nightclub proprietor, sang, appropriately enough, was 'High Hopes'; thirty-seven years later, he still often opens nights at the Embassy with the same song.

The look and atmosphere of the club was set, almost in concrete, on that first evening, and has never changed, surviving even the original structure being burned to the ground in 1987 and the club being rebuilt in the precise image of its original self. The Embassy Club was, and remains, a barely prettified working-men's club, with harsh lighting, Formica-topped tables and hard-working, white-jacketed waiters sweating under the weight of trays of brimming pint glasses. The club has been described as 'an ashtray with lights, the sort of place where you wipe your feet on the way out'. There was a large area devoted to snooker tables, the last remnant of the building's original purpose, except that the tables no longer had any hint of temperance about them, as they were part of what Bernard named the Leisure Bar, a vast drinking den.

Virtually on the opening night it dawned on John Manning, and his son too to some extent, just what an extraordinary business the Embassy was going to be compared to the greengrocery. The roar of the greasepaint, the smell of the crowd were one thing, but what entranced the Manning and Father partnership almost as much were the positively thrilling profit margins.

We went overnight from taking hundreds of pounds a week, to thousands. And the beauty of the club business is there is no waste. With a greengrocer's, you can see cauliflowers deteriorating before your eyes, lettuces going limp, and, if they're not sold, getting thrown away and your profit gets thrown away with 'em. Saturday afternoon, a hot, sunny day, and you'd see food wilting before your eyes. Berries from Poland starting to run and run, and you'd know they were all going to be ballsed up for Monday morning, all got to be slung. Bananas ripening, going yellow, then getting spotted, then they'd go black and they have to be thrown away. With beer, it lasts for months and months in a barrel. We couldn't believe it. With no waste, it's like liquid gold. Me dad and I used to joke about it, the difference in the businesses. All you do with beer is keep serving it. And any bad beer you get, just cork it up, sent it back to the brewery and get credit for it. Magic.

The club was a roaring, seven-nights-a-week success. 'There was money, no depression, you opened your doors, got a good star on, a great atmosphere, a nice club, waiter service, you couldn't miss,'

Bernard says. 'They were queued up at the door at seven o'clock at night to get in for eight. Straight across the board, business people, old people, young people.' From the start, the Embassy evening began and ended quite early. This was another canny Manning calculation. Just because he had his own club – and was shortly to open two others, the Palladium and the Wilton, both demolished after a few years – Bernard's appeal around Lancashire as a performer did not diminish. He was still wanted at other people's clubs, and he did not see the Embassy as an obstacle to that. 'I used to fetch the people in, my name got bigger if anything, and then this agent used to get me jobs at other clubs in Bolton and Preston. In them days club life was really big.' He started travelling on after finishing at the Embassy to do one and sometimes two more gigs a night. At sixty-six, he is still following the same punishing schedule – punishing, that is, to anyone but a workaholic, to whom it is positively therapeutic. In the sixties, when the Embassy, the Wilton and the Palladium were all running, Bernard's routine was almost superhuman. Not only was he playing at all three every night, plus another gig or two elsewhere, but he was spending the days going from one club to the next doing practical jobs – everything from lighting the boiler to putting up Christmas decorations.

The Mannings' guiding principle as far as booking acts for the Embassy and its satellites was concerned was to keep the cost down. But in common with other cheap and cheerful northern venues of the times – the Cavern Club in Liverpool being one – concentrating on economically priced local talent meant that some of the trendiest performers in the country turned up for a few pounds at the Embassy. The club rapidly established itself as hot. The acts Bernard had seen in other clubs recently and made a note to book as soon as the Embassy got going included Matt Monro (£30 a week), Mike Yarwood (£40), Jimmy Tarbuck (£5 a night), Vince Hill (£10), and Freddie Starr, then working as Freddie Stark and the Delmonts (£175 a week to share between them).

Being both the proprietor and a singer and a comic in his own right gave Bernard an unusual, and often highly critical, perspective on the show-business hopefuls that came through the Embassy Club. Although he has repeatedly tried to argue that his famously disparaging remarks about fellow performers are merely part of his act, a gimmick, and not designed to wound, it is probably fair to say that they go a little deeper than that. It took a confident man, or at least one who wanted to appear confident, to break the unwritten rule among comedians not to slag off each other's acts. Being the boss, a theatre manager in effect, before he was thirty encouraged a latent authoritarianism – 'He ran the place like a drill sergeant,' says his son, who was running around the club almost as soon as he could walk. Then there was a big-headedness, which his old Army pal Len Astill, among others, had noticed developing in Bernard. He had packed an enormous amount into the few years since National Service, and enjoyed more ego trips – from getting out of some lousy duties in the Army to marrying the notably pretty Vera to seeing audiences collapse in laughter around him – than any of his contemporaries would ever experience. Bernard's favourite-son-turned-family-top-dog, status, was an important factor too, as was the fact that he had taken a business gamble and won within days, overturning any lingering doubts his father might have had over his son's abilities.

Then there were the more negative, defensive sides to Bernard's character, all of which made his unpopular (but entertaining) role as slagger-off-in-chief of other comedians the easier to explain. The Oscar Rabin episode had not exactly been a fiasco, but it still took some passing off as a triumph. Bernard had enjoyed dipping his toe into big-time show business, but scalded it all the same. After walking out on the band, he had deliberately recast himself as the provincial cousin, and would always find it difficult not to feel something of a show-business outsider from then on. The intensely family nature of the Embassy Club, right down to having his old mum on the till – it was more reminiscent of a circus ethos than that of a nightclub – intensified a waggons-in-a-circle attitude to the broader, and perhaps more sophisticated, outside world of showbiz. Even in 1959, it would have been easy to predict that Bernard Manning would never become a golf-playing celeb with a mansion in Surrey. 'I have nothing in common with surgeons and suchlike,' he would say.

Act after act, they came to the Embassy, to be met by Bernard's increasingly baleful eye and razor wit. Cannon and Ball were hired for a week as the Harper brothers, two ex-welders from Oldham. 'I had to fire them,' says Bernard. 'It's never a nice thing to do. But when an act is dying on its bum, you have to tell them they can't stay on the rest of the week. I had to be tough. They took it badly, but they could see for themselves they hadn't gone down well. They came off the stage to the sound of their own footsteps. I told them they would never get away with all that braces stuff and Come on Tommy and Rock on Tommy. Now when they walk past me, they just raise one finger.'

Little and Large came in 1962 as semi-professionals, Bernard explaining that he was putting them on as a joke, and to find out how good they were. 'I went on stage one night and did all the gags in their act. Then I introduced them, with everyone listening hard. To give them their due, they did very well. But halfway through, Eddie gave up. He said to the audience, "Whatever Bernard says goes for me too," and walked off.' Little and Large, who were earning £44 a week between them in their day job, were staggered to be offered £55 for a week's work at the Embassy – and staggered again when Bernard told them they were expected for their fee to include performances at the Palladium and the Wilton clubs after they had finished at the Embassy.

Yarwood, he said he didn't rate. 'I paid him £40. And I'd give him the same today. He's still doing the same act. No, he's changed. He used to have a Lancashire accent. Now he speaks like an Oxford graduate.' He criticised Tarbuck on almost identical grounds. 'As Tarby walked on to the stage, he knocked a waiter's tray flying, and it went all over the place, so that was a great start. But that was the only round of applause he got. I was paying Tarby £5 a night then. And he can come back for the same amount of money now, because he's still doing the same act too. His father was a bookmaker, and he was one of the first losers.'

Of another unfortunate, Craig Douglas, Bernard said, 'He was diabolical, unbelievably bad. If he can sing I'll show my bum in the Vatican.' Stan Stennett, an actor from *Crossroads* trying a bit of comedy on the side, was another. 'He could have got picked up for talking to himself,' Bernard commented. A cousin of Helen Shapiro, a lad of about twenty-three, came in as a singer. 'He was terrible,' recalls Alma. 'He had the worst voice I've ever heard in my life. He was just working on his cousin's name. When he came off, Bernard said to him, "You're as rough as a monkey's arse. I am sorry, lad, but don't give up your day job." We never heard any more of him.'

The Beatles on the other hand were a huge success, but to the Mannings, just another act on the conveyor belt. 'To be quite honest they were just another group,' recalls Rene, while Bernard recounts:

> The Beatles, aye. They were fourteen quid and they just did a one-off show. It was about three quarters of an hour. I rated them. All nice boys, got there dressed, went on and did the show and buggered off. That John Lennon drove me potty, because he wanted a dressing room with a washbasin. What did he want that for? You come here to work, not to wash. But we used to get a lot of groups from Liverpool. I didn't really think they were going to be that big. Now there was a group called The Chants from Liverpool, an all-coloured group. They were fantastic, and they became The Real Thing and they made it. I saw one of them with his dog who won a prize at Crufts not long ago.

Bernard's comprehensive role in show business made him unique, even then. From booking the stars of the day to dealing with draymen, he delegated almost nothing. 'No matter how late he gets home, four or five in the morning, he is always up at eight to supervise the daily beer delivery,' Vera once told the *Sunday Mirror*. 'He goes down to the club in his braces to wait for the beer to arrive. He stands out in front and waves to people on the buses.'

His daily routine has barely altered, except that the club now operates three nights of the week rather than seven, the club scene today being that much quieter than it was in its glory.

> First of all you had to get there early of a morning and set all the room out from the night before. All the stools were stacked by the waiters, so the cleaners would do the floor and the toilets and get everywhere looking sparkling. Then you'd do the chairs and put the tables out, put an ashtray on, all the drip mats on ready for the night, making it all ready for when the punters came in. We'd stock the shelves up, replenish all the bottles, drain all the dregs from the barrels in the cellar, cork them all up and send them back to

the brewery. Then the brewery would come with more beer, then you would stillage that, because there was no keg beer in them days, very little anyway, and everything was from the wood, so everything had to be looked after. Me dad knew what he was doing, and he taught me. I could run a cellar now. I could go in any cellar in any hotel and run it for them and they would know that the beer would be spot on.

Not very surprisingly, working with alcohol diminished any slight alcoholic tendency Bernard might have been developing as a younger man. 'People look at me and think, he's a boozer, but I don't drink at all, not since the Army. But I let 'em think that I do, because I am in the business of selling ale. When you're a licensee, you can soon become an alcoholic, but it's not business-like to be half pissed talking to customers. I soon found that out in the old days, when I was drinking fourteen bottles of beer a night at one time. It could just push you over the edge. You've got to use your brains.'

Junior

Me serious side is me family. Cut one of us, and we all bleed.

Bernard Manning, when asked what he takes seriously

Inside three months of the Embassy Club opening, Vera was pregnant, and Young Bernard (as Bernard's son now fears he will be known until he is at least ninety) was born in November 1960. It was a routine pregnancy, and a delighted Bernard Senior that rushed Vera into the car and off to Crumpsall Hospital in the middle of the night, when labour started. It being 1960, Bernard naturally was not there for the birth, which was a difficult one.

Next morning, I went in and there he was. I remember going for him too. Carrying him in the little old carry cot. The first time I saw him, absolute magic. It is a great feeling, you know, one of the best feelings of your life when you have a son. He was a jolly little lad. Even when he was born, he was smiling. I remember holding him for the first time. He was eight pounds, as bald as a badger and I couldn't believe he was mine. I was so looking forward to fatherhood I had the lad named before Vera had a look in. She couldn't understand why I called him Bernard. Every time she shouted we both came running.

Bernard did more in the way of childcare than many other fathers of that time. He was neither nervous nor unused to dealing with a small child thanks to his experience of looking after Frank and the girls when he was a boy. 'It made no difference for me. I was used to making the old porridge and sticking a bit of cream in the milk, getting the boiled eggs, right, come on get your clothes on, all that. And Young Bernard was no worry. He was a robust little boy, never ailed. Big blue eyes, blond curly hair, always playing football and wanting to get out and play sports.'

Bernard looks back on the late 1950s and 1960s through a heat haze of sentiment and fondly recalled spoiling Young Bernard – he was an indulgent father and an indulgent, though possessive, husband – and it is not at all difficult to understand the depth of his contentment. 'Young Bernard had a little football team round there, and I bought them all jackets and kits,' he reminisces. 'They were never out of the Clough, the park. There's a putting green and they used to play there, and the top fields where he used to play cricket. You could always see him – I can see him waving now.'

'Our Bernard loves our Little Bernard so much,' Vera said in an early interview. (Although he is now referred to universally as Young Bernard, he was Little Bernard until the age of eleven.) 'Every time our Bernard comes home he hugs our Little Bernard and tells him how much he loves him.' For Bernard Senior, another aspect of love was that, as he puts it, the boy 'always had plenty of money in his pockets'. 'My dad spoiled me rotten with pocket money and presents,' Young Bernard, now thirty-six, confirms. 'My mates got 50p a week and I got a fiver. I always had the best football boots and the best tracksuit. For my eighteenth birthday, he bought me a Daimler Sovereign. Dad loved giving me electronic gadgets at Christmas but he always forgot to buy batteries and transformers. Every year I'd be in tears, and he'd have to ask a mate who owned an electrical shop to bring some over.'

The copious money in the household, his only-child status plus his father's oft-stated attitude that 'My son can have what I didn't have' (even though Bernard Senior's childhood poverty is, to some extent, a myth that has become the hoarier for its frequent retelling) made money a bit of a problem for Young Bernard, a gentle, intelligent and thoughtful man today. 'I could sense how much money was coming in, and I would want things then because I was a kid. So I always had the best of everything,' he sighs. 'I had to learn to handle that.'

Bernard Senior's emotional profligacy spread to the area of discipline. 'I only ever hit Young Bernard once and I still remember it as if it were yesterday,' he grieves. 'He was three and running around the living room. I told him to calm down, but he kept going. Then, bang! He went straight through a pair of glass sliding doors. There wasn't a scratch on him but he could have killed himself. I was shaking with fright. I grabbed him and smacked his legs. It was a reflex action. He started crying and I went to pieces. It was the worst day of my life. I often tell him about it but he says he can't remember. I wish I could forget.'

Bernard's indulgence was directed at his parents too.

Me dad would be on the bowling green if it was a good summer. I'd pass the green, and he'd give me a wave as I was going to the Embassy Club. You see, my dad had trusted me, and suddenly he had the best living of his life. He used to travel the world with me mum, go on cruises. I used to take him on me jobs to the Hilton. He met Harold Wilson – Harold liked his drink. If people knew the things he laughed at, he'd never have been elected. My dad couldn't believe it. He met all the boxers you can think of, James L. Braddock that fought Joe Lewis, Tommy Farr, Henry Cooper, all the big sportsmen's dinners – I used to do them at the Hilton and the Dorchester, Jack Solomons, the big promoter; I used to do all his stuff at the Dorchester. Big suite there, I couldn't believe it, big bureau there in the room, adjoining bathroom and room service. Me dad couldn't believe what it was like.

And Vera got on with everybody. There's never been any trouble in this family with anybody, thank God. I loved her every day. She wanted for nothing. I used to have the house decorated and carpets put in regularly, bought her diamond rings galore. I used to send her on cruises – I don't like going away, lying on beaches in Bermuda shorts; I don't want to know. I like to build and see the business doing right, but her and Bernard, I've got photographs of them shaking hands with the captains on the P&O liners, going on cruises here there and everywhere.

Surprisingly, perhaps, for a nominally Catholic family, the question of having more children never really arose. Young Bernard's birth had been hard on Vera, and she was not looking forward to repeating the experience. Bernard, however, tells it a little differently. 'If they came, they came. I didn't take precautions or anything like that, oh, no, none of that. But we didn't have them. I was never bothered, me. I had a son, one to carry the name on and all that carry on, and the girls – my sisters – used to make a fuss of him. If you took him round to their houses, you couldn't get him home again. "Can he stop the night?" and all that, because they had no children so they used to commandeer him.' Of the five Manning children, only Jack, the eldest, had a brood of children. After Jack divorced, all seven children stayed with their mother and became effectively estranged from the rest of the Manning family.

Bernard's mother remained an enormous influence on him.

Me gran was the only one who could tell him how it was going to be (Young Bernard recalls). She was the only person he was really frightened of. He would probably keep things from her because he was frightened of letting her know something. For one thing, until the day she died she thought he wasn't that rude on stage. I don't think he wanted her to know how bad he was. She worked in the club but she was deaf as a post. Someone told me when the tax men used to come to the Embassy Club to see the books, which she did, she used to turn the hearing aid up so it just whistled and after about ten minutes they would go because they had had enough.

Another thing was that she never liked him gambling, and she would give him a right old telling off for picking the phone up too often to the bookie. He didn't stop, but he would have to pick his moments to ring the bookie, make sure she was in the back. Even though me dad was a bit of a law unto himself, he was very respectful to both his mum and dad. But she used to nag him about it – 'All this hard work you do, and you go and put it on a horse. You can lose, you know.' And he'd say, 'Yes, but you can win.' It's all you get off him – he doesn't tell you about the ones that lose, only the winners.

Vera obviously came under Nellie's jurisdiction as well, but the mother–daughter-in-law relationship was, by Young Bernard's account, a good one.

She just understood that she married into that family and had to go with it, and I think she was quite happy, because she had a good lifestyle. There were never any bust-ups as far as I can remember between mum and gran. They spoke every day on the phone, because obviously me mum was involved with the club as well so they would be talking about the general day-to-day running of the club, people that worked for them, the takings and how things were going. Me mum and me gran were very good at watching what went on at the club, obviously looking at it from a protective point of view, because me dad, when he goes out on stage, doesn't see a lot, and then he'll go on to another club.

Bernard's tendency – in fact the mainspring of his personality – to be a controlling man was as plainly visible at home (even within the constraints of his mother's influence) as it was at the Embassy Club, where he wouldn't even have half a pint, so that he could keep the sharpest of eyes on proceedings at all times. So devoted was he to home that he refused to leave Lewis Avenue at all if he could avoid it. He forbade swearing or even mildly smutty jokes at home. Then, as he announced in a *Sunday Mirror* interview, in which he clearly hammed up a Manning manifesto for the traditional, northern husband, but meant most of it: 'I won't wash pots, I won't go shopping, I won't knock a nail in the wall. My job is to be a comic and bring the money in. You might say it's a caveman's approach to marriage, but at least we're still living together in the same cave.' He was intensely protective of Vera: 'If I found out that anyone had been getting at Vera on account of me, I'd be round their house, and what I'd do to them would make the Kray twins look like a couple of choir boys,' he snarled. (As of his sixty-sixth year, it has to be said that Bernard has yet to threaten anyone with physical violence, let alone to punch them.)

'We had quite a weird family set up,' reflects Young Bernard today. 'Me dad was always on the road, so you didn't see him. Mum was always at home, so they saw very little of each other, a couple of hours a day. So as a kid, I couldn't assess whether they confided in one another. I knew they were very close and did love each other, but he had his lifestyle and did what he had to do to become successful and she was happy at home, being an old-fashioned housewife and looking after me.'

At the club, the received wisdom was that Vera's notably head-down, eyes-averted attitude on the cash desk was the result of Bernard banning her from smiling at people, but the truth was that Vera was simply very shy:

I'm the quiet one, the one who gives in. His home means a lot to him. It's a place where he can escape, where he can loll around in his underpants all day if he wants to (she once explained). I've been a home bird all my life. Bernard's always wanted to know where I was, what time I was going out and what time I was coming in. He's so possessive it makes me laugh. He once joked that the only time he would let me go out of the house without him would be in a wooden box, and even then he would be right behind me. Isn't that morbid? If I didn't like it, I would have cleared off long ago. I knew he had old-fashioned ideas before we married. He told me straight that my place was in the home, and that's where he expected me to be.

The true relationship between the Mannings was built on a more equal, and a more subtle, basis. Vera had total faith in Bernard. He would never stay away and fuel any suspicion she might harbour about infidelity, even if he was performing miles away. 'He has never spent a night away from here yet,' Vera said in the Embassy Club's heyday. 'Even if he has to walk home he'll do it, no matter where he plays, he always comes home at night. Usually it's the middle of the night. He can't stand hotels. And he likes to go to his mother's house nearly every day for lunch.'

'I'm not jealous of the other women who want to know him,' she told a probing *Sunday People* reporter once. 'Bernard says he'd rather have a pan of potato hash. I think when you live with someone you really know them. He might have a little flirt – but it never takes over.' Although Vera was shy with most customers, Bernard, for his part, was quite happy for her to chat to regulars. And, since her husband was disinclined to leave the club for even a moment to take a holiday, she was given the freedom to go away, usually on cruises, with Young Bernard, or, on occasion, with her girlfriends. So used was the lad to the family tradition that dad stayed at home for holidays that, beyond a mild curiosity as to why other people's fathers went on holiday and his didn't, he barely thought about what those cruises might have been like with his dad there.

There was far more to Bernard's and Vera's marriage than him just pampering her ('All this for me, and he wears big plastic cufflinks,' she would say) and her submitting to his quirky whims, such as naming their child after himself. Bernard and Vera shared the same likes and dislikes of TV programmes, of valuing respect for elders, and being straight with each other all the time. 'We're like that young couple,' he loved to say, 'who got married. The fella had terrible stinking feet and the girl had awful bad breath. On the wedding night they both decided to be straight with each other and tell each other about their problems. So the bloke threw his socks into the bathroom, climbed into bed, turned out the light and said, "Darling, there's something I must tell you." The girl interrupted him: "No, darling, there's something I must tell you."

"I think I know what it is," said the bloke. "You've just eaten my socks." '

The heavily done-up semi in Lewis Avenue, abutting as it did a sea of *Coronation Street*-style terraces, along with the interior decor the Mannings chose for their home, always fascinated the journalists – mostly middle-class southerners – who started to travel up to Manchester to interview Bernard when he first made it on television at the beginning of the 1970s. The furniture at number 34 was certainly not G-Plan, which was the contemporary modern look, but neither was it quite the freakish aesthetic nightmare that reporters found it. Joe Steeples of the *Sun* judged that the house looked 'like a cross between the Taj Mahal and the Co-op'. Noreen Taylor of the *Sunday Mirror* wrote: 'The taxi driver had no doubt where comedian Bernard Manning lived. "You can't miss it," he said. "It's like bloody Disneyland." He was so right. The Mannings' home looks like a mini Taj Mahal in the humble street of a Manchester suburb. Inside, it's breathtaking – a sort of palace struggling to escape from a small semi-detached.' Peter Dacre of the *Sunday Express* described Bernard's 'back-to-back corner semi-detached house' (it wasn't anything like a back-to-back, but might conceivably have been mistaken for one by a southerner) as 'a plushy mixture of the modern and neo-antique with a metal chimney piece and tropical fish tanks built into both sides of the electric fire. The wall above is covered with an array of metal shields, swords and reproduction ancient pistols.' Another *Sunday Mirror* reporter on Bernard's trail, Gordon Blair, wrote: 'His home is a modest semi. Or it was modest until he had it painted white and stuck wagon wheels in the garden. Among the terraced houses in this road in

Blackley, Manchester, it looks like a national monument.'

Blair, noting Bernard's habit (and it was hard not to) of receiving visitors in his vest and Y-fronts, brilliantly described him as looking like 'a suburban Sumo wrestler'. Bernard and Vera (who sounds as if she could have been the prototype for Caroline Hook's Mrs Merton) were perfectly disingenuous about sly journalistic inquiries as to the inspiration for their homemaking style. 'The house is just how he likes it – nice and homely. He won't move in case it brings us bad luck,' Vera would say, adding, 'We don't have parties and friends in for a drink. He doesn't like people in our house.'

Bernard's insistence on staying put in Blackley, effectively part of Harpurhey, despite his growing wealth, seemed something close to an affectation to anyone not atuned to his genuine craving to cling to his roots. For Bernard, to stay faithful to his background was not a simple matter of taking the odd, nostalgic cruise in a limousine around the streets of his childhood. Short of living in the middle of a busy road on the actual site of his parents' home, sticking in Lewis Avenue was the finest way he could pay tribute to his roots, as well as stay close to the preoccupations of working-class people – an affinity which would get him into trouble with the wider public before very long. The matter barely needed explanation as far as he was concerned: 'I could have bought mansions,' he said in a 1979 interview. 'Bleedin' hell! What would I do with a mansion? I was born down the road; when I was a lad I used to deliver news-papers to this house. I always wanted to buy it. I've put everything in it, even an electric shower.'

On the quiet, the elegant Vera actually longed to move out somewhere smarter. Bernard would tell her she could have anything she liked, as long as she didn't ask him to move from the house. Because she and Bernard never quarrelled, she would never complain.

Me mum and dad got on wonderfully, and she was very under-standing (explains Young Bernard). She just said, right, that's the way it is. I know she often asked if it would be possible – like somebody going to the headmaster and asking – to move to a nicer area and a nicer house, maybe into Cheshire. But no way. He's so into the area, it's unbelievable. He just wouldn't be happy in

Knutsford or Cheadle. He wants to be on the north side of Manchester, where his business is, where he relates to people. Jack, his older brother, and him used to meet at me gran's house every day for breakfast and talk about business. That would have gone. And you have to remember that he spends all day long bouncing things off people that are on his wavelength, and he can communicate with those people. Honestly, if you put him in the middle of Cheshire, he would be probably lost with those types. He's never been into houses or flash suits. He's just not interested, totally unaffected by it. You know how these showbiz people are – 'Darling, how are you?' and all that   you couldn't put me dad in the same room as those people because he would have to say something.

The fact that he scorned snobbery and insincerity did not mean for a minute that Bernard had a disregard for money. Far from it; he was in awe of cash, and the security it brought as the stuff started to pile up around him, especially after he hit the big time on TV in the early 1970s. His charge for cabaret appearances went up almost overnight from £15 or so to £2000 or £3000. 'It was like winning the pools for him, really, it was like a windfall,' Young Bernard says. He tells a story which echoes how, twenty-five years on from being a paper boy and delighting in handing his tips to his mother, Bernard was doing precisely the same, albeit on a vastly larger scale, for Vera. 'I remember one time getting up in the morning before going to school. Me dad had obviously been out late working, and on this little kitchen table we had, in that modest little house, there was what must have £500 spread on the table where me dad had come in and taken it out of his pockets and thrown it on the table for me mum. And I was there looking at all this money.'

Bernard saw his frugality as yet another quality that set him apart from the showbiz world, of which he was determinedly not a member anyway. As he explained to an interviewer from the *News of the World* in 1976:

A lot of people in show business muddle their way through. They don't pay their tax on time, then turn round, find a bill for £20,000 to £30,000 pounds, but they have blown the lot. That's when the trouble starts – there are rows about money and the home starts breaking up. I always remember Bob Hope's words: 'Show business is a funny business. One day you are drinking the wine, the next day you are treading the grapes.' I'm drinking the wine now, but I'm not going back to treading.

Money and spoiling were obviously a major factor in the father–son relationship, but the drip-down effects of fame also played their part. The most obvious of these, of course, was that celebrity dictated the two did not spend an enormous amount of time together. Home lover though he was, Bernard's punishing schedule, from overseeing the draymen early in the morning to performing at the Embassy Club and others until early the following morning, meant that Young Bernard's upbringing was largely in the hands of a tribe of women, unmonstrous though they were. Mother (herself at the club each evening), grandmother – a special influence, quite a hard woman, although not one Young Bernard remembers very clearly – the childless aunties, Alma and Rene, and a childminder called Jane (who helped him with his homework and watched the telly with him) were the fixed points in the boy's routine; dad was a special, and adored, treat.

Young Bernard's happiest childhood memory is of one of these special occasions when Bernard Senior decided not to spend the entire afternoon resting for that evening's show, but to take Young Bernard to the park.

He took me to Boggart Hall Clough, a very famous park in Manchester, a lovely place then, before it was hit by vandals. We went to the boating lake, about five or six of us little kids and me dad. He was at one end of the boat, and the five of us were at the other, and I still maintain that his end was in the water and us lot were right up in the air, looking down at him. I was really worried, because I thought he was going to go under. There were little bits of water coming over. All me pals were laughing – 'Look at your dad' – and the boat was up in the air. He was pretty good with kids. With my own kids now, he'll spend hours with them, he gets down on the carpet or goes out the back to play football with them, and every day he's got a little present for them.

Young Bernard was five years old when he realised his father was famous.

I always remember him taking us to the football matches, to Manchester City on a Saturday afternoon. We always used to pick up his father outside the Conservative Club, and then we'd go down in me dad's Mark 2 Jaguar – this is the sixties. City were a great side then, with sixty thousand going to watch them and wiping the floor with United every week. I remember the atmosphere and people recognising me dad. He has a lot of charisma in public places, and people were always going 'Hiya, Bernard' and he'd say 'Hello, son' to them, and he would always have a little joke to tell or a quip. Then we might walk through and see a player, Colin Bell, sometimes. Bell would come and shake my hand – and he was my hero. I was quite proud that people knew him. Then there'd be the match, and we'd drive home. One time, me dad had a bump in the car, and he wanted to drag this fellow out of the car – he got out, and he wanted to kill him. He can be very short-tempered, as I can. Those Saturday afternoons were really the only time I had with my dad because he was so busy. But then, as he got busier and busier, going to the match fell by the wayside, because me dad, when he goes to the game, he gets that involved he loses his voice and he screams and shouts and gets mithered with people. So he stopped going because of that.

At this stage, Bernard was still a strictly local celebrity, a well-known Manchester club owner, but that was about it, as far as fame went. Young Bernard helped his father in the business some mornings, much as any willing child might, had the family firm been a greengrocer's rather than a nightclub. He would stack bottles on shelves and hump beer crates, so was perfectly aware of the scene Bernard operated in, and weekly at football saw the result of being well-known in the area, but the idea of his father as any kind of star would have been laughable. He was aware that his father *knew* stars, but that was part of his work, and not very remarkable. When Young Bernard was ten, however, Bernard Senior became a household name himself, whom the boy's mates saw on TV, and things changed.

Young Bernard's friends at school would say, 'Hey your dad was on TV last night,' and an edge of jealousy would creep in. Much of this problem was caused by his father's stubborn, and in every way commendable, refusal to move from a working-class area. In a strange way, becoming rich and famous and yet staying in his own part of town was a warp in the natural order of things, and it distorted life a little for Young Bernard, as it did for Vera, who was so keen to move out to somewhere where the family would not be so anomalous. Young Bernard was a big lad, and luckily good at sports too, which meant he never got beaten up; had he been the fat boy with the finest football boots and tennis racket on the block but no idea of how to use them, childhood might have been a scarring experience. Instead, Young Bernard has grown up to echo some of his father's ethos rather than reject it. He lives in a beautiful and tasteful house, sends his kids to a private school, and even likes alternative comedians, but he still lives and works not far from Harpurhey, and has the same friends now as when he was a boy. 'We still live in an area which is very working class, my friends are working-class people and the people I deal with are working class. We could move somewhere more upmarket, like Bowden (the smartest suburb of Manchester) but we'd be back the next week. I couldn't live that way. I can mix with people like that. I could go out for a night in Bowden and talk "Bowden". Unlike my dad, I could adapt, but I don't want to.' (Whether Bernard Senior – who has boasted that he has always lived, worked and will die within 300 yards of where he was born – would agree that his son has kept the geographical faith, is debatable. For Bernard Senior, his son's move to Rochdale, all of a twenty-minute drive away, must be akin to the boy having emigrated.)

Young Bernard has adjusted to fame: 'Every day I'll hear someone say, "That's Bernard Manning's son." I don't suppose it will ever be "That's Bernard Manning", will it, but I have learnt to live with that. Rather than making him bitter or tortured, being Bernard's son has left him philosophical. He talks about writing his own account one day of growing up as the son of Bernard Manning. 'I've been very, very lucky, but I know in my own mind, without being big-headed, that I have had a different life from most people in this area, from the normal son of Joe Bloggs. It's really been very strange.'

One of the oddities was that although Young Bernard could grasp the concept of his father being a star – indeed, was surrounded by reminders of the fact – he did not truly understand how good Bernard was at his job until his late teens. Bernard Senior will say that his son didn't tell him how good he was until he was sixteen, and saw him play the MGM Grand in Las Vegas. Young Bernard places the dawning of this realisation almost two years later when he was seventeen.

He was working at a club in Leeds, Batley Variety Club, I believe, which held about two thousand. He never asked me whether I wanted to go at that age but, for whatever reason, that night he asked if I wanted to come, and I said, 'Yeah, I'd love to go.' I was backstage, and he was doing his act, and I could hear the crowd laughing, and I thought I'd have a peep through the curtains. I was directly behind the drummer, who was just to the right, and there was this little slit in the curtain. I got behind it and peeped through, and it really dawned on me how brave you have got to be as a comedian on your own. There was just him and this audience, two thousand heads beyond him, and he had them in the palm of his hand, screaming for more. It really brought a lump to my throat. I was so proud. I have never told him that. We don't talk about feelings – he finds it just as difficult to talk about personal things. He'd rather make a joke of it. But I have got every respect for him. He does things the way he does them and, although I don't agree with everything he does, he has been a success.'

The question of Young Bernard's own prospects for success inevitably surfaced at about this time, and Bernard's shadow loomed over them. Young Bernard's education was skeletal and, by being lenient as ever, Bernard Senior did remarkably little to help put any academic flesh on the bones. Young Bernard came out of school with nothing apart from a cycling proficiency badge. 'All I did was play football and swim and go to the clubs at night, so I didn't really come out with a great education, just a bit of savvy really, common sense.'

There was no question that he had ability and application. Although at senior school he was hopeless at maths and English, he got good marks in subjects that interested him, especially history and geography. While he now downplays his academic ability, Little Bernard had done well enough at primary school to be close to the top of the class, and only failed his Eleven Plus by one mark. The headmaster of his primary school recognised Little Bernard's ability, and came straight round to Lewis Avenue to talk to Bernard and Vera when the bad news about the Eleven Plus came. The story Young Bernard relates of that visit could serve as a warning to any parent tempted to be too benevolent to an adored child.

> The headmaster was a lovely fellow called Jim Kelly, and he said to me dad, 'Look, we can't understand why Bernard has failed, but it doesn't matter, because if you want him to go to a grammar school, or to pay for him to go to a boarding school – we're talking public school here, because he realised me dad had a few quid – he can go wherever he wants. I can sort it out for you. What do you want to do?' Me dad sat there in his underpants and said, 'What do you want to do, son?' And I said, 'I want to go with me mates round the corner,' because I just wanted to play on the same football team – that's all I could think of. The decision should have been made by me dad really and he didn't make that decision; he put it all on me at eleven years of age. Mr Kelly was a bit perplexed, a bit, like, oh, all right, OK. Me mum was happy for me to go where I was happy, so I ended up at St Anthony's, which was literally fifty yards round the corner. It was a little secondary modern, pretty rough type of school and, although I loved it there, with hindsight I think maybe I should have made the decision to go a bit better than that. Of course, I would have hated boarding school, but I could have gone to a grammar school in the area which might have given me a little better education. As it is, the only education I have got is the school of life through me dad, even though it really doesn't matter any more, because I've not done bad.

When it came to education, Bernard continued to be hands off in the extreme as a parent, rarely if ever attending open evenings, and only once turning up to see Young Bernard in a school play. This,

1939: Bernard, Alma, Nellie,
and Frank the baby.

Chirpy chappie: Bernard as a greengrocer's
lad and part-time singer, aged 16.

Bernard and Vera's wedding, 1956.

Nellie and John Manning,
1956, at the wedding.

Lads out on the town: Jimmy, Bernard, Don and Harold.

(below) The loyal subject: The Queen meets Bernard, the London Palladium, 1972. Lord Grade looks on.

Margaret Thatcher meets Bernard.

(right) Vera and Young Bernard in the place Bernard Senior would never venture if he could help it – abroad. They stopped off in Venice on a cruise.

The house in Lewis Avenue, where Bernard and family lived for 30 years. Abutting Coronation Street terraces, the ornamental wall, he says, cost more than the house.

Young Bernard and Dad.

A Friday night out in the Embassy Club, Manchester, July 1996.

(left & below) Bernard Manning in Las Vegas, 1978. (*Scope*)

Ironic or what? Bernard and the
'World Famous' Embassy Club,
July 1996.

(right) Bernard hits the London
alternative nightspot, Jongleurs:
he got a standing ovation.
(*Mike Lawn for Sky TV*)

World famous at last: Bernard's photo adorns an Amsterdam bus shelter. The Generale Bank took to his 'cynical face'. (*Marje Alleman*)

I laf, you pay. Bernard and his Roller.

Bernard and DJ Lainey D, whom he spotted in 1995 and hired. 'If people have a problem with Bernard Manning, that's their problem,' she said. (*Kevin Fitzpatrick*)

Alma (left) and Rene, Cornwall, 1996.

Bernard with Young Bernard, daughter-in-law Julie, Chloe, Hayley and Ben, July 1996.

Bernard and Mum on her 90th birthday.

Frank Manning with son Billy – who is now down for Eton.

Thoughts from the green chair.
(*Jillian Edelstein*)

(right) Mr Bernard Manning at home:
dressed to impress. (*Jillian Edelstein*)

A winter Manchester gloom descends in
sympathy on Bernard Manning Drive,
Duncraig, Western Australia.

Young Bernard says, was at his own insistence. He was uneasy about performing in front of his father. 'I was a sensitive teenager, and dad's stardom niggled me, especially since I wanted to be an actor. I banned him and my mum from coming to see me in school plays in case I was terrible and he was disappointed. I know my aunties came with my mum, but they did it under cover, and me gran came too. But me dad didn't apart from once, when he sneaked into one. I was fourteen, and playing half of a comedy duo in *Viva Mexico*. He said I was brilliant. I was secretly touched that he took the trouble to come but I couldn't find the words to tell him.'

The funniness factor had become another consideration in the father–son relationship; Young Bernard was expected to be funny among his friends – a duty he discharged admirably and enjoyed – but the possibility of being assessed by his father's professional eye and, worse still, criticised, was a daunting one, so he baulked at being funny on stage, got nervous and, he says, nearly lost his bottle. Teenagers' sensibilities being what they are, he also found his dad's funniness embarrassing. Bernard Senior once came to the school to do a presentation, cracked a few gags and left him blushing with mortification. Then again, his father *not* being funny was his other nightmare. 'When you have got a father who is a comedian, who is expected to be funny, you are hoping he is going to be funny because you don't want all the other kids coming round saying, "That was stupid, that joke." '

But before long, the still chubby lad became tired of playing the fat, jolly kid, always cracking jokes, and bored of fat-man cracks about his father, too. As sixteen, and the inescapable school leaving loomed, there were two rather diverse options open to Young Bernard. He really wanted to be a professional footballer, but weighed sixteen stone, which did not endear him to the talent scouts. His other hankering was to be an actor, or at least something in entertainment, and this frightened Bernard Senior. 'He is a good impressionist and is very funny, but I knew he wasn't tough enough for show business. Then I had a worrying time when he was eleven. He wanted a drum kit, and then he wanted drumming lessons but he soon got tired of it, thank God.'

Once he was sixteen, football seemed to the top choice, so he started a crash diet and exercise regime, which succeeded in whittling his sixteen stone down to a shade over eleven. Because he was genuinely talented, this earned him a place with Stockport County in the then Fourth Division. 'It was only very limited, a season and a half that I played there. They were in the old Fourth Division. I didn't really enjoy it. I was out of my depth to be quite honest, I wasn't quite good enough. I'm not one of those that say, "I could have done it." I knew I'd never be a star, so I chucked it in. Like dad, I want to be the best at what I do.' (After many false starts and experiments, Young Bernard eventually settled into becoming a club owner himself, and proprietor of the Fun Factory, a children's roller-skating rink and entertainment centre in Rochdale. He is also chairman of a local non-league football club.)

Bernard as a father was not a hard man or a vicious authoritarian, but nor does Young Bernard remember him as being a joker at home. He could, however, be as embarrassing as the next parent. 'Dad was often over the top. He could make me cringe. I'll never forget the day my first girlfriend phoned the house and asked for me. Dad answered and asked who it was. When she said it was Louise, he twigged it was a girlfriend and blew his top. He gave her a mouthful, and then I got one. "You're only fourteen and you have bloody birds on the phone," he yelled. I could have killed him. He went around the house for weeks singing, "Every little breeze seems to whisper Louise". He knew he'd been out of order and was trying to make a joke of it.'

What kind of man was the still young but now highly successful Bernard Manning turning out to be? What, apart from being fleetingly jealous of a first girlfriend of Young Bernard's, did he take seriously? His standard answer to the question is to cite family – 'cut one of us and we all bleed,' every member of the family says – but he has as many serious concerns as any intelligent man. Interestingly, given his reputation, when he is asked to speak seriously, even in off-guard moments, the question of race does not come up. And until late into his career, when he was already enormously rich, drove a Rolls-Royce and was renowned for his dodgy 'racist' jokes, he was a solid Labour voter, and something of a class warrior. Although he told Harold Wilson, at a dinner at the London Hilton soon after he retired, 'Some Prime Minister you were. You got rid of the idle rich and you've replaced them with the idle fucking poor,' he was massively insulting, and, one suspects, with a little more meaning, to aristocrats and Royals. He has described the Duke of Kent, whom he met, as a 'gormless bastard', and, sitting on a top table with the Duke of Westminster, said to him, 'I've got a message from Tony Benn for you.' 'What is it?' the Duke replied. 'Get fucked.' For months afterwards, the Duke would tell people how Bernard Manning told him to get fucked. Bernard still finds it amazing that he repeated the humiliation to others. (He is not rude about the Queen: 'She put her hands in mine and said, "I thoroughly enjoyed your performance." Nice old dear.')

I used to vote Labour until the Winter of Discontent and all that carry on (he says). I've not voted since, not Tory or anything. I think politics and religion are something you can argue all day about and get no further. They're best left alone, especially in my game. You can have a quip at them all, bounce a few lines off them, have a go at the John Majors and Tony Blairs. But really, I think it's a carve-up. Most of these politicians are having dinner with one another, and the next minute they are slagging one another off, and then they go to dinner the next night. Unbelievable. I like equality. It's nice on paper, like everything else it's nice if it works out, but then you get the thieves and the vagabonds and the people that aren't straight, and you can't run it then. Hypocrisy also annoys me. I can't stand two-faced people. I don't like anything like that. I have no time for them kind of people. Have a good row and then finish it all, clear the air. Say, 'I don't like the way you did that,' and then you can go on from there.

Bernard has never been an observant Catholic, and tells plenty of jokes that would once have seen him prosecuted for blasphemy. ('A priest fell over this cliff, and he's hanging on with his fingertips, and he looked up and said, "Lord, can you please help me?" And a voice said, "Let go of the cliff, your body will be dashed on the rocks below, and this time tomorrow you will be sat on the right-hand side of God." And the priest said, "Is there anyone else up there who can fuckin' help me?"') Nevertheless, Bernard still prays.

Sunday is a day for being lazy (he insists). But I pray. I pray many a time. But I don't know who to pray *to*. I'm not giving it all up. I pray at night. Whether there is a God or not I don't know, because some of the fairy stories they tell you about heaven and hell ... well. It's barmy. But there has got to be something, somewhere. There's this great big world, and you see beautiful new-born babies, and you see people grow up, and people become stars, and there's a world full of nobodies, and a level of clever people ... there has got to be something, hasn't there? I don't know what it is, and I wouldn't try to guess what it is, but I do pray just in case there are any loopholes, as W.C. Fields used to say.

Another thing that is deadly serious about me (Bernard concludes, back on the earthly plane), is that I have to bollock people. Young Bernard is just having his club refurbished now and we have got workers in there and I have to go round and give them a bollocking every so often to make sure everything is ticking over. That's when my serious side comes in. All the comedy stops then, it gets serious. If a customer comes up and says he's not seen a waiter for ten minutes, I have to get down the bar say, 'Get that table served over there, don't piss about, no time for acting the goat here, get 'em served now.' They know when I go overboard, but you have to get things done, you can't be a muggins. There's a time for laughing and there's a time for business.

The Comedians

He's the main man, he's the main man of all my life.

Bernard on Johnnie Hamp of Granada TV

It is often said that Bernard's effective exclusion from performing on television in the 1980s and onward – the result of
the raw offensiveness and racial content of his act – demolished
his career, reducing him from being a promising, respected, nation-
ally recognised comedian to a marginalised provincial performer.
However, it is more likely that the break with television was as
advantageous to Bernard Manning as it was necessary to the TV
industry.

It was not just that Bernard had become unsuitable broadcast
material. By the eighties, TV had largely moved away from carrying
stand-up comics. Bernard had used the medium brilliantly while it
benefited his career. By the time he was deemed inappropriate for
family (or almost any other) viewing, appearing on TV no longer
mattered a great deal to him. He was famous enough because of
television to pack out any club in the country. The fact that he was
no longer seen on TV added significantly to the Manning mystique.
The highly successful Bernard Manning videos would not have
been such big sellers if he had been available at any time on popular
programmes. As the Establishment came to be perceived as anti-
racist, anti-sexist, anti-fun prod-noses, this effectively turned
Bernard into an underground comic.

Yet you have to be something before you can quit it and, at the
time, Bernard's late-in-life TV debut – he was forty-one – and the
enormous amount of television he did through the 1970s was the
greatest turning point for him since the opening of the Embassy
Club twelve years previously. In many ways, TV stardom was more
important in the early seventies than it is now. With sixteen million
people regularly watching top entertainment shows, and just three
TV channels to choose from, if you appeared a couple of times,

you were a national star, and big news too. Pop music was in the same position, of course; if Gerry and the Pacemakers knocked The Beatles off the top of the *Hit Parade* the *Daily Mirror* would carry the news on its front page, and people would talk about it in bus queues. In today's vastly more dissipated media, a Top Ten story would never make it beyond the pop columns, if at all. A national TV event is almost unheard of – one of the few in modern times being Princess Diana's *Panorama* interview.

It is probable, then, that a new Bernard Manning appearing now, especially if he were restricted to cable channels (as he would be), would be far less of a 'story' than Bernard ever was. But *The Comedians*, the programme that discovered and made Bernard, was not a minority-interest, marginal show, but a major mass enter-tainment series, and was made by the mighty Granada for the full ITV network.

The man who discovered Bernard Manning for television was a Granada producer, Johnnie Hamp, a southerner from Streatham, London, who went north with the company shortly after Granada moved from theatres into TV. Hamp, who has since retired from Granada, but is still producing TV and videos from his adopted city, became a major show-business figure. He came from an enter-tainment family. His father was a magician, he the blond, blue-eyed boy who assisted his father. He won a talent contest when he was a teenager, with a Danny Kaye impression, joined the RAF, and then Granada Theatres, in the same year, 1952, that Bernard was with the Oscar Rabin Orchestra. He progressed from office assistant to running the stage shows in Granada Theatres, booking acts such as Little Richard and Jerry Lee Lewis for the one-night-stand tours. He drifted into TV, putting acts who were already touring the theatres into the flagship programme of the time, *Chelsea at Nine*.

In 1962, he came to Manchester to start the local magazine programme, *Scene at 6.30*, his particular brief to find new local talent. It was a propitious time to be doing such a job in the north-west. Hamp's was the first TV programme to air The Beatles, Gerry and the Pacemakers and Freddie and the Dreamers. He went on to do entertainment specials, bringing performers including Jerry Lee Lewis, Woody Allen and Burt Bacharach to Manchester. He was Granada's head of light entertainment when, in 1971, he created

The Comedians, with its simple, but knockout formula of re-creating on national TV some of the atmosphere of northern, working-class clubs like The Embassy. *The Comedians'* concept, although based on working-men's clubs, was really new and innovative, because it involved several comics on the same show, firing off jokes one after the other in a sort of relay race. 'I used to spend half my life in clubs, looking for other artists, and that's how the idea of *The Comedians* came,' Hamp explains. 'I would go to so many clubs, usually to see the top of the bill, which was normally a singer, but there was always a comic on, and a lot of them were good. It struck me that if I got enough of those together, that would make up some sort of comedy show, because they were all unknown at that time, all on ten quid a night or so.'

In 1970, he sort of came across Bernard at the Mannings' soon-to-be-demolished Wilton Club in Manchester, where he had gone to meet Adam Faith for a drink.

> Someone told Bernard that Johnnie Hamp from Granada was in, so apparently he went out there and worked his balls off (recounts Hamp). I say apparently, because after I'd met Adam, I pushed off, so Bernard had worked for an hour thinking he was impressing this producer from Granada, but I didn't even see him. I didn't know anything about it. But a little later, when I started *The Comedians* and was looking for at least thirty comics to bring in, ten a night for three nights. Bernard was very well known in Manchester – in fact, he was *the* Manchester comedian, and was one of my first choices. I saw him working at The Embassy and a couple of other places, and he was quite blue even then, so people sort of warned me off and said you can't use him on television.

Undaunted, Hamp went backstage to see Bernard, who recalls: 'He told me, "If we take you on, you'll have to go through your act with Daz. I'd end up in jail if I let you tell some of your gags on telly.' Bernard, eager for a TV debut, reassured Hamp that he could clean up.

> While I was thinking about this, Bernard said, 'Well, come out with me and see,' so I did, and he actually did four shows that night. I

couldn't believe it. We started off in a Catholic club, run by a priest and a few nuns, and of course he was as clean as a whistle. Then we went on to a British Legion Club, and he was a little bit bluer, then on the posh cabaret club which was right bang in the centre of Manchester. It was the place where all the artists used to congregate. You could go in there almost any night at midnight or one in the morning and find people like Tom Jones and Bruce Forsyth after their shows. Then we went on to a gay club – it could have been Bunny Lewis's or Fou Fou Lamar – at about one in the morning. The great thing was that Bernard changed his routine for every different location for every type of audience and, for me, he is a brilliant stand-up comic, one of the very best in this country. I have never really seen Bernard die, never seen him go other than well. (Bernard Manning at a gay club sounds a little unlikely, but Hamp recalls Bernard being perfectly at ease there, simply adapting the routine to include a couple of gay jokes.)

The criterion for appearing on *The Comedians* or any TV comedy show is the face, (Hamp expands). Bernard does have a good comic's face. Then it's the delivery, and Bernard is perfect at delivering a gag. I have heard people do the same gags as Bernard but they just get the words slightly wrong. Bernard had a knack for banging the tag line in and getting it just right. Thirdly, it's the material. The series had an insatiable appetite for material, and Bernard was one of the few who could keep coming up with new stuff all the time. Whether he invented it, or someone had rung him with the gags, I don't know but he delivers it beautifully. He is a grafter. He knows whether jokes are funny or not. As far as clean was concerned, over all the years, he probably did over a hundred and twenty shows for me with not one blue gag. Not one. You couldn't in those days and I wouldn't want to put any blue stuff out on the air. *The Comedians* was a family-time slot – it used to go out about 7.30 on Tuesday night.

The three nights of back-to-back stand-up comics Hamp set up at the Granada studios provided the raw material for episodes one and two of *The Comedians*. The show, interestingly now, was billed as a launchpad for unknown *young* comics; in its own fashion, it could be argued, the show paved the way for the stand-up alternative of a decade later. Hamp was immediately struck by Bernard's intelligence and professionalism. Knowing the tapes would be edited, Bernard would do a string of three clean jokes that he knew Hamp would use, then craftily slip in a blue gag, which would surprise the studio audience, and get a huge laugh. He would then go back to the clean jokes, with the now more responsive audience in the palm of his hand.

While Hamp was still recording hours of raw comedy to edit down into a usable couple of pilot editions, there was considerable opposition at Granada to his project.

Everybody at Granada thought I was potty (he admits). What I had to do in those days as a young producer was to show edited tape to my bosses, Lord Bernstein – he wasn't a Lord then, he was just Sid – Cecil Bernstein and Sir Denis Forman, who wasn't a Sir at that time either. They had to approve it. The first gag that came up was Frank Carson, and he did the one about his brother Sammy, who had two wooden legs and, when his house caught fire, the fire brigade managed to save the building but Sammy was razed to the ground. Bernard was next, and it was the joke about the Jewish Santa Claus who comes down the chimney and asks, 'Do you want to buy some toys?' The third on was Dougie Brown, who did the gag about the fellow who goes into a pet shop and said, 'I want to buy a p ... p ... p ... p ... parrot,' and the fellow says, 'H ... h ... h ... how much do you want to p ... p ... p ... pay for it?' 'How much w ... w ... w ... will that one cost,' and he says, 'f ... f ... f ... four quid.' 'C ... c ... can he talk?' asks the bloke, and the parrot says, 'A bloody sight better than you two can.' It was only at this point that I realised that Sidney and Cecil were both Jewish, Cecil had a bad stutter and Sir Denis had a wooden leg.

The big three at Granada sportingly overcame any personal objection they felt to these kind of gags and approved the show, but not every comedian thought *The Comedians* would work, either. Frank Carson, the Ulster comic, told Hamp he thought it would fall apart when the comics started arguing. Instead, a friendly leg-pulling kind of rivalry grew up backstage on *The Comedians*, but nothing unpleasant. Bernard's great rival in the first series was George

Roper, a fat Liverpudlian comic, slightly less abrasive than Bernard. All the comedians used cue cards with a series of single words to remind them of the gags. (Bernard had not used memory aids of any sort in nearly twenty years, but the necessity to tell clean jokes nearly threw him. Blue gags were his bread and butter and ran off his tongue by the hundred; clean material required concentration.) During the first recordings, there was a technical breakdown in the studio while Bernard was on, and Hamp asked him to fill in, expecting Bernard would relish the chance to do some blue gags. Bernard, however, had spotted Roper's cue card, knew all the gags and did his rival's entire routine. Roper, waiting backstage, had no idea this was happening, and happily came on stage when Bernard introduced him with, 'Here he is, a very funny man ... George Roper.' After two gags met with a muted response and shouts of 'We've heard it', Roper twigged. 'Has Bernard done these?' he said, 'Yes, well, whatever Bernard says goes for me too,' and walked off – a repeat of the occasion a decade earlier when Eddie of Little and Large had walked off the stage at the Embassy with the same face-saving line after Bernard had done his act for him in advance.

The first episode of *The Comedians* was broadcast in the early evening on Saturday, 12 June 1971. To watch it in the light of later developments in television, of Bernard Manning's career, and of society in general, is a fascinating experience; because, while Bernard is entirely clean and could only be construed as being offensive by the most hypersensitive of prudes, many of his fellow comedians would be utterly unacceptable to today's viewers – albeit in a way that seems still curiously innocent.

The show opened with a joke by Ken Goodwin, an innocent little taster of the quick-fire, working-class – but generally earthier – material that was to come: 'This fella come to our house, he said, do you believe in free speech, I said, I do, he said, OK then, can I use your telephone?' then came an introduction sequence, with Vaudeville-style music by a band called Shep's Banjo Boys, who were dressed in white trousers, pink shirts and pink neck scarves. They got the audience to clap along, until they got to the point of introducing the main acts with drum rolls and a cymbal tish. The audience was comprised mainly of women wearing bouffant seventies hair, nylon dresses and cardigans. Some of the men were in regulation early-night-out gear of black shirt, white tie and white shoes – the kind of togs John Travolta would immortalise a few years later in *Saturday Night Fever*. The big, comfortably bosomed women cackled and wiped their eyes on handkerchiefs during the show in an 'Ooh, isn't he naughty, but you have to have a laff' kind of way. Indicative of the time, members of the audience were smoking.

The Ulsterman, Frank Carson, was the first comic on screen after the musical introduction, with an involved Irish joke. Carson was immediately followed by Bernard. For his first appearance on TV, Bernard had his back to the audience, and was smoking a cigar held aloft between thumb and forefinger. He was wearing a black suit, a frilly shirt and a bow tie – and looking very much like Young Bernard does today. The spot lasted ten seconds, and the viewer did not even get to see him full-face. Yet the perfectly timed pause before he started, combined with that cigar, gave a powerful impression of unhurried, self-assured professionalism, of a man who had been waiting for this moment for many years and was going to savour it.

There was no warm up or preamble in that gravelly voice when it was heard by millions for the first time. There wasn't even a definite article: 'Irishman, up in court for maintenance. The Judge says to him, "We have decided to allow your wife £7 a week." He says, "Thanks very much, I'll try and send her a few shillings myself." ' The next joke, by George Roper, had a drunken Irishman telling a policeman who asked where he lived that he was of no fixed abode; a Scouser with the Irishman is then asked where he lives and answers, 'In the flat upstairs from him.' Then there followed the extraordinary sight and sound of Charlie Williams, an elderly black man with an exaggerated, slightly whiny, Yorkshire accent. His joke concerned a friend of his – 'a Jew boy'. (The phrase Jew boy, it must be noted, rarely heard or seen today even in neo-Nazi pamphlets, is every bit as offensive as 'nigger' or 'coon'. It was a favourite of Mosley-ite fascists in the thirties, and has probably never been broadcast other than by Williams before or since, let alone before the 9 p.m. watershed.) The Jew boy, as Charlie Williams told us, went to the dentist and asked for all his teeth to be taken out. The dentist told him this would cost twelve guineas. Shocked, the Jew boy replies, 'Here's a dollar. Slacken 'em.'

Within a few moments, the comedian Mike Coyne swore – only a 'bloody', but a pioneering 'bloody' none the less – and told a racist joke: 'I knew a fella once who spent thirty years in darkest Africa looking for the lost Masazuki tribe. He eventually found them over a chip shop in Bradford.' At this point, by way of a link to Charlie Williams, we saw Williams cracking up with laughter, as if at Coyne's joke. The effect was very much that the black man was giving any white viewers who might feel uneasy about laughing permission to guffaw. 'Immigration', as the race issue was then labelled, was clearly the key issue of the day, just three years after Enoch Powell's 'Rivers of Blood' speech. But although Powell had made the issue a sensitive one, in 1971, the crudest stereotypes were still perfectly suitable family material. 'The new Corporation toilets in Birmingham are losing a fortune,' cracked Mike Coyne. 'All these Jamaicans are doing the limbo under the door.'

Then came Charlie Williams again, telling a variation on the one-liner that Bernard would use a quarter of a century later for the benefit of Yomi Mambu, chair of the Manchester City Council equal opportunities sub-committee – 'I didn't see you when you walked in until you smiled.' 'So what, is there a colour bar on, or what?' Williams continued. 'I'm a Yorkshire lad, y'know. There's not many of us left. We're a dying race.' Then, to a black man in the audience: 'Greetings, cousin. I didn't realise you were in, I've just seen you. Are you settling down OK in this country? We take over on Monday, so it's all right.' (After watching him for a while, it occurs to one that, far from being an Uncle Tom, Charlie Williams was in a sense quite a subversive comic. He told a joke in this first episode about going into a restaurant and being served by a waitress who says, 'Excuse me, young man, we don't serve darkies.' He replies, 'That's all right. I don't eat them.' Later he refers ironically to 'Our Saviour, Enoch Powell'. Williams's material was, in fact, not dissimilar to the gags a young Lenny Henry was practising for his emergence on TV four years afterwards.)

Bernard had his full set in the second half. He stood out for his dead-pan manner and the way he didn't laugh at his own jokes, as a lot of the other comedians did. He did not interact with the audience directly, but just fired gag after gag, punctuated by a lazy drag on his cigar:

A fella went to the doctors and he said I've examined you and I can't find anything wrong with you. You must have Alice. He said, what's that? The doctor said, I don't know, but Christopher Robin went down with it ... A fella selling seagulls on Blackpool front for half a crown each. A bloke walks up to him and says, I'll have a seagull. He said (pointing skywards) take that one there ... Fella went to the optician and said, my eyesight's failing, something wrong with me eyes. He said, come outside, look at the sky. What can you see? He said, I can see the sun. He said, well, how much further do you want to see? ... Two attendants on a boating lake. One shouts, come in number 91 your time is up. The other said, we've only got ninety boats. Oh, he said, are you having trouble number 16? ... Little Lancashire woman walks into this Jewish fella's shop. She said, have you any of those fans they have in these foreign countries when it's warm like this. He said (adopts Jewish accent), fans, fans, I've got fans. I've got fans at £2, fans at 30 shillings, I've got fans at £1, fans at 10 shillings and threepenny fans. She said, give me a threepenny one, it might rain tomorrow. (Audience laugh as though this is the joke). She gets outside and does this (shakes it from side to side) and it all falls to bits. She said, Mr Cohen, this fan you've just sold me, it's all fallen to bits. He said, what did you do? She said, I just went like that (shakes it from side to side) He said, how much did you pay? She said, threepence. He said, for threepence you don't do that (shakes hand) you do this (shakes head from side to side).

The run of gags, it has to be said, seems innocuous and bland enough when read, but with the full weight of Bernard's twenty-stone presence behind them, they had the audience in stitches.
The Comedians was immediately a stunning success, rapidly gaining ratings second only to *Coronation Street* for the two years it ran. The shows made stars out of Carson, Williams and Roper, of Dougie Brown, Ken Goodwin, Tom O'Connor, Stan Boardman, Mike Reid (of *Eastenders* fame, and a seventies children's quiz show called *Runaround*) and Jim Bowen, later compère of the TV darts quiz

show, *Bullseye.* Ken Goodwin, whose *Beano*-style gags (exemplified by his opening 'Do you believe in free speech?') worked so well by virtue of their charming naivety, was regarded at the beginning of the series as *The Comedians*'s great new discovery. But it was Bernard Manning who did best out of *The Comedians,* who sent audiences rushing into the Embassy to see the droll ex-greengrocer from Harpurhey.

Bernard's gratitude to the Londoner Johnnie Hamp was unequivocal. '*The Comedians* was my gateway to the world, and he's the main man, he's the main man of all my life. He took me from a £10 compère in the clubs to what I am today. He said, this is what you are doing wrong and this is what you are doing right. I listened to him. I called him the Cecil B. de Mille of television because he knows exactly what he is talking about. He has made stars out of Cannon and Ball, Paul Daniels, myself, everybody, made us household names. You could say, Johnnie Hamp made the water for me to walk on.'

Sadly for Bernard, however, his elevation to the big time had come immediately after the death of his father. The man, whose faith and trust in his son had been so vindicated by the success of the Embassy Club, missed by a matter of weeks Bernard's greatest moment.

He died of a heart attack on the bowling green where I used to see him and wave to him every morning (Bernard says). It was heartbreaking. I went home one day and my mother said, 'Your father's not come home for his dinner,' and the phone rang. 'Get down to Crumpsall Hospital right away,' they said. I shot down there, and they said, 'Your father's died.' 'Oh, no, that's bleeding terrible,' I said. 'You've got to get him on a machine. He can't be dead, he can't have died.' The doctor said, 'Sit down, son,' because I was going berserk. He offered me a sedative and said, 'Your father's gone.' I had to come home and tell me mam. I don't know how I did it. I was crying all the way home. I drove home, I don't know how. She came to the door and said, 'Where's your dad?' and I said, 'He's died.' You can imagine what that moment was like for both of us. We had to go down to the morgue. And the young policeman who came with us was marvellous. I suppose he'd done it before, but he was someone to talk to.

Bernard was haunted by his father's death, and years later would still say how the one thing that distressed him was that the old man had not quite lived long enough to see him hit the heights. When Hamp first approached Bernard, the comedian was at his lowest-ever ebb, both personally and as an entertainer. Bernard's boyhood friend, Sammy Dardick, remembers bumping into Bernard at Boggart Hall Clough (the park in Harpurhey) at this time, and Bernard bringing the subject of his father up immediately. 'He said it was such a pity,' Dardick recalls. ' "I've just about got almost to the height of my fame," Bernard told me, "and the old man has died and not been able to enjoy the fruits of it all." '

Just as he did years later, when both Vera and his mother died, Bernard honoured engagements despite his devastation. 'My Dad and I were so close. I had a booking that night. How I got through it, I'll never know. My eyes were as red as beetroots from crying. I did an hour, came off and went to pieces. Believe it or not, I couldn't eat for three weeks. I lost two stone through grief.'

There is no doubt that *The Comedians*, apart from sending his career into the stratosphere, also helped Bernard – a man who is so deeply tormented by death that he will cry (as he has done recently) openly at the funeral of the mother of one of his staff at the club – to overcome the depression caused by his father's death. The new success did not end with *The Comedians*, either. A long-held ambition of Bernard had been to perform at the London Palladium, as opposed to his own club of the same name in Manchester. In April 1972, *The Comedians* had a six-week run at the massive London theatre with a stage version of the TV show – it was extended to five and a half months – while another posse of *The Comedians* team played Blackpool and toured theatres across the country. Each show involved various permutations of six of the comics (plus special acts and dancing girls), and Bernard appeared in both the Palladium show and the tour, staying whilst in London in what was then style – at the Hilton on Park Lane. One of the production numbers Hamp devised to flesh out the Palladium show was the 'Wheeltappers and Shunters Social Club', a scenario in which all the acts were deliberately lousy; before long, that fleeting idea too was turned into a hit TV show that ran for several years, with Bernard as the first choice comic compère.

While at the Palladium, *The Comedians* also did a Royal Command performance, after which Bernard shook hands with an appreciative Queen. Bernard appeared with Des O'Connor, Richard Attenborough and Mike Reid. 'The Queen told me she liked my show,' Bernard told reporters. 'I love meeting famous people, so being introduced to the Queen was the greatest thrill of my life.'

It was during the Palladium run that some of Frank Carson's predictions that the comics would inevitably fall out among themselves began to come true. It was the first time in the history of variety that six starring comedians – Bernard, Mike Reid, Ken Goodwin, Charlie Williams, Dave Butler and Jos White – had shared the same theatre stage, and competitiveness had to raise its head eventually. The *Daily Mail*'s Linda Lee Potter was prompted to investigate the tensions between these six big-league northern egotists. She found that White sometimes ate with Williams in the Pancake House next door to the Palladium and that Reid and Bernard sometimes drank together but that, mostly, *The Comedians* kept themselves very much to themselves. Dave Butler was upset to get the smallest dressing room, so Hamp had it redecorated and recarpeted. Ken Goodwin, the most popular with the TV viewing public, had the top-of-the-bill dressing room, which everyone seemed to resent a little, as, they would bitch, he was renowned principally for laughing at his own jokes.

Ken Goodwin confided in Lee Potter: 'I'll be glad when I'm out of this show. On the opening night I went on for a couple of minutes too long and, when I came off, all the others started having a go at me. When I went on at the end, I was so upset I forgot to thank certain people I should have thanked. Psychologically, I've got to feel happy-go-lucky before I can go out on stage, and I've lost a lot of that in this show. I went straight home that first night just to get away from the unpleasant environment.'

Williams was less inclined to bitterness. 'All in all, I think the six of us get on very well,' he said. 'A little jealousy, it's a natural thing, but Ken has a hard task here. His brand of humour, it's *Jackanory* stuff, and people do love a nice spicy gag. It's in us all – it's human nature.' Mike Reid, meanwhile, boasted to Lee Potter: 'I've had the training. I've played audiences none of these have ever seen. I've had a tremendous schooling. I've done pubs, stags, I have done four hundred skinheads one night. I've had no one to push me, babe. Everything I've done, I've done on my own bat, which I do feel a little bit cocky about. According to one critic, on the opening night I nicked the show. I'm well known around East End clubs, but being in a real production is new to me, baby. I'm the only boy. I mean, take Bernie Manning,' Reid said sarcastically, 'he's got his own club in Manchester, but he's a diamond of a man. He's real eight-carat gold, is Bernie.'

'Bernard thinks he is the greatest comic in the world,' Reid told another interviewer from the *Sunday People* when asked about his drinking companion from the Palladium days. 'He couldn't kiss my arse as a comic, and I have proved it dozens of times when we have been on stage together. When we did *The Comedians* I got on with Bernard better than anyone. He gives everybody a lot of stick, he shouts and screams at them, has a go at them and makes them feel small. He's like that. But I gave him just what he gave me, so Bernie and I got on very well.'

In this mental war of attrition, Bernard was in his element. 'I like to be top dog,' he readily admits. 'I've always wanted that. When I was doing the Palladium, Milton Shulman, the *Evening Standard*'s theatre critic, reviewed it and said, "But for the professionalism of Bernard Manning, the rest of the comedians are a wasted journey." I went round and pinned it on all their dressing-room doors. Ever since me mother went to see that gipsy in Blackpool who said, "You're going to see your son's name in big lights," I knew I could top that bill.'

When Ken Goodwin complained about the 'unpleasant atmosphere', it was Bernard he was referring to principally. Bernard felt he had good reason to grumble: 'When we were doing a run-through for the Royal Command performance at the Palladium, Ken was doing more than his time on stage and I told him, "I'm not wearing that," and told him to come off on time like everybody else. These people seem to have lost their common touch. Yes, I put him in his place. Sorted it out. There wasn't any more trouble,' he told the *News of the World*.

Johnnie Hamp, obviously aware of the sparks flying, was not deflected in the least in his assessment of Bernard as a man. 'He is a kind and generous and good-hearted man,' he would say, even while Bernard's reputation as a Mr Nasty was growing. 'There is no doubt about it,' Hamp insisted. 'He was never temperamental, and caused no problems at all. Maybe that's because I was the boss, but I don't think it is. We have always got along very well. He's just a pussy cat really. People seem to be scared of him, and I don't really know why.'

Within a few years of the Palladium, Hamp gave Bernard his own show on Granada, his first solo TV spectacular, ironically entitled, as a way, perhaps, of capitalising on his new notoriety, *Mr Nice Guy*. Bernard appeared with supporting acts that included the Three Degrees, Acker Bilk and the Syd Lawrence Orchestra. 'Tonight, you will see the other side of my character,' Bernard announced just before the show. 'The stories will be nice, clean ones, suitable for all the family. But most of the show will be taken up with me singing ballads and golden oldies ... I want to prove I can be this sort of artist. After all, I don't have to be blue. But most of my living comes from club and cabaret work. You can't tell fairy stories to those customers. They just won't stand for it.'

Bernard still recalls finally getting his own show with delight:

Loads of names on it, and you're the main one – absolute magic. You don't get scared by that either, because you're not an overnight star, you have come up. I would have been terrified at eighteen or nineteen, but then I was about thirty before I got the first of my big breaks, so I had built up to it. It means you're not stuck for a word and you know a million songs if you are. I'd sung with the dance bands, I knew exactly what these conductors wanted, so it just spread and blossomed like a flower. If you had thrown me in at the deep end with the Three Degrees, I would have been shaking, but being a household name and doing good things, working hard and doing all the clubs and places, there's nothing you haven't done – you click.

Johnnie Hamp was at the time one of the most influential men in British show business, and remains a close friend of Bernard, organising his enormous sixtieth birthday party in 1990, visiting him at home and speaking to him regularly. Was Bernard Manning, then, his favourite member of *The Comedians?* It is a question that Hamp, a charming and diplomatic man, clearly finds awkward to deal with, even today. 'It is very difficult to say that he is a favourite,' he says. 'For example, I've known Frank Carson longer probably than anyone else, back from the early fifties, and I see in Jim Bowen's book, he says someone told him that *he* was one of Johnnie Hamp's favourites. But then Bernard *is* a favourite, and everyone will know that. So perhaps the answer is yes.'

Las Vegas

I'm not interested in that. I've got me own punters.

Bernard on being offered a £750,000 contract to play in America and Australia

Young Bernard confesses that he was seventeen before he appreciated the extent of his famous father's talent to beguile an audience even though, in his early teens, he had already come to realise how genuinely funny Bernard Senior could be on a day-to-day basis. If humour is an indicator of intelligence – and there are few more complex functions of the mind than the ability to make humour – Bernard must have been a genius all the time he was making a minimal impression at Mount Carmel School. As described by Young Bernard, his father's everyday funniness, whether expressed in on-stage ad libs, at home or in the running of his business, suggests a man of extraordinary quickness of mind, eccentricity, as well as that Quixotic ability to see a funny side to situations that other people miss.

I find him much funnier talking about the old days, when he was setting up the business with his dad, than any of the jokes he tells (Young Bernard explains). For example, my dad says the funniest thing that ever happened at the Embassy Club was right at the beginning, in the first few weeks, when they wanted everything to go right, and they had a magician on. The magician, my dad describes, walks out on stage and he is meticulously dressed. You have got to picture this working-class audience looking at this fellow, with the girl at his side, and as he walks out on to the stage, twelve birds fly out of him. They are flying out of his pockets and from up his sleeves and everyone realises that he can't control them and they have just decided to fly up into the trellis ceiling they used to have. The birds are just sitting in the trellis work looking down, and the magician is on the end of the stage, whistling pathetically.

There's another story about when they bought a new grand

piano. They'd paid £400 for this, a white piano. Now his father was one of the tightest men. He really was shrewd me grandad, and he couldn't believe they had paid such an amount of money for a piano, but me dad said, no, we had to have a decent piano. It sets the room off, and it's proper backing for the singing. So they put the piano in. Well, they had had it one night and they had an act on – an Indian axe-throwing act. And, of course, one of these axes went straight into the piano. Me dad couldn't believe it, and me grandad is on the stage having a fight with this Indian. He got him by the throat and was saying, 'I paid four hundred quid for this piano.'

The other story was one which Mike Harding used to tell. Me dad was a stickler for not having bands or groups on who were too loud, and they booked this group called the Cherokees from America. They had a hit record in the late sixties, so they were obviously going to be quite popular, and the club was packed out. Me dad said specifically to them, we don't want it too loud, so they said, OK, yeah, yeah. So they go out on stage and set off, and the roof nearly lifted off. Me dad is, like, 'What's going on here?' and he just pulled the plug, straight out. So this Yankee turns round, and me dad walks out on stage and, the bloke says to him, 'Don't you know we're the Cherokees?' And me dad says, 'Well you'd better fuck off because Custer's arrived.' And they had to go. I can just picture now, how he would have reacted walking out on the night, I know what his face would have looked like, I know what attitude he would have adopted.

When, in 1989, the Embassy Club was destroyed by fire – it was rebuilt in a magnificent four-month effort by Bernard's friend Barry Clark, who is, among other talents, a builder – Bernard gave a sterling display of the kind of eccentricity that would be regarded as ridiculous in a TV sitcom.

Me dad decided he wanted everything put back in exactly the same place as it had been. I said, 'Dad, why don't you make it a little bit longer now, a little bit different?' But he said, 'What for? I'm a success as it was.' So the stools went in the same spots, everything on the walls, everything was the same. He started going around with a whistle, and if he wanted something in particular doing, everybody had to know. He'd whistle and announce, 'Anaglypta. I want anaglypta on that wall.' Now, he wouldn't just tell the decorator. The electrician had to hear it, the plumber had to hear it and the joiner. This whistle would go again, and me dad would say, 'I'm just telling him to put anaglypta on that wall.' Unbelievable, it was.

Now there was something else from that time I didn't see, but a guy pulled me in a pub and told me about it. He said, 'Your old fella's a bit of a card isn't he? I tried to rip him off with some windows when he was redoing the club after the fire.' Now, if you look at the club, it's got these Georgian windows outside, and this guy said, 'Your dad said to me, "I want toughened glass in them windows, because the kids round here, they're bastards. So put toughened glass in them windows." So we thought he won't know the difference, you know, and we put ordinary glass in, which is a lot cheaper, and we'll charge him for toughened. Anyway, we went into the club after, and said "Bernard, we've done the glass, go and have a look." And Bernard said, "Ah, marvellous, let's see it." And he trundles out there. "Is it toughened glass?" he asks. "Oh, ay, it's toughened glass, all right," we said. "Marvellous," said Bernard, and picked a brick up and threw it straight through the window. "I said toughened glass. Now, get 'em out, and put 'em in," and he went back inside.'

Just as he could handle them on stage, Bernard had just the right touch for dealing with truculent young men on the lookout for trouble. Even in quite undignified situations, as Young Bernard recalls, he had the wit and charisma to deflate, defuse and assert his will; it is sometimes easy to imagine Bernard as a wonderful teacher.

He was sitting in my snooker club one morning (Young Bernard says). He would come up for his breakfast there sometimes – and there used to be a load of local lads that used the club before breakfast for a pint before time. Me dad would be sat there eating his poached egg on toast, and there was one particular lad that I could see me dad didn't like, because he had a little bit too much to say for himself – probably a little bit like me dad, you see. And he came in one day, and me dad was there with his vest on, a pair of old trousers, a dirty old belt with a horrible buckle on, and half his breakfast down his vest. This fella looks at me dad, and, a bit snide, says, 'Got your best gear on again Bernard, I see.' So me dad turned round, and he said, 'Well, son, you like nice trousers, shoes and jumpers, and I like Rolls-Royces and Lincoln Continentals.' Everybody thought it was brilliant, because nobody else liked this fella either.

The seventies, from the moment he appeared on *The Comedians,* were Bernard Manning's heyday. Everything he did was big and brash, and reported in detail by newspapers local and national. His love of big, expensive cars – incongruous as it was when he still lived in a small, modest house – was finally consummated in January 1973, a few weeks after the Royal command performance, when he bought a new Rolls as a belated Christmas present to himself. At £20,000, the car was worth almost double the value of the family house, and the arrival of the Silver Shadow in Lewis Avenue was duly noted by the press. Three weeks later, the *Daily Telegraph* made space for a report on Bernard being prosecuted for speeding a short while before he bought the Rolls, on the way to a club date in Blackburn. He was fined £20. It was his third endorsement, but he escaped a ban – and the frustration of not being allowed to drive his expensive new toy – when the Bury magistrates accepted that he needed to be able to drive because of the late hours he kept and the difficulty in finding chauffeurs prepared to work so late.

A few weeks later, the menswear chain High and Mighty, which specialises in clothing the man with the fuller figure, had the clever idea of getting Bernard to open their Manchester shop. The event was covered by the tabloids amply enough to make a lucrative deal out of High and Mighty's investment in shirts to pay for their star's personal-appearance fee. Other fatness-related publicity stunts included one whereby Bernard, supposedly to lose weight, went into training with Manchester City. The club manager, Tony Book, commented in the *Daily Mail*: 'At the moment, the only position Bernard could play would be in goal. He isn't very mobile, but at least he would reduce the target area.' Bernard responded:

'Footballers have it easy. You have got to be fit to face two thousand people and the Queen at the London Palladium all by yourself. I don't have ten team-mates backing me up. But I found the training quite hard. I think I'll go back to my own training schedule – winding my watch up in the morning.'

Bernard in his forties was now on the sunlit plateau of national fame. With Johnnie Hamp's confidence in him riding high, plus a range of contacts across the TV world, he did what he wanted to do. After a couple of years of *The Comedians*, he felt that the show did not quite reflect the true atmosphere of northern clubs. The idea that had been minted for the London Palladium show, the 'Wheeltappers and Shunters Social Club', an authentic reproduction of a real club, right down to the lack of requisite apostrophes in the title and genuine (if untouched) pints of bitter nestling at the compères' elbows, consequently came to life as a TV series. Bernard co-fronted *Wheeltappers* with Colin Crompton. As a *Daily Express* preview announced: 'The new show will bring in high-powered artists who are normally worth £500-a-week at the clubs, all the way from Matt Munro to Tessie O'Shea. Manning says: "I am breaking a bit of new ground with this variety show. There will actually be real beer for the audience – something very special on TV, where it's usually cold tea. Scampi and chips and bouncers and, at last, the real atmosphere of the famous northern clubs which so many people around the country know nothing about. I'll be right back where I started."' (This last thought was quite true in more than one sense. At forty-four, Bernard was at last allowed to return to his artistic roots by singing on TV, one song per show. Within months, he had an LP in the charts. He has sold 800,000 records in his career, and, as he says, 'Nobody's getting their money back.')

By the end of 1974, Bernard's Rolls-Royce, registration BJM 1, was a Manchester landmark; he was doing private shows in London in front of notables such as the Duke of Edinburgh and Sir Charles Clore, and planning the £250,000 extension of the Embassy Club. 'We have to expand. Our Embassy Club can only take about three hundred. And it's due to come down. The new place will seat eight hundred and even then it won't be big enough. We've got thousands and thousands of members,' the *Express* quoted him as saying.

Against the run of play for Bernard in 1975 came the embarrassing business of a *This Is Your Life* appearance that had to be scrapped, for reasons never clearly explained. According to the *News of the World*, reporting with not a little glee (being a professional nasty man had its pay-off in that any career or personal setback was seized on with extra relish by the media), the Thames producer Jack Crawshaw pulled the plug only five days before the programme was due to be screened because the material was too thin, and not enough people could be persuaded to appear on it. Originally, the show was going to be postponed to improve on the material, but the *Daily Mirror* got on to the story and sent a reporter round to Lewis Avenue to put it subtly to Bernard; as Vera recalled it, he did this by asking, 'How does it feel to be rejected as a *This Is Your Life* subject?'

Because he was told about the show, it had to be cancelled completely. What emerged was that the family gossiping – and more specifically Bernard's mother gossiping – must have alerted the press. Bernard's brother Frank, who by now ran his own club in Newquay, had travelled up for the show with Alma and Rene, who had also settled in Cornwall, 'We are all terribly disappointed,' Frank said. 'But I think Thames Television must bear a heavy share of the blame. They telephoned our family on Friday and said they would not be going ahead with the show as planned because they did not have enough material. We all thought they were cancelling the programme, not just postponing it. They should have made the situation clearer.'

Bernard's mother, it emerged, had spent six weeks working with the researcher, and even bought a long gown for the programme. 'It was such a terrible let down when they rang me on Friday and said the programme was not going ahead,' she said. 'My son has such a wonderful story to tell, how from a greengrocer on a bicycle he became a famous name. I really wanted that for Bernard.' Johnnie Hamp recalls what would have been the ruined show's format. 'We were going to do it out of the *Wheeltappers*,' he explains. 'As the resident compère, Bernard would be stood by the bar and introduce some Irish act with a phoney name, and it was Eammon Andrews who would come along with the red book.' Some dignity was retrieved by Granada by throwing a special evening on the

Wheeltappers set, which was televised, as a sort of compensation even though by then everyone was taking the mickey out of Bernard. George Roper came on with a red book and blew the dust off it.

(More than a decade later, Bernard finally received the *This Is Your Life* accolade. 'Young Bernard was doing all the dealings with *This Is Your Life* this time,' Alma says, 'Me mother knew nothing about it because she would have told Bernard. So what we did was, we went to London and bought my mother an outfit. Then we went up to me mother's and told her we were taking her out to the Midland Hotel for a dinner. We told her a load of lies. We had her hair and her nails done at the Midland. She told everyone we were going to a party. When we got there for the rehearsal and found out what it was really about, she was annoyed with us because we hadn't told her. She really was mad. She said, "I don't think this is right, I should have been told about this, I don't like it." We said, "Look, mother, there was no use telling you because you would have given the game away." '

In TV terms, the wait had been worth it. John Fisher, now head of entertainment at Thames TV, and then in charge of the series, recalls: 'There was a moment towards the end when Bernard's daughter-in-law came on with the as-then baby grandchild, Ben. We all know that show can be phoney at times, but if ever – and I really mean this – there was a moment of genuine love, it was from Bernard to that kiddie. Forget the cameras – the defences came down, and you just saw this big softie. You just sense on those occasions how people really feel. (A few weeks before, the pro-gramme team had done a show with Zsa Zsa Gabor, whose daughter came on and shook her mother by her hand.')

Another classic show-business accolade came Bernard's way in 1976 and 1977, in the form of two appearances on the *Michael Parkinson* show, also produced by Fisher. Bernard's co-guests on the 1977 show were Esther Rantzen and Magnus Magnusson. As Fisher recalls, 'Esther is a consummate professional and is never lost for the right word at the right time, but on this occasion, she didn't know where she was.'

Rantzen tried to corner me into a situation about some of my jokes about coloureds (Bernard explained in an interview with the

Guardian). I don't think she knew anything about my background. After twenty-six years of being heckled, there was no way she was going to upset me. Anyway, I suddenly went all serious and started to say something like, there was nothing I would like better than to see all the world – the Irish, the Jews, and so on – come together, united . . . And she was lapping it up. Then when I said, . . . to attack the Pakis, her face fell. Magnus Magnusson, who was also on the show, and whom I had expected trouble from, just fell about laughing. But I didn't know anything about Esther Rantzen. I hadn't seen her programme because I'm always working at night, but somebody told me she takes the mickey out of small firms who can't make deliveries on time. And you know, if you're going to hand it out, you've got to be able to take it. It's like, if I see a fat man in the audience, I'll say something like: 'Don't worry about being fat. You can fight it. I did.' But I have to take it too. The audience is always shouting to me, 'Do you get your clothes from Rent-A-Tent?' and, 'I suppose you have to go to the car wash to have a bath.' I can't stand these holier-than-thou folk like Esther Rantzen and Jess Yates. They bring out the devil in me. I like to see them squirm.

Bernard's ultimate moment of 1977 – the summit of his career, he maintains today – was in November, when he played the MGM Grand in Las Vegas. It was a one-off visit, as well as being Bernard's first trip abroad since he left the Army. (Subsequently, he has been outside Britain just twice, on three-day working trips to Benidorm in 1990 and again in 1996.) To put it in its proper perspective, Bernard's Las Vegas appearance was arranged as a TV stunt by Johnnie Hamp, who made a brilliant documentary for Granada on the expedition. The stunt part of it, as he explained to Bernard at the outset when he suggested the idea in the sitting room at Lewis Avenue, was that the film would be shown even if Bernard's act was a complete flop. The very premise of the film, indeed, was that British comics hardly ever succeed in America, and the idea of Bernard Manning, the most esoterically English of them all, being the first to attempt stand-up at the MGM Grand, no less, was a very clever one. Hamp's film, directed by Baz Taylor, was shown as the week's main ITV network attraction on a February Wednesday evening the following year. The *TV Times* gave Bernard Manning in Las Vegas a front cover, with a montage photo of Bernard on a fluorescent-lit Vegas strip, under the meaningless but magnificent headline: 'My Great Gamble, By Bernard Manning'. It scarcely needed explaining that the only thing Bernard was really gambling was his pride.

To further enhance the pre-broadcast hype, Bernard bought a somewhat eccentric centre-page spread of advertising space in the *Stage* to alert people to his triumph and update them on his general wonderfulness. The advertisement declared: 'Advice to up-and-coming young artists: I have never appeared on *Opportunity Knocks* or *New Faces*. Take note: if you've got talent, good agents and managers will find you.' The ad, although it stopped short of saying as much, was a collective 'Up Yours' to the entertainment industry, as well as a demonstration that, if Bernard was aware that Las Vegas was a deeply ironic exercise, he chose to turn a blind eye to that implication. As far as he was concerned, he made it in Las Vegas – and, in a substantial sense, he did.

In going along with the Las Vegas idea, Bernard placed a quite touching faith in Hamp, especially as the Granada man had said openly that he would have been quite happy – for strictly televisual reasons, at least – for Bernard to die the death in front of an American audience. He did not shield Bernard from this view, and told him it would be just as good a film had he died on his bum – 'Not so good for him, maybe,' he adds today. Bernard confessed he was scared by the possibility of an embarrassing flop, but went ahead anyway. He had dreamed of playing Las Vegas for many years. In the event, the show he did, albeit on a quiet afternoon in the Nevada desert, was not a flop at all, and ended with Bernard being offered a contract to play in a more starring role. The contract could have been worth up to £750,000, but would have kept Bernard away from home for six months. He turned it down.

'Bernard got very excited about Las Vegas,' Hamp remembers. 'It was a funny thing really, but he has always put great trust in me. Whatever I suggested, he'd say, "If you think it's going to work, I'll do it." When I asked him to do his first special, to show him as a comic, as a singer, and as someone that had good repartee with other artists, Bernard said to me, "Thank God you didn't ask me to do sketches or acting. I'd have done it because you'd asked me, but I am glad you haven't." '

The beauty of the Las Vegas project, of course, was the sublime incongruity between Bernard's blunt, abrasive northern English humour and the more sophisticated comedy that an American audience might expect. He stocked up on Jewish, Irish and Italian jokes, but was not prepared to dilute the earthier aspects of his act for sensitive American ears, even though his mother's parting comment when he left home was, 'Now, our Bernard, don't be rude.' In theory at least, Bernard's form of insult humour was not entirely new in the US, anyway. He had for many years been fascinated by the Californian comic Don Rickles, who is equally rude to ethnic minorities, and happened to be on in Las Vegas at the same time as Bernard. One of his great treats while he was there was to see a Rickles show and meet the comedian backstage.

Bernard has since always compared himself to Rickles although in truth Rickles's act is far more intellectually sophisticated than the nightly bearpit maulings at the Embassy Club. He tends to be regarded as risqué and adult by middle-class audiences, rather than beyond the pale as Bernard so often is in Britain.

Now, I'm not saying life has to be a fucking Coke commercial (Rickles ranted in a recent TV appearance) but it would be great if I could tell a Polish joke once in a while without a horde of them descending on my house and unscrewing all my fucking lightbulbs ... You know, if you're gonna insist on telling me it's natural for all people of all races and ethnicities to get along, well, you're living in a fantasy world full of elves and fairies. And, incidentally, elves and fairies didn't get along either. They hate each other. Elves refer to fairies as 'flying Tinkerbell Nancy boys' and fairies call elves 'rainbow-humping suckpots' ... Human beings always have and always will actively look for people to not get along with. And, this is true even within groups – northern Californians don't get along with Irish Protestants, circus clowns fight with birthday-party clowns ... Begrudging someone else's existence just happens to be the most convenient way to validate our own ... Bottom line, America is a polyglot, bastardised culture. It's been settled by wave after wave of immigrants who assimilated and became part of the establishment so that they could one day look down their noses at the next wave of immigrants. Therein lies the paradox of this great land of ours – freedom of beliefs also means freedom to make fun of the 7–11 guy's sandals.

Interestingly, Rickles, who is certainly as outrageous, even if he is a little upmarket from Bernard, has been welcomed far more into the mainstream of American comedy than has Bernard in Britain. He has been a lifelong friend of Frank Sinatra, and has had his own prime-time situation comedy (*C.P.O. Sharkey*, in which he played a Navy man whose character was substantially based on Rickles's stand-up routine) and was hired as the voice of the grumpy Mr Potato Head in the Disney film *Toy Story*. In 1988, Rickles was even – and here Bernard could surely not even begin to compete – named by the Tailors' Council of America as the best-dressed man in comedy.

Bernard, considering himself to be the Don Rickles of Harpurhey, was going to be launched on to the greater stage of the USA. Although he was completely unknown in America, Bernard felt able to make a relatively brash, showbiz-like entry to the USA, as the £40,000 budget allocated for the film allowed him to bring an entourage with him that included his younger brother Frank, Young Bernard, who was sixteen, and Barry Clark, who is Bernard Senior's best friend. Vera, however, stayed in Manchester. The trip was designated by Bernard as a strictly boys' outing.

Bernard's journey to Las Vegas started, as did Hamp's film, with him saying goodbye to his regulars at the Embassy. The film opened with a moody view of Manchester in the winter. At the club, Bernard's farewell evening was going well. Signs said '*Bon Voyage Bernard*' and the crew circulated among the club regulars to ask how they imagined their local hero would do in the States. As ever, northern honesty prevailed, even on camera: 'I don't think he'll go down very well,' opined one woman. 'I think the Americans will be offended. Like when people walk in the club and he insults them, that goes down great here because of the sense of humour of the northern people. But in America I should imagine that the type of people who go to Las Vegas are the type with plenty of money, who like gambling, and will probably take offence.'

'The American sense of humour is not like ours,' said another Embassy customer. 'I see American programmes and I don't know what they are laughing at. I don't understand what they are laughing at because I just don't laugh at their sense of humour. And they won't at our sense of humour – especially Bernard Manning's.'

Hamp, meanwhile, was already out in the States cranking up the media machine for Bernard's arrival. He recalls a situation which happened minutes after Bernard landed, a scene which – thankfully – never made it into the film.

I was out in Vegas in advance lining things up, and arranged to meet Bernard in Los Angeles, where we were going to stay overnight and fly in the next day to Vegas to meet the film unit and have the big welcome and all that (Hamp recounts). I went down to LA airport to meet him, and I was leaning over and watching them come through customs. Bernard came out, this big, unshaven man with a pink shirt and red braces and virtually the first person he saw on American soil was this enormous black porter, walking by. He had this huge pile of suitcases on a trolley, and one under each arm, and he was sweating like a pig, and I heard Bernard shout, 'Hello, my friend, free at last, free at last!' But the guy took it very well. If someone else had done that, he would have thumped them, but this guy joined in and said, 'Yeah, free at last, look at this.'

What was televised however was the welcome fit for a star at Las Vegas airport, with the mayor on hand to greet the man who had been promoted ahead as Britain's biggest entertainer (not entirely a fib). It was a funny sort of big-time showbiz star who was travelling on a brand new passport, because he had not been out of Britain since doing military service, but the Americans were not to know this. 'It's my very first trip to America and it won't be my last I can tell you,' he assured his hosts, though as it turned out, it was his last to date. Outside the terminal building was an open-topped red Cadillac, from which Bernard waved like Prince Philip as he passed Caesar's Palace, the Flamingo, Circus Circus, The Sands – 'names I'd only seen before on American TV movies, and now were right there in front of me.' The Yanks cheered and waved at a man most

109

of them had never even heard of until the publicity had started rolling a couple of weeks earlier.

As they were driving along, Bernard asked his American hosts how much the car cost. He was told $40,000. 'You'd think for that sort of money it would have four doors and a roof,' he quipped. 'It wasn't the most brilliant joke I've ever cracked, but the Americans were repeating it gleefully to each other as our convoy of Cadillac, film truck and fleet of taxis wound its way slowly along the famous Vegas Strip.' The party ended up at the MGM Grand, the world's largest hotel and entertainment complex. Bernard, now temporarily renamed American-style as 'Ber-nard', and his room-mate, Young Ber-nard, were booked into a penthouse suite on the twenty-sixth floor, which had been decked out with flowers flown in from Hawaii. The suite, where Elvis Presley used to stay, had a private bar twenty-five feet long and three bathrooms with gold taps. Bernard found the huge bed uncomfortable: 'It takes you ten minutes to walk round it,' he said. 'You need rucksack rations to sleep in it. I miss the wife's elbow.' He took instead to sleeping squashed up on the chintzy Louis XV-style sofa. 'Young Bernard and I looked at each other,' he recounted in a *Sunday People* article. 'I said, "Well, old lad, your dad's come a long way since those days on the back of a greengrocery cart." And Young Bernard replied: "You sure have, dad. I just hope these Yanks can understand your gags." '

On the first occasion he was required to crack a joke in the line of duty, as British comedy's ambassador to Las Vegas, the Yanks understood it all too clearly. As part of the publicity package Bernard was interviewed on the local radio station KLAV 1230. Here, he tried a Jewish joke, aware that in America Jewish stories are far more mainstream than in Britain. He told the story about Hymie and his wife who wants to bathe in champagne. After she has her bath, they re-bottle the champagne and find there's some extra. 'Becky, you didn't . . .' says Hymie. The DJ laughed – a lot – then added, 'I've got to warn you that we're on live radio here, I've got to watch your punchlines because you're liable to knock us off the air.'

There was plenty to amuse the boys from Harpurhey besides filming. They drove out to the state line to cross into Arizona and larked about changing their watches forward and back, Arizona being in a different time zone from Nevada. The gang all dined together in a three-dollars-for-all-you-can-eat joint: 'I'm telling you, real grub. Chunks of beef, chicken, cod, hake, apple pie and custard. Can't be bad, eh?' Bernard enthused in the *TV Times* article. (Custard? Was he mistaken, or had the stuff made its first-ever appearance on the American continent in his honour?) Bernard enjoyed seeing so many fat people in America. 'From what I can see, I'm average size here,' he said. 'The shops are full of underpants my size. I've sent Bernard Junior out to buy fifty pairs.' In this manner, Bernard and his party had a magnificent four days before the afternoon he was booked to appear. In between doing bits for Hamp's film, they took in shows by Tom Jones, Liberace and Paul Anka. One night, Hamp and an expatriate, Charles Mather, who ran a show-business management agency, organised a barbecue at Mather's home for Bernard to meet American comedians and pick their brains. He told one of them his old story of the man with two wooden legs being burned to the ground. The American loved it, and said he was having dinner with Paul Anka and would tell him the joke.

During this lull period, there was a last-minute change to the line-up at the theatre. According to the huge MGM Grand sign, which Bernard was photographed in front of repeatedly and Hamp even hired a helicopter to film from the air, Bernard was supposed to be appearing with Shecky Greene, a comedian. Greene, however was caught up at the last minute in a legal case, and Joan Rivers took his place. Rivers featured briefly in the film, reclining on a sunlounger alongside Bernard, chatting. To Bernard's regular clientele in Manchester, this sight of Bernard, complete with deafening Hawaiian shirt and sunglasses, hobnobbing with the stars, would convince them that he had 'arrived' and that their envoy had been accepted in Vegas, even though to the trained eye the Rivers–Manning interchange was perhaps a little stilted and tense, with Bernard saying very little. Yet if Harpurhey needed further confirmation of Bernard's stardom overseas, it came in the next shot of three very pink, sequined and feathered Las Vegas showgirls welcoming and kissing Bernard in his dressing room.

On the day, Bernard was given Dean Martin's dressing room. 'I made my mark by peeing down his sink. It's an old show-business tradition. But that didn't relieve my jingling stage-nerves as I marched out on stage to the stirring notes of "Rule Britannia" to face two and a half thousand Americans.' (Although Bernard was told it was a full house, the *TV Times* reporter estimated there were more like 500, but it was still a remarkable turnout for an afternoon show by a British unknown.)

In the film, Hamp added the nice touch of the 'Also Sprach Zarathustra' music from *2001* to the Bernard-coming-on stage sequence. Bernard, bedecked in a red velvet jacket, a red bow tie and a frilly shirt, was probably more anxious than he has ever been in public. He sniffed hard, licked his lips, and the muscle in one cheek tensed involuntarily. He was seconds from going on, and the compère announced, 'And now, direct from Harpurhey, Manchester, England ...' Bernard Manning was finally playing Vegas.

Forcing himself into a laugh, he walked on, seeming relaxed and happy, leaving Johnnie Hamp nervously smoking a cigarette backstage. Bernard immediately had trouble getting the microphone off its stand. 'That's a good start,' he muttered, but it wasn't a problem at all. Curiously, he tried to start with some racist hard-fire material, which sounded a little laboured. The first thing he said to the audience was that he had spotted a Pakistani over from England in the audience. 'I didn't see you till you smiled,' he said. When he relaxed into his other gags he was much better. He hadn't had a woman in ... he began distractedly, then asked, 'Is $5 too much for a hooker?' They laughed. Taking care to turn birds into broads, tramps into hobos, Bernard soldiered on.

The Jewish kamikaze pilot who crashed his plane in his brother's scrapyard was a hit with the Americans. The old one about a fat man in the audience who doesn't take a bath but goes to the car wash got a laugh. 'Long live the Queen – well, she's cost enough, she should do,' was a hit. Then Bernard went back again to race, and lost it in linguistic confusion. He picked out a black man at the back and asked, 'You're a long way from home, friend. Where are you from? (pause) New Jersey? (pointing at the sleeve of his jacket) This is a new suit.' No one understood that at all. It seemed from early on in the show that Bernard, having been sold as controversial, felt he had to get in some racist material, but soon realised it got a muted reaction. Once he felt unfettered by what he was expected to produce, he was genuinely funny and generally benign. The crowd did not seem to like the Irish rapist who tied his legs together, but loved the woman who went to the hairdressers and said she wanted to look like Barbra Streisand – so they hit her on the nose with a hairbrush. They roared at Bernard talking about his friend who was an unorthodox Jew – 'He's a Nazi' – even though it was Woody Allen's line. He broke his own golden rule by telling a joke about a cripple: the night after a party, a man finds a bloke on the floor. He stands him up. The bloke falls over. He takes him home dragging him down the path, stands him up, he falls over again. He gets the bloke home. His wife is there. 'Oh, he does get pissed,' she tuts. 'Now where's his wheelchair?'

Political gags were a success: Israel has declared war on Egypt. The Italians have surrendered just in case. George Wallace [the ex-governor of Alabama, a famous racist] knocks on heaven's gates. 'Who dat?' says a voice. 'Oh, forget it,' says Wallace. (That gag was adapted from one that worked well at home by the simple substitution of Enoch Powell for Wallace.)

The Irish–Polak jokes worked well, but received best of all was Bernard's enormous stock of Jewish jokes. The first he told was about a frummer – an Orthodox Jew – whose business is failing. He asks his brother what he should do, and the brother says he must become more westernised. The frummer buys a Savile Row suit, has his beard neatly trimmed and is immediately run over by a bus. 'Lord, what have I done to deserve this,' he howls. 'To tell you the truth, Schloimy,' says God, 'I didn't recognise you.'

In an almost experimental routine, more reminiscent of alternative cabaret than regular Bernard, he performed over a minute of silent comedy, a piece about a group of conscripts waiting stark naked for their Army medical and eying one another's willies. The routine was done extremely well, and showed how he felt sufficiently confident for a slow, quite subtle, gag that could have been excruciating had he done it badly.

One of Bernard's favourites, the double-joke whammy, where the audience laugh thinking it is all over, and then he carries on, worked well.

Two lunatics escape from the asylum and arrange to meet in the centre of Las Vegas. One arrives in a big Rolls Silver Shadow. The other says, where did you get that from?' The first one says, this bird – or broad as you call them – turned up with this car, wearing mink and diamonds and asked if I fancied a trip to the countryside for half an hour. She took me right out into the desert. She took her knickers off and said you have what you want now, so I took it. (Here, Bernard mimics a steering-wheel motion, the audience laughs. He pauses and then bangs in the tag line.) So the other said, 'You're not a bad judge, because the knickers might not have fit you.'

Bernard got plenty of singing into his act, a brave idea, again, with an American audience. He did a stirring 'Without You', finishing with a buoyant exclamation of 'Yeah, Dawgie' in a passable Yankee accent. He seemed, at last, relaxed and to have got his bearings. He ended the afternoon on a positively resounding 'Be My Love', a Mario Lanza song, before a genuinely happy farewell to the audience. 'Good Afternoon,' he beamed, 'God Bless You All For Coming, Thank You Very Much.'

They took just about five minutes to decide they liked Mr Ber-nard Manning, (Bernard continues in his own account of the show). I sang my finest version of 'Be My Love', moved easily into my jokes, and literally held that audience in my hands for nearly two hours. In a way, they were an easier audience than some of the boozy customers in the clubs back home. Of course, I had to switch my jokes around a bit. In the Irish stories, the Irishmen are Polaks to the Yanks. I told the gag about the Polak who was arrested for rape. He went on an identity parade and, as the victim was led into the room, the Polak shouted: That's her! But the story that went down best of all was the one where I told the audience they should never have impeached President Nixon, or even considered it. All they needed to do was get Teddy Kennedy to give him a lift home. That sent them falling about laughing. Then, at the end of my act, I sang my favourite, 'Without You', blew a stream of kisses to the standing, shouting, applauding Yanks, and walked off in blissful ecstasy.

Johnnie Hamp's film confirmed that Bernard's own perspective was more or less accurate. He did get a standing ovation, if a rather polite one. He was warmly received by the early afternoon audience, tempted in from the gambling tables and one-armed bandits. There was a definite sense of puzzlement from the Americans at times, as viewers back home saw, but the Vegas public unquestionably laughed – by no means a common experience for British comics trying to work in the US.

To mirror the earlier vox pop in Harpurhey, the crew went out again into the crowd to ask what people thought of the show. 'Oh, we thought he was fantastic, tremendous,' said one woman. 'He had an outstanding voice. I think that he would fit in with the type of entertainment that's presented here. His jokes I liked very much. His singing was beautiful.' 'I thought he was very funny. I really enjoyed his jokes but I was surprised that when he sings he doesn't have an accent,' said another. A man was similarly enthusiastic. 'I loved him, I thought he was very talented, very funny, very warm and confident, he had a great singing voice and he blends it all together very nicely. I think if he would come to this town as an opening act, he would do very well.'

After the show, a stream of other comics came into the dressing room to tell Bernard they hoped he realised how good he was. A Lancashire woman who knew his father's shop on the Rochdale Road dropped in, and Bernard called for champagne as he handed out LPs to his new fans. The champagne didn't come, as there were only soft drinks available. 'Never in me wildest dreams did I think I'd be doing all this,' he said, still a little dazed. 'Seeing my name on a big sign, having a helicopter taking pictures of it all for the TV. That was really summat. All those years of poverty really did flash by me then.'

Young Bernard, who in Las Vegas told his father for the first time how brilliant he thought his old man was (although he places the moment when he truly appreciated Bernard's talent a little later, at a show in Leeds), was keeping an alert, quizzical eye on the whole spectacle.

He loved every minute of it (he says today). I was analysing him as we went around, and he was definitely taken aback with Las Vegas. He was, like, 'This is *it*', absolutely full of it, and I know that in his

115

own mind he was very proud of the fact that he had got there and he was going to make the most of it. Because he did, he made them laugh. This guy waved a piece of paper in his hand and said, 'Have I got a contract for you,' and me dad wouldn't take it up. The fella couldn't understand it, but me dad said, 'I've got a club to run, the Embassy Club, and I can't be away for three months, six months touring the west coast of America and Australia.' It was mega money, and he said – I remember him saying it – 'I'm not interested in that. I've got me own punters.' They were his words.

Other than that (Young Bernard concludes), I don't think he has got any desires to go abroad at all. I think recently he was offered work in Dubai, but he wasn't interested. 'Too hot for me,' was all he said.

More Mr Nice Guy

All I wish is that he'd let himself go a bit. He's outrageous when the cameras aren't on him.

Vera Manning, 1976

On a summer's afternoon in 1996, Bernard Manning, looking oddly like a Michelin man at the wheel of his pale blue Rolls-Royce (registration number 1 LAF) turns from the Rochdale Road into Westbourne Grove, the short cul-de-sac at the bottom of which lies the main entrance to the Embassy Cabaret Club. Drivers toot on their horns at him as he turns, and people on passing orange Manchester buses wave. He beams and waves back. All this recognition and adulation – and just a few yards from the site of his father's now demolished greengrocer's shop – are the routine, day-to-day thrills that make it all worthwhile for Mr Bernard Manning. Then, as he gets out of the car, his voice lowered confidentially, he describes something even more wonderful that sometimes happens when you used to be poor, but now are worth millions and are on to your seventh Rolls. 'You wouldn't believe what it's like when you drive up to the Dorchester down in London and places like that in this,' he says. 'Everyone shows such respect. And you know that all these people in their little Montegos feel inferior to you. You can't beat that, I'll tell you.'

It was an unusually transparent sort of comment, but Bernard has never had any inclination to hide his mission to outwit, out-earn and out-do the rest of the world. Even detractors, of whom, to put it mildly, there is no shortage, grudgingly admire his honesty in the matter. When you combine Bernard's gargantuan, indomitable ego with the bumptiousness and determination to take the piss, which comes as standard issue with every northern English male, some explanation begins to suggest itself for the extraordinary business of Bernard's turbulent relationship with his fellow comedians.

On the stage, he is breathtakingly rude to members of the public. He has been known to greet a black man with, 'I'll tell you something mate. If you don't laugh tonight, we'll cut down the trees. Then how will you get home?' Elderly couples are told, 'Bleedin' hell! Look at that – a trainee corpse. Give our love to Elvis when you see him.' 'They come here to be insulted,' Bernard explains. 'They want to laugh at themselves, and I help them do it. They know I don't tell fairy stories. When I'm on TV, people see a nice little fat chubby fella who doesn't rock the boat. But that's not me. That's why I don't do so much TV any more. I'm at home in a club.' This insulting behaviour is, as Bernard is at pains to point out, a joke, an exaggerated version of the regular cut-and-thrust of northern people having a laugh together, which generally takes the form of them maligning and belittling one another. (His repartee with the public went spectacularly wrong only once: 'This chap walked across the front of the stage while I was on,' Bernard relates, 'and I broke off and said to him, "Who cut your hair? Tell us who it is, and we'll get him for you." This fellow stopped, lifted his hair and waved it about. It was a wig and he was as bald as Yul Brynner underneath. Then he replaced it and carried on to the gents. I was dumbstruck. There was no answer to that.')

The public seem to enjoy being slighted by Bernard, but with his colleagues in the entertainment industry, however, he is in a permanent state of war. Some of this is an off-stage extension of his act, but frequently the attrition is so fierce that it starts to appear ugly and embarrassing. Bernard has cast himself as the black sheep of comedy, and nobody knows quite how to handle him. Fellow comedians and performers are more than often shocked by the things he says, and react in a distinctly non-comedic way.

'He insults everyone,' observed the gentle and sweet-natured Vera before she died, 'especially the young rock group fellas. He introduces them by saying they shouldn't have got dressed up. The dustbins are round the back.' Bernard's professional insults seem to be an unstoppable, knee-jerk reaction, a ready method, like the Rolls-Royce, of making people feel inferior to him. And whereas his scatological and racist humour have emerged only late in life and accelerated with each personal tragedy that has befallen him – a process that will be examined later – Bernard's foulness to his

peers goes back decades, and gives every impression of being not
so much a pose he strikes, but something more personal.

Asked whom he admires in comedy, Bernard answers:

'W.C. Fields. I love sarcastic comedy. It was him that said, "The first
thing I do in the morning is smile. Get it over with." I loved that.'
(The idea of Bernard actually laughing at another comedian may
be an unfamiliar one, but there is an authenticated record of this
happening. The Harpurhey local historian, Joe Kay, recalls in the
fifties being at the Palladium cinema, close by where the Embassy
Club now stands, and seeing Bernard a few rows ahead, watching
W.C. Fields and 'laughing his head off'.) 'Don Rickles, I love.
Tommy Cooper. Groucho Marx – a genius. Jackie Mason is very
funny. Laurel and Hardy. I like Billy Dainty. And Benny Hill. Eric
Morecombe, Ronnie Barker and Bobby Ball also make me laugh.
The rest are all fucking wankers. Les Dawson? Fucking hell, no.
Ken Dodd? No, they're childish comics.'

Bernard has also expressed his admiration for Frank Carson, Jim
Bowen and Johnny Hackett. 'These are down-to-earth characters,
and they and one or two others and myself meet, have a few drinks
and tell blue gags. They are not big-headed and still lead normal
lives ... give me someone like Eric Morecambe was, any day. Totally
untouched by it all, by show business, anything. Once you start
cutting yourself off from the people you are trying to entertain,
you're finished.' Bernard was especially upset, he says, by the Surrey-
isation of Mike Yarwood.

People seem to change when they get to the top. Mike comes from
up this way. I knew him as a lovely, natural lad but, as soon as he
made it, he started speaking all posh. 'Why the hell are you talking
to me like that?' I asked him. 'It doesn't wash with me' ... The only
impression I'd like to see him do now is one of the Invisible Man.

'Most of the so-called comics of today are lazy buggers,' (Bernard
insists). 'They do the same act over and over again. They're bone
idle. I do more work preparing my act for one night than most of
them do in six months. All they can think of is getting out on the
golf course. And you don't learn to entertain by hitting a golf ball.

119

Bernard is in his element being rude about competitors. It is part of his act and image, and he plays up to it as much as he can. Of Colin Crompton, with whom he co-presented *Wheeltappers and Shunters*, Bernard said: 'He hasn't got a clue. In my opinion, he's about as funny as typhoid fever. Colin could never put me in the shade ... and Tommy Trinder's about as funny as woodworm in a cripple's crutch. But he's still quick on the uptake. When he was recording a *Wheeltappers* show, Colin Crompton interrupted him. Trinder said, "Do you get the same money as a professional?" It brought the house down.' (During the show, Bernard had introduced Trinder thus: 'Here's a very funny man. Tommy Trinder is to comedy what Danny La Rue is to all-in wrestling.' Trinder later declared, 'That remark about getting the same money as a professional was made to Bernard Manning, not Colin Crompton. And he tried to have it cut out of the show ... But if Manning says he's the best comic in the business, then he must be right and my sense of humour's wrong.' 'Tommy Trinder', riposted Bernard, 'he's the star of the film *The Foreman Went to France* – and that was made forty years ago.')

Frank Carson, although an old mate and one of the select band of performers Bernard admires, has never been immune from a harsh word. 'He's doing quite well these days renting his mouth out to stunt motorcylists to jump over,' Bernard said in 1980. 'He opened a hotel in Blackpool, too. They tell me it's an ashtray with music. The IRA sent over a squad to attack it, but when they saw it they thought it had already been bombed. Frank has imposed a 10p cover charge at his hotel to keep out the riff raff.' Towards another *Comedians* veteran, Ken Goodwin, with whom Bernard clashed at the London Palladium, he was equally disagreeable. 'As a comic,' Bernard said, 'he's a good banjo player. I've hired him at my Embassy Club. But he's about as funny as a hole in a parachute ... Do you wonder whatever happened to him? Well, I saw him three weeks ago. I bought some shoelaces from him.'

Max Bygraves, a particular *bête noir* of Bernard's since he saw him at Blackpool as a boy and thought he could sing better himself, has been the prompt for some spectacular Manning invective.

I was thinking of Max the other day (he said in the early 1980s) and it occurred to me what a great help he could have been to the police during the miners' strike. He could break up a picket line with one song. He's known in the theatre as the neutron bomb of comedy. He gets rid of the audience but leaves the theatre standing. I should hate to leave this world and be remembered only by my Singalong records. When he took his son, Anthony, for a show in the Channel Islands they held a referendum there a few weeks later on whether the islanders would rather have Max and his son back or the German occupation forces. The Germans won by a big majority . . . He's working in Oldham this week, but there'll be more people in the doctor's surgery next door than in the theatre.

Bruce Forsyth was another old stager subjected to a stream of Bernard's insults – disparagement that seems to go a crucial step beyond mere teasing: 'He's a classic example of someone who shouldn't be a success,' Bernard says. 'He worked to half empty audiences in London in *The Comedy Man*, and he died on Broadway. But there are always jobs for the boys. Brucie can't sing. He dances like a poor man's Fred Astaire. And I need his type of humour like a reindeer needs a hat rack. In this business you're only as good as your last show. Well, his was terrible. I keep the tropical fish so I have something entertaining to watch when Bruce Forsyth is on telly. He should buy a taxi and earn a decent living.' When it was pointed out that this attack on Forsyth was a little unprovoked, Bernard explained his philosophy on the matter to a reporter; 'My motto is, "Never hit a man when he's down. Kick him – it's easier," ' he said.

Leslie Crowther and Arthur Askey fared no better: 'I see them on TV and they are supposed to be funny men – I think.' Of Ronnie Corbett, Bernard expressed the view: 'He couldn't make it on his own. He's a little passenger for Ronnie Barker. I wouldn't pay Ronnie Corbett in washers. I really don't know how these people made it in the first place. He's what's known in the business as a comedian's labourer. He's got a face that even Snow White couldn't like ... managements only use him to make their drinks look bigger.'

One by one, Bernard demolished colleagues with a crafted, and sometimes not-so-crafted piece of insolence. Asking Bernard for a pithy, free character reading on fellow show-business stars and others became a Fleet Street standby that still, to a large extent, remains popular. Ken Dodd, he said, 'Looks like a cross between Bugs Bunny and a Brillo pad. Anybody who is so ugly abuses the privilege of belonging to the human race. If there is such a thing as reincarnation, I hope he comes back as a comic.' During Dodd's prosecution and trial for tax offences (Dodd was acquitted) Bernard enjoyed nightly jokes about the proceeding court case. 'He's stage-struck and won't come off . . . if he gets two years he'll do four.'

On Hughie Green, the sixties game-show host: 'I don't think he has any talent and has nothing to offer me whatsoever . . . God knows where he got his acts from. I think he advertised for them in the *War Cry.*' On Bob Monkhouse: 'He's got no personality. It grates on everyone who watches him . . . he's just been hired by Gerry Cottle's Circus. The lion's going to put his head in Monkhouse's mouth.' On Des O'Connor: 'He runs a close second to Hughie Green for having no talent at all. He's even meaner than Jack Benny was. He pulled out a packet of fags the other week, and a cigarette card of Stanley Matthews fell on the floor . . . Flashing his dimples at his age, pretending he's still seventeen. There's nothing worse, is there? Trying to be something you're not. Bloody pathetic.' On Tom O'Connor: 'The clean-cut, never-tell-a-blue-story comedian. Did you know he's been nominated for the next Pope? I'm sure when I get to heaven, peeping through the pearly gates will be Tom O'Connor and all the other clean, boring-as-hell comics.'

Some show-business stars got sharp, one-line put-downs at Bernard's hand – George Roper: 'He's modelling now for Toby Jugs. When he was a baby he was so ugly they had to tie a Choc-drop round his neck so that the family dog would play with him.' Esther Rantzen: 'I can't stand that toothy smile. She's about as funny as a burning orphanage.' Tony Blackburn: 'He has all the charm of an unflushed toilet.' Mike Reid: 'I understand he's giving elocution lessons to Arthur Mullard.' Stan Stennett: 'I'll never have him at the Embassy again. He's about as funny as rabies in a guide dogs' home.' Terry Wogan: 'A Jack of all trades and master of none. I'm sure he'd love to be in show business.' Jimmy Savile: 'People won't go by train in case he's on it.' Julian Clary: 'I don't know what people see in him. His type of humour is bitter and twisted.' Even

Frank Carson, his mate, merited a quick stab in the back: 'I've always enjoyed Frank's show. His joke is very good,' Bernard says.

Other notables got longer shrift. Freddie Starr was subjected to such a tirade. 'Freddie's a good mimic, but I don't rate him as the superstar. I'll tell twenty gags while he's thinking of one. His act today is practically the same as when it cost £175 a week ... he's the only man I know in show business who has become a star by doing the same act for fifteen years. He's always talking about going to America, but talking is as far as he gets. He's the only man the Samaritans hung up on.' Then, in a phrase fascinating to anyone who believes Bernard must, surely, be a supporter of the far right, he added: 'Freddie Starr is such a nutcase, he was refused membership of the National Front.'

Of Charlie Williams, with whom he had appeared on *The Comedians*, Bernard commented: 'I don't know what it is about Charlie, he tries to be Yorkshire, but his accent comes and goes when it takes him. I go to Yorkshire, and not many people there talk like he does, with thee and thou and my old flower, my old son.' On TV, Bernard once introduced Williams by saying, 'Charlie's a very funny man. He's black, but he can come and live next door to me any time. I happen to live next to the Southern Cemetery.' ... 'Of the ex-*Comedians*, the wrong-coloured comic made it for my money,' Bernard said in 1976. 'I don't think Charlie Williams should have gone as far as he did, but he took a knock when he appeared on *The Golden Shot* and it didn't do him any good. In my opinion, Josh White is more polished than Charlie Williams and should have succeeded internationally.'

Jimmy Tarbuck was dealt with with relative briskness:

He appeared at my club many years ago and we are still open despite it ... my New Year resolution is to drop six stone – on top of Jimmy Tarbuck. That man is to comedy what Woodbines were to Sir Winston Churchill. He should stay out on the golf course and let Tony Jacklin do the comedy ... I saw his act last year. It was like watching a coffin on its way to the cemetery. He opened up with, 'You lucky people'. The only thing lucky was that they hadn't locked the theatre doors and people could get out – which they did in large numbers as it went from bad to worse. Some people never know when to give up.

Rolf Harris was the honoured recipient of one of Bernard's funniest slights, a jibe that could easily have come out of Ben Elton's mouth: 'My mum, Nellie,' he said, 'thinks he's a painter and decorator. And tying kangaroos down ... what's that all about? I can tell from the audiences at my club the people they don't like as soon as I start talking about them. Rolf's one of them. And so is Arthur Scargill.'

Enjoying the notoriety he garnered by being so rude about comedians whenever a reporter was within earshot, Bernard again went for maximum effect when, in 1982, he won the national Club Comedian of the Year award – as he did a second time, in 1985. To celebrate the award, he sent 'get well' messages to Max Bygraves, Jimmy Tarbuck and Les Dawson. 'A lot of comedians were jealous that I got to Las Vegas,' Bernard says. 'Des O'Connor for one. They were going to book him at a top hotel but cancelled him. They installed automatic roller towels for excitement instead.'

Of the newer, more modern comedians, Jo Brand has been a subject of particular astonishment – bewilderment, almost – for Bernard, as well as something of a godsend. A surprising number of Bernard's critics in recent years have, in quite a childish way, picked on his fatness and, as if they were in the playground, added to critiques of his racism the observation that he is ugly too. Brand, as a less than classically beautiful woman, put herself among the 'Bernard is fat and ugly' school of opinion, and Bernard was waiting for her. He maintains: 'I have got a lot to thank her for, because I sell alcohol and I get half my living out of alcohol. She had a go at me the other week, so I said the only reason they invented alcohol was so that ugly women could get a fuck. The only way she'd ever get a fuck would be to get the vibrator pissed. That'll knock her bleeding sick ... Jo Brand with her sick toilet humour. If she was in India she'd be sacred. Do you ever hear me talk about sanitary towels? I talk about sex, about what people do.'

Les Dawson, with whom Bernard is continually confused, even by other comedians, was equally the butt of Bernard's abuse. (Frequently, critics complain about Bernard's 'mother-in-law' jokes, yet, perhaps because of his reverence for family, he has never told one – 'They're just not funny,' he says.)

Les Dawson doesn't tell gags,' Bernard said on one occasion. 'He just refreshes your memory ... When he's telling jokes, it's like having a tooth pulled out without anaesthetic.' On another occasion, he said of Dawson, 'Watching him is like watching a coffin walk.' In 1992 Bernard's act included a routine about the death of Les Dawson, which Bernard (rightly, as it turned out) implied might be imminent. Off stage, he was asked by an *Observer* journalist to comment on Dawson's stated philosophy 'Be kind'. 'Yeah, well, he'll wind up fucking skint, won't he?' Bernard responded. 'He's not in my fucking league. He's third division. He dresses up as women.'

When Dawson died the following year, however, Bernard was lavish in full, sentimental tribute.

> Les Dawson was the last of the clowns (he said). He used to amble on, something like myself, with all the fat bouncing, and people laughed because they were glad they didn't look like you. Les and I first worked at a social club in Harpurhey when we were both semi-pros. I was a greengrocer and Les was on the knocker, selling Hoovers door-to-door. That's where he got a lot of his material. In those days, we were paid two guineas for half an hour. It was working-class humour. We all lived in back-to-backs in those days and had dragons for mother-in-laws, and you'll never hear material like that again.

It seems highly unlikely that Bernard's kind, regretful words on Dawson's death were insincere. He would have been quite capable of refusing to comment, or even telling a joke at Dawson's expense, when he heard the news. Bernard is massively sentimental, but shedding crocodile tears has never been a failing. Yet he is by no means consistent in his views. Just as he swears he doesn't tell 'sick' jokes about cripples, but then promptly does, he sometimes justifies his revilement of other comics as being simple honesty, and at other times claims, disingenuously perhaps, that his attacks, like his racial jokes, are 'just a joke'.

'I don't give a damn about any of them. I don't owe them anything,' he told the *Sun* in 1975, after a session of piling abuse on colleagues. 'I can hold my own with any comedian in this country – especially in cabaret, the most lucrative of all work. Most television comedians are no good in cabaret ... If I met comics I didn't like, I couldn't possibly say, "Hello, how are you? I like your show." I'd have to say, "I think it's a load of bloody rubbish and in my opinion you're about as funny as a hole in a parachute.' He used his Las Vegas adventure as an opportunity to have another dig at his fellow comics: 'I just hope that all those old guys who used to be with me in *The Comedians* will be watching the TV, so they can learn what comedy is all about,' he crowed. 'I'd like to see them in Vegas.'

Asked in 1978 why he persisted in insulting other comedians, he said, 'That's what I honestly feel about them. I'm the kind of man who speaks his mind. I can't stand phonies and I dislike the comedians who go about calling themselves superstars.' And when, in 1980, one tabloid's readers voted Bernard 'the most hated man on TV', Bernard was positively boastful:

> I'm not worried. It's never been my style to make myself liked. I want audiences to pay close attention to me, and think hard about what I'm telling them, certainly. But as for liking me, I couldn't care less. I'm a blue comedian through and through, an attacking, often vicious, comedian ... Everybody knows that. What I like about this country is that it's free. We can all say what we like. The people who want to knock me can call me a big fat slob with a mouth as big as Jaws. That's fine with me, as long as they don't get the wage packets mixed up.

Just a year previously, however, in a *News of the World* interview, Bernard insisted: 'I don't hate anybody. Never have. People are potty if they think I mean it. I've worked with most of them as well, the Yarwoods and the Tarbucks. Almost all are great entertainers ... All that attacking the other comics has ever done is put bums on seats and provide some free publicity for all concerned.' In 1984, he continued on the same tack in the *Sunday Mirror.* 'People know what kind of bloke I am,' he said. 'They know I'm just geeing them up. I've always had a jokey way of being rude. I don't hate anyone.' Bernard admitted that Max Bygraves loathes his abuse, as did Bruce Forsyth, but said, 'It's because they take themselves so seriously. They are full of their own importance. Their attitude says more about them than it does about me. All they do is make me have a go at them more. I can't stand that side of show business – the snobbery, the big I Am.'

Whatever his reasoning – or excuses – may have been, with Bernard in such provocative form, and his determination to place himself outside the show-business mainstream so plain to see, it is not surprising that rivals tried to hit back at him. Some have succeeded, yet there always seems to be a critical edge of venom missing when showbiz victims of Bernard's spite try to bite him back. In 1975, for example, he appeared at a working-men's club with Ivor Davis. 'I was never allowed on first,' Davis complained in the *Daily Star.* 'Maybe he was afraid I'd spoil his act. The truth is he can't work without being blue and the truth is he's not as funny as me.' (Davis nevertheless appeared with Bernard in 1991, when Johnnie Hamp got as many of the original Comedians as he could together for a twentieth-anniversary charity show.)

Throughout the seventies and eighties, other comics lined up to take a pot shot at Bernard. 'They tell a joke in the business,' Mike Reid said. 'If Bernard Manning and a hippo fell off Blackpool Tower, who would hit the ground first? Who cares?' Freddie Starr was barely more charitable: 'He is a funny man in his own club – fantastic – but that is where he belongs ... He is fat, ugly and has no talent. In my view he's one of the worst comedians in the country.' 'I always love Bernard's act,' Lennie Bennett said. 'It saves me having to take a sleeping pill.' Charlie Williams's assessment of Bernard, as canvassed by the *Sunday People* in 1976 was: 'If slagging people off is a gimmick, then it's a poor gimmick. And he has enough talent to do without that. He just wants to rule the roost.' Jimmy Tarbuck said: 'He makes me laugh, but he couldn't be mentioned in the same breath as some of the people he has been known to have a go at, like Arthur Askey.' According to the *Sunday Mirror,* Tarbuck put it about that Bernard had always wanted to have an affair with Joan Collins, but Wimpey wouldn't put up the scaffolding. Ken Goodwin joked that, 'All the Comedians clubbed together to buy Manning a chair as a token of appreciation. We'll have to wait until he sits in it before we plug it in.'

Colin Crompton combined a joke with an observation: 'Manning gave his old clothes to Oxfam, but they're still looking for a twenty-four-stone starving African,' Crompton said, then added, 'The trouble with Bernard is that he engages mouth before putting brain in gear. I'm surprised that someone hasn't clocked him before now. He made it because he started nicking other people's gags and then found he could tell 'em a lot better than they could.' Even George Roper, whose photo Bernard today keeps on his dressing-room wall at the Embassy Club and who is a frequent visitor to Bernard's house, could not resist administering a dose of poison: 'He's the king of the toilet comics,' Roper sniped, 'an oddity like the fat lady in the circus. But he's not fit to lick Bob Monkhouse's boots.' Monkhouse himself said: 'If Manning was in the condemned cell, he'd ask for two last meals.' George Melly said of Bernard, 'Beneath that cold exterior beats a heart of pure crap.' Also from the left, Ben Elton, the then emerging genius of stand-up (and a favourite, by this time, of Young Bernard) said: 'I don't want to sound like a preacher, but we can make people laugh without being racist or sexist. Bernard Manning's mother-in-law jokes and jokes implying that all Irish are stupid are out.'

(Colin Crompton's charge that Bernard 'nicked other people's gags' might seem to border on the libellous, yet it is almost a matter of pride with Bernard himself. It is not just that jokes are not subject to copyright, and therefore can be plagiarised at will. Borrowing jokes and then improving on them by using them more skilfully is, curiously, an honourable tradition among comedians. 'This is a cut-throat business,' he says. 'Sometimes I steal a gag because I can tell it much better than the other fellow who is putting it over ... Don't forget that other comedians are always using other people's jokes. It's bloody hard to be a good comic.')

A less fleeting and arguably more wounding attack on Bernard than any of his British colleagues had launched came from Joan Rivers, whom he had met and got on with rather well in Las Vegas. The two clashed whilst recording a BBC series for Rivers. She was incensed when Bernard told jokes about AIDS, used four-letter words and said the idea of homosexuals sticking their tongues down each other's throats was disgusting.

Bernard Manning is very formidable, very, very smart (Rivers said) but I thought he was a tremendous hypocrite. I'd like another go at him because it was my first show and I was being too polite. If he's going to be that much of a sonofabitch then OK, at least we know where we stand. I was trying to be nice to the fat pig. I thought maybe he didn't mean what he said about homosexuals. He's hypocritical – don't say it's all in fun if it's not all in fun. In the States, bigots aren't allowed to speak like that on television. I have a feeling that he is secretly homosexual anyhow. He was wearing a pale blue suit with brass buttons and is crazy about his mom.

Ignoring the most obvious line of counter-attack – the bit about his suit and his mother was probably as narrow-minded and stereotyped about homosexuality as it is possible to be – Bernard appeared genuinely, and uncharacteristically, hurt. 'I thought it was a fantastic show,' he said in response to her attack. Bernard typically disarms criticism by making his opening response to the press about any contretemps a very positive statement. This in turn undermines critics by making them seem uncharitable and he the generous one. Then his usual format is to go on to defend himself.

Joan said I looked like a fat pig and I told her that with the price of bacon these days that wasn't an insult. Then she asked me if I was gay and I told her that if all women looked like her, I'd certainly turn. I kept on nailing her and she didn't like it. She was out to destroy me and it backfired. She was very upset. But people like her who dish it out should be prepared to take it.

They'll know who Bernard Manning is when they see it (he concluded). I don't know how Joan can grumble. I've heard her use four-letter words in her club act in Las Vegas. They lined her up to destroy me and she failed. But I am not going on with her again. You only get one chance at the champ. If I went back she'd have gags all lined up against me on cue cards. But to say I am a secret homosexual is going too far. That makes me very angry. My mother is eighty-five and that sort of thing could really upset her. I admire Joan but if she says things like that I don't want anything to do with her. (Bernard claimed at the time that the astrologer, Russell Grant, dropped out of the recording.) He was due to come on Joan's show but he knew he was going to get a hiding so he chickened out. I honestly believe he can see the future. He knew what he was in for.

These star-studded ding-dongs seem in retrospect to be a droll by-product of the public relations industry, and Bernard certainly does his best to explain away the exchanges as hype, and yet there is evidence that the comedy world really did take Bernard's sniping seriously. A clearly exasperated Mike Reid responded at length in the pages of the *Sunday People*:

Bernard talks a lot of old rubbish. Who in their right mind can say people like Ronnie Corbett and others he mentioned are not funny when ninety-eight per cent of the population think they are – their shows wouldn't be so popular if that weren't the case. How dare he? What gives him the right?

People in the business were absolutely choked when he first made his outburst. Everyone's phone got red hot talking about it. It's terrible the way he names people. He certainly shouldn't have a go at his own artists. He worked with Colin Crompton for years – now that's not right. He has done himself not one ounce of good in the business – in fact, it has done him a lot of harm. But he doesn't care, he couldn't care less. He doesn't care about anything or anybody – he seems to have no feelings. Some people just don't want to know him. When you say Bernard Manning, they say Bernard who? The man is wealthy and I suppose that is partly why he doesn't care about anybody, because it doesn't matter. Bernard Manning – that's all he's worried about. If it wasn't for Johnnie Hamp, the producer, he wouldn't get a day's work on the box. Look at his track record – everything is for Johnny Hamp and Granada. Bernard thinks he is the greatest comic in the world. He couldn't kiss my arse as a comic, and I have proved it dozens of times when we have been on stage together. When we did *The Comedians*, I got on with Bernard better than anyone. He gives everybody a lot of stick, he shouts and screams at them, has a go at them and makes them feel small. He's like that. But I gave him just what he gave me so Bernie and I got on very well.

Freddie Starr too joined the spluttering counter-attack.

Bernard has talent (Starr said). God gifted him with a big mouth. He knocks everybody in the business and says nobody should be on the same bill as him. He is laughable. God gave *me* talent. I'll walk on stage with Bernard any time. He can name the place – in his own club if he likes. I don't fear him. I'll even go on after him. He knows I will, because we worked together once and he said to me, 'You'll never be able to follow me.' He went on and he made me laugh, but he was so blue – filthy four-letter words every few seconds. So my strategy was to go on and do a one-hundred-per-cent-clean act. I did and got a standing ovation. He talks a good fight but when he comes into the ring with me, he is not in the same class ... Bernard put British humour back fifty years when he went to Las Vegas. He has stopped a lot of good British entertainers going over to America since. He does a lot of talking and he thinks he is the greatest thing – but he is nothing. He's just a hit man for the Brownies.

While Bernard's relations with the comedy mainstream appear to be on the poor side, to put it generously, Johnnie Hamp, his guru and mentor at Granada TV, who knows both Bernard and the show-business world better than most people, believes the real picture is actually different from that. 'I think all the other comedians treat Bernard with a bit of respect,' Hamp says. 'They all stand back. They might call him names, but they respect what he does. He is a funny man. He comes out with such wonderful lines. There was a well-known comedian who died – I can't say who it was – and someone came into a Variety Club lunch and said, "Oh, so and so has died." And Bernard came out with, "Well, how did they know?" It is a Dorothy Parker line, but the fact that this brash, northern comic had come out with it, I think, is wonderful and he is full of those.'

Strangely, that latent respect for Bernard sometimes comes more from younger, newer comedians than from the old guard. Bernard's views on 'alternative' comics are predictably uncharitable. ('There is no such thing as the new comedians,' he says. 'You mean alternative as in not funny. They're all right for three minutes on television, and then they slowly go downhill. If they were to go on stage, they'd be pinched for talking to themselves. My material is clever good material. I am a wealthy man from my material.') Yet there is a strange reluctance among young comedians to argue back, perhaps because simply to call him racist is a little obvious, while to go down the 'fat and ugly' route is both puerile and just a little politically incorrect as well.

The Bernard Manning–Stephen Fry spat of 1995 was the best example of this unexpected, almost secret, admiration for Bernard. In 1991, Bernard had commented in the *Daily Star* that, 'Stephen Fry has the wit of an unflushed toilet,' but the immediate cause of the public argument-by-newspaper-quote four years later was when Fry was quoted in a magazine: 'I've always found that the real joke is the sight of Bernard Manning going on about how fat and ugly his mother-in-law is. I defy anyone to find me anyone fatter and uglier than Bernard Manning. It's like a perfect joke – like a person covering himself with green paint and saying, "My wife's a funny colour." When I hear him I think, hang on, has this man seen himself? It's the arrogance of it, this huge man – there's a sea of Bernard Manning when you look at him.'

Bernard retorted with the salient point that Fry was probably confusing him with Les Dawson, and added a couple of fairly average jokes, by Bernard's standard of invective, to deflate Fry. 'He's got a face like a bulldog chewing a wasp, but he wasn't brought up at Eton – he was eaten and brought up,' Bernard said, adding, 'I work seven nights a week, I doubt if Mr Fry does. He'll never live to be as old as he looks.'

There is nothing more embarrassing to a meticulous and intellectual man like Fry than to realise he had got his comedic references wrong, and he immediately contacted Bernard to apologise. 'I wrote him a letter to smooth things over,' he told the Manchester *Evening News*. 'I hope there are no hard feelings. I wrote that it was very funny of him to come back with three good gags in a row.'

Bernard was delighted by the letter, and can still quote it word for word, although he threw it away. Fry, however, confirms that it was sent, and adds, when asked if he really had some regard for Bernard: 'I do indeed admire Bernard Manning's ability with a joke. Few comedians I've ever seen have been able to make the art look so simple. I had said something about how amusing it was that such a large and less than prepossessing figure should tell ugly-women jokes, and referred to black pots and kettles and so forth. His reply was along the lines of, "That Stephen Fry, he wasn't so much brought up at Eton as eaten and brought up," which tickled me.'

A Manchester comedian of a radically different nature from Bernard, Steve Coogan, referred to Bernard in oddly less than scathing terms in the Manchester *Evening News*. In a diary item, he discussed how Bernard had unwittingly funded him when he was a struggling unknown. 'I used to serve in the petrol station which Bernard used,' Coogan said. 'It was one of the old-fashioned garages where you fill up the cars of those who can't be bothered to get out. If the petrol came to, say, £36, he would give me £40 and say, "Keep the change." But if it came to £40 there would be no tip. So when I filled up his Rolls-Royce, I always made sure that it came to just about £36. He'd always tip me the rest.' Bernard, in response to this excellent item of trivia, told the newspaper's diarist, 'I wish him well. I certainly don't condemn him. That's how life goes.' Pressed for a view on Coogan's show of the moment, Bernard allowed himself a small dig – 'It's awful. Shocking.' Coogan refuses today to elaborate on his views on Manning – either to condemn or praise him. The other vogue Manchester comedian, Caroline Hook (Mrs Merton) has told a *Guardian* journalist that she has been to the Embassy Club, but declines to be drawn into discussing Bernard's comedy.

The Perrier Award-winning comedian, John Thomson, who for a while included a character called Bernard Right-On in his act similarly avoided going wholeheartedly for the Manning throat when offered the opportunity on a 1996 Granada programme, *Funny Business*. Bernard Right-On was a Manning pastiche with a twist; he would say things like, 'There was this Irishman, a black man and a Jew sitting in a pub ... now isn't that a nice example of interracial harmony?'

I am having a go at two people (Thomson explained of his creation).
I am having a go at Bernard for being racist and for not realising

what the score is these days, and I am having a go at what I call futon socialists, who are the people who make a big deal out of the fact they had a mung-bean casserole last night. It's a difficult thing to talk about because people say to me about Bernard Right-On, 'Are you on a soap box, are you trying to preach to change people?' Well, you can't teach an old dog new tricks. The older generation are not going to turn and change, to accept the new movement of comedy because they don't understand it, they know what they are stuck with and they don't know any better. They don't read *Spare Rib*. I was approached to do *The Time, The Place* as Bernard Right-On, and have Bernard on too, but I said categorically no. I wouldn't do it because he is very witty and he would tear me apart – he would *tear* me apart. I know he would.'

If anything, it is journalists of radical sensibilities that have been more condemnatory of Bernard than comedians. Over the years, dozens have been attracted up from London to interview Bernard, and he has been the inspiration for some powerful prose. Sometimes, Fleet Street baits Bernard, although he is too clever to fall for simple tricks; the *Daily Mail* sent a young female Asian journalist to interview him, and he was charm itself, as her subsequent piece reflected. For white middle-class writers and readers, Bernard Manning is generally excellent value, however, and makes exceptionally fine copy. Furthermore, Bernard appears to know it, and plays up to whatever beastly image is required of him. Not only does he not seem to care – he seems positively to relish being verbally disembowelled by day-tripping feature writers.

The use – a mutually satisfying use, one suspects – of Bernard as a journalists' scratching post precedes the more recent racism controversies by at least two decades. In the mid-seventies, in a TV review in the *Daily Mail*, Peter Cox wrote: 'For some obscure reason, possibly his wife, that fat heap of lard Bernard Manning made a misguided attempt to become an all-round entertainer on ITV last week. He is extremely good at being nasty and should abandon all hopes of becoming lovable. He is far more successful as himself.' At around the same time, Cynthia Bateman visited the Embassy Club on behalf of *The Times*. She described the (pre-fire) club wonderfully: 'Sticking out like a sore thumb among the rubble is something like a giant war-surplus Nissen hut painted for the blackout.' She added, 'The sheepskin-furnished white Rolls-Royce stands in the half derelict side street like a mayoress in a chip shop trying not to be noticed.'

A decade on, the *Observer*'s John Sweeney, then writing for the Edinburgh magazine, the *List*, was on the same train up north to take a fine and eloquent tilt at Bernard. The article was also published by the Manchester *Evening News*:

A squat toad of a man eases his fat out of the limousine. Two lithe associates follow. They fuss with the toad's stage clothes, while the object of their devotions slowly, plumply, self-importantly, waddles to the tatty tangerine door of the club. Bernard Manning is not a pretty sight. And I thought that before he took his clothes off. Well, not all his clothes. He kept on a pair of baggy underpants which long, long ago had been white but were now the colour of an old cat's teeth. He claims his vital statistics are 56:56:56. There was no doubting it when he stripped in a office-cum-dressing room. No creeping, crawling slug, no alien thing dripping in green slime, no ritual disembowelling or despicable act of torture can match it: Bernard Manning semi-nude. We chatted as he oozed into his stage clothes, purple trousers and a blue marquee of a shirt ... Oh, what company he is. We rattled through his early career at the Oldham Empire. It was hard to tell who was more uninterested: him repeating the facts, as smooth as old pebbles, me jotting them down in largely unreadable shorthand ... The voice is soft, Mancunian: the delivery quick. The feeling behind it was genuine enough ... 'The two most useless things in the world are a write-up in the *Express* and the Pope's bollocks.'

In spite of myself, he was making me smile (Sweeney continued, an honest admission of the feeling so many middle-class, professional people have at the Embassy Club when faced with the dilemma of how to respond to Bernard's most outrageous jokes). And so the conversation edged slowly along. I felt like being aggressive but it felt like bouncing puffed wheat off a hippo's back. He's not stupid, and he sensed my hostility, weakening by the minute though it was. 'My motto is never say anything behind someone's back that you can't say to his face.' It was a sort of challenge, so I

BERNARD MANNING: A BIOGRAPHY

looked him in the eye, 'You're a fat bastard.' 'No, son, you've got it wrong. I'm a fat rich bastard.' Then out it popped from his wide toad's mouth, 'Enoch Powell would have been the man. If he had gone through with it, he would have had ninety-eight per cent of the country behind him, but he missed his way.' ... With that, the atmosphere changed and became just nasty enough to leave a certain unpleasantness in the mouth. His act is obscene, cruel, malicious, racist, sexist and degrading. And worst of all, he makes people laugh.

Sweeney still admits to feeling, he says, that Bernard is a funny man. Jim Davidson, on the other hand, who tells similar race gags, none the less fails to make him laugh. Chrissy Iley, writing in the *Daily Express* a further ten years later observed: 'He comes from the kind of close-knit Mancunian working-class stock whose attitude to life is that it is a great achievement if you can live without taking a day off sick and if you can begin it and end it in more or less the same place ... Bernard is good on sentimentality. He is rheumy-eyed. But it's not an act, it's for real.' Iley concluded: 'Manning has no irony. He's stupefyingly, idiotically sincere when he says: "It's only a joke, it doesn't upset them," because what he sees is only the laughing.'

In the summer of 1995, in the wake of the *World in Action* programme, Lesley White went to see Bernard for the *Sunday Times Magazine*. Again, Bernard triggered a *tour de force* from an upmarket southern writer.

Like many public monsters, he is, in private, a pussycat, obsessed with the idea of family loyalty, marshmallow-soft about his late wife, Vera, whose early portrait adorns the cramped corner at the club he calls a dressing room, his son and grandchildren ... Manning sighs and stares at the tropical fish in the aquarium that is part of a wonderland of kitsch and memories. It is all preserved in the same cultural aspic that makes its owner one of the most outrageous museum pieces you are ever likely to meet. While the world around him bows to the demands of political correctness, he is locked in his own historical niche; the Embassy Club is a time warp where a spade can be called a spade, a nigger a nigger, and the crowds love it.

This kind of fascinated squeamishness – not to mention outright revulsion – at Bernard and his comedy is most marked among writers for national newspapers who are less used to, and as a result many times more shocked by, the rawness of Bernard's act. In Manchester, there is, even among some of the intelligentsia, an uneasy acceptance – but enjoyment, nevertheless – of Bernard's style. His insults and ruthless mickey-taking are part of a familiar, everyday scene; they are the stuff of pub friendship, factory banter and office chat. The swearing is taken for granted and unremarkable, and even Bernard's racism is understood and accepted, albeit uncomfortably, as something that happens in working-class culture. It is endemic in white people of Bernard's class, and there is little point therefore in wringing one's hands about it.

The Manchester *Evening News,* as sister paper to the *Guardian* and in the same liberal tradition, but at the same time a gutsy tabloid evening paper aimed at a broad public, is forced into a schizophrenic attitude to Bernard both by Bernard's immense popularity and its own judgement that he is a very important and significant local notable. It is inclined to report his doings in a friendly manner, since he is a cornerstone of working-class Manchester culture; on the other hand, it is pulled equally by a need to treat him objectively on the not infrequent occasions that he goes outrageously over the top. (The newspaper is not alone in this problem; Granada TV has been instrumental in building Bernard up for nearly twenty-five years, and he still regularly appears on the company's programmes. Yet the 1995 *World in Action* programme, in which he was secretly recorded telling racist gags to an appreciative audience of policemen, and which led to the Prime Minister John Major condemning Bernard in the House of Commons, was also a Granada product.)

The acceptance of Bernard as a Manchester icon extends beyond mere tolerance. Mike Summerbee, the former Manchester City footballer, explains that Manchester people 'know Bernard for what he is. They love him for his entertainment and his charity work. If you took a vote among them over the recent controversy (over the *World in Action* film) they would be overwhelmingly in Bernard's favour.' Many middle-class Mancunians go out of their way to see Bernard at the Embassy Club. As Danny Harris, a young surveyor and property agent from Hale, Cheshire, and three times a visitor to the club explains:

> Going to a working-men's club to see Bernard Manning is a novelty in itself. It's all a bit dated now, but that's part of its appeal. I've been to two stag nights and a Jewish charity event there. The first time was when the first of our crowd got married. We were all trainee lawyers, accountants, dentists, a guy in advertising, someone else who's a senior buyer for a chain – all graduates. We sat at the back in the hope that he wouldn't pick on us. Everyone said if you go near the front or move you get picked on. As it was, it was quite obviously a Jewish stag night, so as he walked past, he crossed himself. There was a black guy there, which I thought was particularly brave. Bernard said, 'Fucking hell, whose job have you got?' But he's offensive to everyone really. There was an old guy there, and Bernard said, 'Have you got grandchildren?' The chap said, 'Yes.' And Bernard said, 'I hope you've bought them some Easter eggs, 'cos I don't think you're going to make it till then.' It's all bad taste, but you've got to go with the flow. We were looking forward to having a real laugh and we did. At the charity do later, I think some people weren't very amused – perhaps they didn't know what they were going in for. I think Bernard Manning is very much a cult thing now. I can't see people taking it seriously because it's so broad. I'm not aware of any group or religion that he doesn't slag off. Whether someone's fat or Jewish or black or whatever, he'll have a go irrespective. He's anti everything and everyone. He'll laugh at himself too.

In fact, Bernard is not quite anti everyone, although his list of heroes, it has to be stressed, is a short one. It is also a somewhat eclectic group. The first idol he always mentions is Mother Theresa, 'that woman who looks after all 'em starving fucking kids in India. Mother Theresa is there in the slums of Calcutta without two bob to rub together, handling dirty, scruffy babies, risking God knows what disease. Fantastic! ... I can't stand people who do charity work and wind up with money for themselves. All that Mother Theresa has in the world is what she stands up in. I'd love to meet her. It would be a great thrill. Being the type of lady she is – and she loves everybody – she would probably think I was all right.' Johnnie Hamp is another, closely followed by Enoch Powell. Bernard thinks Powell's 1968 'Rivers of Blood' speech, in which he warned about the dangers of Britain being 'swamped by immigrants', was 'great'. To this day, he keeps a painted wax candle in the form of Powell among the treasures on his mantelpiece, along his jungle of family and career memorabilia. 'That candle was a present off somebody,' Bernard says. 'I can't remember who sent it to me. But it's Enoch Powell strangling an Indian. Enoch is a very intelligent man, there is no doubt about that, and all he has said has come true – ghettoes in every city, trouble, fighting, it'll get worse too.' Another prominent hero is the jockey Pat Eddery, who caused Bernard to win £25,000 on Dancing Brave in the Prix de L'Arc de Triomphe race in France.

A final Bernard icon probably worthy of a mention alongside Mother Theresa is Adolf Hitler, a bust of whom Bernard used to keep at home 'as an investment', he said. As ever, there may be several layers of irony, both witting and unwitting, to strip away before getting to the core of this unfashionable fancy. It would be unfair to assess what he said about Hitler in 1980 without, for example, being aware that Bernard is, by his own boast, partly Jewish, a charitable friend of the Jews and Israel, and a confirmed lover of kosher salt beef. It is also highly likely that Bernard's expressed admiration for Hitler would not have been reciprocated. He did, however, say the following and has yet to sue the newspaper for having misquoted him, so it has to stand on the record, albeit, possibly, as a PR non-starter.

I am an admirer of Adolf Hitler (he informed the *Sunday People*). Not everything about him, of course. I deplore his gas chambers and Gestapo as much as anyone, but I admire him for the things he got right, which I reckon was about fifty per cent. He took over a nation with six million unemployed, with no hope and very little national pride. He set Germany back on its feet and swept its industry back to prosperity by cleaning out the work-shy parasites and spreading the message that it's a fine, rewarding way of life when you work hard for your family and your country. I can't help feeling that that's what Britain needs today.

Bernard later conceded that perhaps he shouldn't have said all this, but continued to deem Enoch Powell the greatest living Englishman. Asked in 1996 about the bust of Hitler, he looked mystified, as if this was truly a trivial detail from his past, and then recalled, 'That's gone years ago, that. I bought it from a cinema operator. He said it was from the Bunker, and he had some glasses from the Bunker, too – genuine, so he said. I got rid of it. Me mum didn't bother about it. I never had it on display. It was just there.'

Those who maintain a high personal regard for Bernard also make an oddly mixed group. Johnnie Hamp is Bernard's leading admirer, although he has tried unsuccessfully to influence his friend to drop his racist material. 'Bernard is a kind and generous and good-hearted man,' Hamp maintains. Bernard's friend Melville Davies is a prominent and respected north Manchester Jew.

> Bernard and I have an equal relationship. He looks on me as a pal (Davies says). Bernard is the kind of guy that, do him a good turn and he wants to do ten for you. He bends over backwards, nothing inconveniences him if it is to help a friend. He is extremely loyal to all his friends – to Stan Boardman, George Roper. They all love Bernard. I have never fallen out with him in forty years. I have never had a cross word with him. I find it very difficult to have a wrong word with Bernard because he is a very affable type of man. When we meet he'll say to me, 'I must tell you about this fellow so and so,' and then I'll come back at him with one and it'll be a joke session. You can't fall out when you're laughing with a fellow. It's impossible. He sees humour in everything. Larry (Larry Jason, better known as Josser) was lying in hospital and Bernard got news. Bernard had to make everyone laugh and Josser used to laugh at everything Bernard said. So Josser said to me, 'Have you seen this what Bernard has sent?' And there was the most massive basket of fruit – as big as the ward – and on it a card. It read, 'Joss, whatever you do, don't snuff it before I get there.' And he roared with laughter.

In the summer of 1996, Melville Davies sadly suffered a disabling stroke. Ironically, he was telling a new Bernard Manning joke when he collapsed. 'Everyone listening thought he were laughing, but it was Mel having a stroke,' said Bernard, shaking his head sadly.

Asked if he had any idea which joke it was that had 'caused' his friend's stroke, Bernard was obligingly able to tell it.

These two Irishmen went for a job (he said, brightening up perceptibly). And the first one goes in and sees the bloke interviewing him has got these two ears, one on his forehead and the other on his chin. He sits down and the fella says, 'Now, do you notice anything at all unusual about me?' So the Irishman says, 'Yeah, you've got these funny ears, look, one's on your forehead and the other one's one your chin.' The fella says, 'You cheeky bastard. How dare you be so insulting. Fuck off out and send the next bloke in.' So he goes out to his mate and says, 'Listen, be careful not to mention his ears. He's a bit sensitive about them.' So the second bloke goes in and the interviewer says, 'Good morning, now before we start, do you notice anything at all unusual about me?' So the fella says, 'No.' 'Are you absolutely sure?' He says, 'Well, sor, I can see you wear contact lenses.' 'How on earth can you tell that?' the bloke asks. 'Well, you'd never get a pair of spectacles to fit over them fuckin' ears.'

A less predictable personal admirer is Julie Brown, of Chadderton, a mile or so from Bernard's house. Four years ago, aged twenty-seven, Ms Brown starred in a tough, left-wing film, *Raining Stones*, which was directed by Ken Loach with the screenplay by Jim Allen, who previously wrote *Days of Hope*. Ms Brown was picked by Loach when he spotted her as a nightclub singer, an evening job she does under the name of Roxanne. The film was a huge success, winning the Jury Prize at the Cannes Film Festival. In the same week as singing at the Embassy Club, she received a twenty-minute standing ovation from the audience at Cannes. Although the idea of Bernard giving his blessing to a Ken Loach film seems a little unlikely, he was, Julie Brown says, wonderfully supportive. 'He introduced me every night for a couple of weeks with a plug for the film. He'd say, "You've got to go and see this lady's film. I've seen it, it's fantastic, she a local girl, go along and see it too."'

Another fan, perhaps more extravagant in his praise than any other in show business, is John Fisher, an Oxford classicist, writer on comedy and currently head of entertainment at Thames Television.

I have the utmost admiration for Bernard as a technician (Fisher says). I actually think Bernard has come closer than anybody in this country to having what at a particular time in his life Groucho Marx had – the ability to deflate a type of pomposity, a type of affectation, with the sharpest edge possible, but without it becoming offensive to the wider audience. One of the jobs of the comic is to deflate pomposity, and if you think of the people around at that time who might have gone on and done similar things, you can think of Kenneth Williams in one sort of style, of Peter Cook, or of a veteran like Tommy Trinder or Ted Ray. But Bernard came on, and you knew he meant business.

All humour is politically incorrect at some level. Humour only works on contrasts and if you are going to have contrast, there is going to be a minority somewhere that comes off badly out of it. Virtually every comic I know who is supposedly politically correct will endorse political incorrectness because it is funny. Yet I can remember in the early eighties saying to Bernard, 'Look, you are going on, you are going to do ten minutes for me, and you are going to keep it absolutely clean. There are going to be no four letter words.' And he would go on and do that and be brilliantly funny. Sadly I think it would be very difficult for a television producer to say that, to instruct him in that way, today. I think he is more and more living up to his tabloid world of the rebel, and obviously that is very valuable to him, but at the same time it deprives a much wider audience, whether through television, or through a wider theatre audience that might be there for him. I think it is a great shame that so much of his popularity has been compromised by his racist angle, and also by an attitude that more and more disregards the advice of producers. It saddens me that with his talent and timing, and his aggression and his attack, that he is not getting a wider audience.

The quintessential Bernard Manning genius for John Fisher was on his first *Michael Parkinson* appearance in 1976, which Fisher, then at the BBC, produced.

If anyone wanted a definition of how brilliant Bernard Manning was, just watch that (he advises). He was on with A.J.P. Taylor (the famous socialist historian) and Fanny Craddock (the feisty TV chef of the day). I think Taylor and Fanny were already on, and Bernard came on last. They all stayed on the sofa, and Fanny Craddock was the type of person whom no one was ever going to be able to upstage. Yet Bernard demolished her and ended up with A.J.P. Taylor as his greatest fan. A.J.P. had carried the stick from Fanny while they were sitting there as a twosome opposite Michael, and of course she had torn into him. But then Bernard had come on like the hero in a western movie to save A.J.P. He dominated the final twenty minutes and left Fanny Craddock speechless, then Bernard and he went off as bosom buddies. It was as unlikely a relationship as you could imagine, and it certainly extended into the hospitality room. I'm sure they never met again, but you could imagine the unimaginable, of them carrying on a friendship.

There is evidence that John Fisher is not alone in his assessment of Bernard as the British Groucho Marx. During the late forties and fifties, Marx was almost as well known in America for a game show he compèred, first on radio and later on television, called *You Bet Your Life*, than he was for the Marx Brothers' films. The show, which Bill Cosby has since hosted, was based on the simple premise of people coming on, chatting to Groucho, him asking simple questions, and if they got questions right they got the money. There was also a device in the show where each episode had a secret word and, if contestants used it, they got a bonus prize such as a holiday. The formula was so successful for Groucho that Associated Redifusion even brought him to England to do a series in the fifties.

Twenty years later, Southern Television in Southampton recognised the parallel between Groucho and Bernard Manning which Fisher had noticed and bought the rights to the show. It was renamed *Under Manning*, but the schedulers slotted it in on Sunday afternoons; a sign that the show did not quite have the faith of the ITV network, and it collapsed – along with Southern TV – after a series. 'Granada should have been doing it,' Fisher believes. 'It could still have been running. It was done in Southampton, and you can imagine the audience, all the old-age pensioners. You didn't get the trust that Manning would have had in Manchester, so he didn't quite gel, and anyone looking at it would say, this isn't good casting. But it could have been the perfect casting had the situation been different.'

Fisher believes Bernard's mistake in recent years has been that he fails to editorialise. After his experience with Bernard at the BBC, when Bernard responded to his briefing and kept the act completely clean, Fisher came to Thames and invited Bernard on to a variety show in 1990. 'I said I wanted it just like he had done the previous time, but he was no longer disciplined enough, with the result that the "fucks" and the "cunts" kept slipping in. This was a show which was going out at eight o'clock. Now, I'd always allow him something a little extreme, because I knew that he would need that to get the audience with him, and then he'd know I would edit it out. But he never understood that if you were doing fifteen minutes and I wanted seven, and every other line had an expletive in or something that was objectionable for a mainstream audience to watch, you could hardly edit it. So therefore the word got around and I think people got a little scared.' (The Thames show was recorded after Vera Manning died, a watershed after which many of Bernard's recent problems over taste began. It is almost as if the ability to censor himself disappeared with her loss.)

'Like so many great performers,' Fisher concludes, 'Bernard acts a part. I think away from all the bombast and the bravado, there is a very decent human being there.' Fisher, interestingly, gives the lie, if a little cautiously, to the universal belief that Bernard is banned from British television. 'We had him on the *Des O'Connor Show* two or three years back, and we would have preferred him not to have said some of the things he did with that audience, but when you are editing an interview, it is easier to take material out than if you are editing a stand-up spot. I see no reason, on the strength of that performance, of what eventually went out, for me to say that on a particular Thursday afternoon in 1996, when we sit down and finalise the bookings for the next series of *Des*, that Bernard might not be considered.'

Like Fisher, Johnnie Hamp has despaired a little over Bernard's increasing self-marginalisation. He sees Bernard's 'blueness' and the racism as two sides of the same coin. For the first twenty years of the past three decades, the principal area of controversy over Bernard was the now slightly dated question of his being 'blue'.

144

Although he was doing racial jokes back in the 1960s, the hot topic then was swearing and scatology, the racism practically ignored. The realisation in the early 1990s that this dinosaur of a comedian was still telling race gags in the age of political correctness almost instantly demonised Bernard – while at the same time making him more famous than he had ever been. The racism is a new angle on an old story, but has led to there being two separate perceptions of Bernard Manning; for younger generations, he is Manning the racist comedian, for older people, Manning the notoriously blue comic. 'Bernard has always been a bit blue,' Hamp says, when asked about Bernard's racism, 'But then again so was Max Miller, who was one of the greatest comics for timing. You listen to his stuff now and it is so tame, yet they used to bring the curtain down on him.

'I think when other blue comedians started to become biggish, like Chubby Brown selling a hundred thousand videos in the late eighties, and it seemed to be required to be a blue comic, Bernard followed the trend,' Hamp continues. 'I just think it was a progression, or regression I suppose, based on what the punters want. If you get a few blue gags and people laugh then the next week the guy who comes in has got to top that and next week he has got to top that and top that. It is very unnecessary really. I have often said to him, "You don't need it," and his mum used to say that to him, "Now don't be rude, Bernard." But he just said, "Bollocks. It's what the punters want." ' ('My gags are very blue and strong and aggressive,' Bernard elucidated in a 1995 interview with Chrissy Iley for the *Daily Express*. 'If you want Ken Dodd talking about jam butties, *Jackanory* stuff, that's for little children. If you get macho men, they want a nice cabaret. They want the F-word. They love it.')

Hamp points out that the progression/regression has been more accelerated in the nineties – again, in Bernard's post Vera period – than most people realise. 'Even ten years ago, in the mid-eighties, he wasn't saying "fuck". Then it would be "This chap was giving his bird one ..." and that was very blue, because a few years before that, it was, "This guy was making love to his girl in the car ..." and that was blue. There weren't many F-words even in barrack-room humour, back in the National Service days.'

The northern comedian Ricky Livid (real name Steve Lee) who

has known Bernard for thirty years and is his first choice stand-in if Bernard is away from the Embassy Club, confirms this. Lee, who like the occasional Embassy Club singer Julie Brown/Roxanne had a straight acting part in *Raining Stones*, says, 'It's amazing how the scene has changed. When I first knew Bernard, an audience would get very edgy if he said a word like "bleedin' "". It was a world away from what you get now. Parents don't seem to mind their kids swearing.'

A symbiotic, yet mutually loathing, relationship between Bernard's kind of comedy and the young alternative variety becomes especially evident when it is pointed out that Bernard only started saying 'fuck' and 'cunt' in the 1980s. Alternative comedy and northern club stand-up cabaret are often seen as being at opposite poles, and present themselves as being implacable enemies, yet the *Comedy Store*-type acts clearly have their roots in people like Bernard. And it was only when performers like Billy Connolly started using 'fuck' in front of young, educated audiences, that the foulest of language was somehow legitimised. Not only did comics across the board, including Bernard, begin using it, but parents, as Steve Lee observes, began to tolerate their children swearing. Stand-up comedy, we are told repeatedly, is the new rock and roll, and deeply hip. Yet it is arguable that the release for audiences of hearing obscenity on stage has been infinitely more important in the explosion in popularity of the 'new' stand-up comedy than its more novel tradition of vetoing sexist and racist jokes. Bernard and Jo Brand may choose to believe that they are opposites, yet they owe much to one another. It was revealing that when Bernard was invited in 1996 to play an alternative venue in London, the Jongleurs club in Camden Town, the young audience gave him a rapturous reception.

Curiously, it was at the opening of the same club a few years earlier that a PR man had the idea, which gained wide publicity, of throwing a burning effigy of Bernard into the nearby Regent's Canal. Once new comedy became the established creed, and Jack Dee was Granada's stand-up heir to the tradition of *The Comedians*, Bernard was at last seen as what he has perhaps been all along – an iconoclastic, underground comedian.

Bernard might balk at the description of himself in 1996 as

'alternative'. Otherwise, the burning effigy didn't bother him. As he is fond of saying, 'I don't mind these modern comedians – just so long as you don't mix up our wage packets.'

Family Business

I love family life. Everybody should love it. It keeps your feet on the ground. I can't understand kids leaving home these days. If you're getting well looked after, there's no one like your mum and dad.

Bernard Manning explaining how, a widower at fifty-six, he moved back in with
his mother

The eighties saw Bernard moving into middle age, and with this passage came the health problems inevitable in a man of his weight, diet, smoking and Stakhanovite work rate. Money had never been a problem, his marriage was stable, his family supportive and his career solid. If he were a man subject to stress, the tension between Bernard and his professional colleagues would have put years on him, but he gave every impression of genuinely not giving a damn. Deaths and family problems distressed him deeply, and there were to be a few in his fifties; they took their toll. Vera's death in 1986 particularly tormented him, even though the show went on, and he was singing and joking on stage the next night, as he had managed to do when his father died. Appearing immediately after Vera's death was perhaps the one time the show should not have gone on: it was a disaster. It was health, however, that came closer than any of his other afflictions to stopping the jokes; he has been sentenced to death by worried doctors on several occasions.

Naturally, his fatness had its upside. He has said he gets away with his jokes, 'because I'm a big fat slob of a bloke. I'm not a handsome bastard. I take the mickey out of myself as well as out of everyone else.' He often says to a table full of women at the Embassy Club: 'I bet I know what you're thinking. You're thinking, doesn't he look like that Richard Gere?'

He is not entirely joking when he asks this. At a sylph-like eighteen stone, he is now a quarter lighter than he was at his 1980 peak, when he hit twenty-four stone. Bernard's gentle but effective fight against the flab used to provide a movable feast – whole banquet, indeed – for the tabloids who, before Manning racism stories became the vogue, charted his weight changes with delighted, if erratic, fervour. In 1972, tabloid readers learned, he dropped two stone from his twenty-one after the death of his father. 'I've put it back now,' he reassured fans, 'but at one time, before I stopped drinking, I had more chins than a Chinese telephone directory. If I sat in a chair, I used to rock myself to sleep trying to get up.'

In 1974, he said he weighed twenty stone. 'My trouble is I love grub. My doctor has given me a million diet sheets. But it's no use. I have no willpower. My secret is I never worry – not even about being overweight.' In March 1975, the doctor told Bernard he could die if he did not lose weight. 'I am at a dangerous age,' he said. 'It was a choice of either losing weight or risking a heart attack. There wouldn't have been much point in buying any LP records if I had stayed at twenty-one stone.'

In 1980, Bernard's doctor told him to lose five of his by now twenty-four stone, or he would die before his fiftieth birthday that August. Bernard, who had a sixty-inch waistline, went on a low-calorie diet and said he was prepared to have his jaws sealed if necessary: 'Yes, it's as serious as that,' he said. 'Part of the trouble is that after all these years on stage I still get nervous before a show, and this gigantic nervous need for food after when it's over. I get my chauffeur to stop at a likely-looking late-night caff and wade through the menu. Giant steaks topped with fried eggs are a big weakness. So is Indian curry, but I don't have it too late because I like to sleep in most mornings. My mum, who's eighty, has always made me steak and kidney pud. She wept when she heard I'd never eat it again, but she understands the situation.'

Vera, who was a fine cook, did her best to help. 'I love Bernard as a chubby hubby,' she said. 'He was well rounded when we wed. I'm determined to get him below twenty stones. He'll still have plenty to cuddle. But I do worry about his willpower away from home. When he makes his mind up about a thing he usually sticks to it though. After all, it's his life at stake.' (It remains sadly ironic that it was Vera who died – and of a heart attack – six years later, while Bernard, at the time of writing, continues chomping ever onwards.)

Bernard found the 1980-model diet unbearable, however. He got irritable: 'I'm nasty enough as it is without getting worse because I'm hungry,' he snapped to a reporter. 'That was the trouble with all the diets in the past. I used to get ratty because I wasn't getting my grub. So I'd have something to eat and promise, I'll start the diet again tomorrow.' So he began eating properly again; in 1984, he explained to the *Sunday Mirror*, 'I know the score. I realise that I'm putting my health in danger. But it's no good worrying about it. If I go, I go. I'll tell you one thing, though. My pallbearers will know they've carried a coffin. With my weight, they'll think I died of lead poisoning.'

The public impression of Bernard was not only as a big-league trougher, but as a drinker too. It was not an image that was in any way discouraged at the Embassy Club, where the customised beer mats supplied by the brewery, Lees of Oldham, depict a thoroughly bacchanalian mine host, beaming cheerfully from behind a pint of keg. This has always been a slight deception, although not one ever likely to trouble the Advertising Standards Authority. Bernard's non-drinking rule still held strictly – one of his many mottoes is, 'We're here to sell ale, not to sup it.' 'I know it's difficult to believe, but Bernard never drinks,' Vera would confide. 'He stands in the club with a glass in his hand, but it's only water. He always had a pint of bitter at his elbow for *The Wheeltappers*, but he never touched it. It was just there for show.'

Bernard's closest friend of over thirty years, Barry Clark, a plumber from Middleton, near Bernard's home, adds: 'They all think he is a big fat cigar-smoking, beer-swilling moron, but he's not. He's exactly the opposite. He'd rather have a pan of tater hash and a pot of tea, and he's a happy man. People also think he's a crude, rude, arrogant man, but that's just his act.'

In March 1984, Bernard's health saga took another turn for the worse. Not only did he start to suffer from a painful gallstone, which the doctor said could not be operated on because Bernard was too fat, but he also developed diabetes shortly after being mugged outside the club.

I came out one Monday morning with £7000 in a bag, and they

must have been watching me (he recounts). They had pick-axe handles, guns, and were masked up. They never found out who did it – even though I offered a reward of £5000. Now we use Securicor. It's shutting the stable door when the horse has gone, but we all do that. We got a burglar alarm once we'd been robbed – barmy. The mugging was over in three minutes – and I even got a gag out of that. Harry Dowd, Manchester City's ex-goalkeeper, who was a traveller for the brewery, was going out with me that morning. I had the satchel, and when they started about me, I threw it to him, and he dropped it, City's goalkeeper. So I got a laugh out of it, and then that weekend I won £5000 on the National, so the bookmaker paid in the end.

The shock of the robbery seemed to set off the diabetes. He started drinking water and fizzy drinks voraciously, and was soon diagnosed with the disorder. He has been able to control it to date without taking insulin by injection, but often suffers giddiness. 'I worry about dad because of the dizzy spells,' Young Bernard says today. 'You tend to think he should slow down, but he's one of these who have never been inside a hospital, and he doesn't believe he is ever going to die. He won't have a doctor when he feels bad. I've called the doctor out on a couple of occasions without him knowing, because if he knew you were doing it, he'd go mad. Once the doctor's in, dad can't refuse you see. He's sixty-six, and still twenty-odd stone and smokes and the doctors don't believe that he's as healthy as he is.' (Bernard has in fact given some consideration to how he intends to die. 'I'll be like Tommy Cooper, drop dead on stage,' he told the journalist Chrissie Iley in 1995. 'I will never stop. All these people talk about how hard they work. If Michael Barrymore spent a week with me, it would kill him. He'd be on his knees. Me on stage, it's just natural, it doesn't feel like work.'

As it is for many overweight people, diabetes was a minor blessing in that it forced Bernard finally to watch his diet. February 1985 saw him down to seventeen stone (and from a fifty-six to a fifty-inch waist). Warned that he would have to start insulin injections if he didn't lose weight, he submitted, and introduced a new and unfamiliar element to his regime – exercise. A friend told him about a model Debbie Benson and her partner Annabel Cushnir who ran a clinic called Fatbusters. 'When you meet gorgeous birds like that, you're at a bit of a disadvantage,' he explained. 'You have to try to haul in your stomach and look manly. Debbie looked me right in the eyes and said, "You're vastly overweight but I can lose it for you." Before I met Debbie, weighing machines used to jump into doorways when I walked down the street. Or if I actually stepped on one it would wheeze, "One at a time please." It was quite expensive, too. I mean, I couldn't go for a bath, I had to use the car wash.'

Soon, he was something approaching a born-again health bore. 'I'm the healthiest I've been for twenty years,' he chirruped. 'I feel a treat. I don't feel tired now. I can stay on stage much longer. This new system is great. Food no longer tempts me. Mind you, I'm not too keen on the exercises. When I'm down on the floor, I feel a right Humpty Dumpty.' He even sought help of a distinctly un-Bernard type for some injured nerves in his neck. He met the Irish faith healer Finbar Nolan at the BBC Television Centre. 'He started working my neck with his fingers,' says Bernard. 'There was a warm glow. He stopped, and I was cured. I've never been a religious man, but now, well, it makes you think.'

The newspapers' fascination with Bernard's alimentary canal continued, meanwhile, after he lost weight. In 1994, the *Sunday Mirror* went shopping with him at his local supermarket, Morrisons in Chadderton, which he visited every week to bring in supplies for him and his mother, with whom he had been living again since Vera's death. It seemed from Bernard's purchases that he ate healthful mountains of apples, bananas, sprouts, carrots and cauliflower. 'I always have lamb, beef or pork on Sunday,' he expounded. 'If it's pork, I get a big Bramley cooking apple, which my mother does in the microwave, and we make apple sauce with the pork.'

In the matter of potatoes, it appeared that the habits of a green-grocer died hard. 'Every Monday morning we have a fifty-six-pound bag delivered, and that does us for a week,' he said. 'My mum still does all the cooking. She's absolutely marvellous.' To avoid any image-damaging accusation of gastronomic correctness, with all those sprouts and carrots and green stuff on the shopping list, Bernard ascribed his mother's long life to a diet of chips. 'They keep you going.' If there was any room left on Bernard and Nellie's doorstep with that monster bag of potatoes in the way, it was taken up by milk. 'Our milk bill was £24 last week,' Bernard revealed. 'That's ten pints a day, and I drink about eight of those. But it's skimmed milk. I used to drink the other stuff, but I had to change because I was ballooning up. I ended up having no neck.'

The physical aside, mentally, Bernard was unusually fit for a comedian. No trace of depression or angst had ever clouded his mind. One slight peculiarity of Bernard's, however, was his dogged refusal to stay overnight when he went away to work. 'He is mental, you know,' says his son. 'If he is appearing tonight in Southampton, he'll be home tonight. He just likes his own bed. I have known him to go to Ireland and then to Jersey and then to come home in one day without stopping. That's how he is.' (On one occasion in 1996, his exhausted driver, Tony Sharkey, confirms, Bernard had two consecutive dates in Swansea, and insisted after the first on being driven through the night back to Manchester, so he could sleep at home before setting off back to South Wales for the second engagement. It is not surprising that the Lincoln Continental he uses for day-to-day travel is currently on its third engine.)

Before Bernard employed a driver for these marathon trips, Barry Clark used to ferry him round the country. It was a mutually beneficial arrangement, by which Bernard got the company and Barry, who admits to a weakness for fancy cars, especially American ones, got to drive them. The friendship between Bernard and Barry was forged on some of these long car journeys. Barry says: 'When you have travelled around the country for nearly thirty years together, you develop a love–hate relationship. It's like being married to a person, although we are not queer. Sometimes I get a bit protective of him. I have had words with people over the years where they have been shouting rude obscenities from the audience at him and I have gone over and said, "Do you mind? Just leave him alone and let him get on with his act." I can call him names, but I don't like other people doing it.'

In return for his loyalty, Barry got to hit the high life: 'I enjoyed meeting all different people, I mean in my walk of life, as a common builder, I have met a lot of the Royals at various dinners, and sportsmen and entertainers. You name them and I've probably met them. There are not many people who can say they have sat and dined at those kind of tables. They are all experiences I would never have had if it were not for Bernard. I was there on the Vegas trip, when Charles Mather offered Bernard £750,000 to do a three-month tour of America and Australia. He said, "I'll pay for all your mates to go as well." I couldn't believe what I was listening to, me, because I had been used to working for thirty quid a week.'

Being Bernard's best friend meant Barry Clark got to take liberties that other people could not. When Bernard first bought the number plate BJM 1 for his Rolls, Barry altered the registration with a bit of sticky tape to make it read BUM 1. Bernard drove around with this on the car for quite a while, until people finally pointed it out. Another time, Barry pulled an elaborate stunt at the Embassy Club. He recalls:

> I have always had a set of keys for the club, for doing bits of repairs and I got a set of walkie-talkie radios and I put one of them in the roof. Now Bernard always did a bit of a sketch in which he goes, 'Oh Lord ...' and then he'd answer himself saying, 'Yes, my son ...' Well, I stood at the front door, and when he came to this part of the sketch, I answered 'Yes, my son' down the walkie-talkie. He looked up and he couldn't believe it. Every time he said this line, I answered him. This went on for a few days, and I couldn't tell him it was me. Bernard was going mad. He thought it was the taxi drivers outside and he kept going out and shouting at them. In the end he found out and laughed at it with me.

Getting one over Bernard was a light-hearted preoccupation amongst Bernard's friends. One of these friends, Eddie Haughton, tried a little sleight of hand on Bernard down in London, with embarrassing results.

> Eddie used to be on the committee of a local club called VASA – Victoria Avenue Ex-Servicemen's Association (recalls Barry). He was a smashing old guy, one of these reet old Lancashire lads as they call them. We were all staying at the Regent Palace Hotel in London and Eddie was with us. Now Eddie went out to buy some extra food and he said to me, 'Don't let Bernard see this food

154

because he'll wolf the lot,' and with that he tied the whole lot up in a plastic bag and hung it out of the window. Next thing we know there's this knock at the door and it's the manager who says to Bernard: 'Mr Manning, are you hungry at all? Is there anything wrong with the food here?' Bernard said, 'No, no, why?' and the manager said, 'Well, what have you got a bag of food hanging out of the window for?'

The manager may have suspected before he saw the bag of grub that Bernard was not quite happy with the cuisine. Posh or, worse still, international cuisine has never been one of Bernard's loves, although he tends to overplay the 'give me good English grub' card a little for patriotic effect. 'Foreign food, oh no,' he says. 'It's awful. I only had Chinese food once. There were eggs floating about on the top. Why people eat it, I'll never know.' He also says he hates Indian food – 'Them curries, they burn your bloody tongue out. I'd rather a nice chocolate roll and a cup of tea' – but in fact, he frequently goes for a late curry. And, although he conveniently forgets that Italian food is actually foreign too, he is very fond of a pasta restaurant near his home. 'I have been going there for years,' he confessed to the *Independent on Sunday* in 1993, the obsession with Bernard's sustenance having, in the ironic 1990s, spread to the upmarket broadsheet newspapers too. 'The service is good and very quick, the staff are extremely friendly and genuinely nice. The food is always excellent and there's plenty of it. I love their spaghetti bolognaise. If they don't serve me a good meal, I take them prisoner.'

He was by now, of course, a master of winding up reporters from posh papers. 'Immigration has to be stopped because there is not room in Britain for our people,' he obligingly told the *Observer* at the same time, when they too got on to the subject of foreign grub. 'You have got Aborigines eating worms and beetles and shit. And they're covered with shit. And mud all over the place. And dust, and blowpipes ... It makes them unintelligent. They should not come to our country. We have a bath every day. And a shower every day. And we do not eat beetles, or anything like that. We eat rice pudding. We eat potato hash. We eat hot pot. Good food. In thousands of years those people will learn; they will be eating nice food and realising that you get diseases if you don't have a bath and wash yourself.'

Another aspect of Bernard's personal life which has attracted more than its share of media attention over the years has been money. All working-class northerners who do well seem to go out of their way to give the impression of being tight-fisted and, for comedians, such an image is practically mandatory. Bernard does nothing at all to dissuade the public that he is rich and mean – he plays on both in his act – and he has never had any compunction in driving around some of the less choice areas of Manchester in a succession of flashy cars with personalised number plates. He has owned a fleet of Rolls-Royces, a Cadillac, a Ford Fairlane and a Lincoln Continental, and never attempted to suppress a tendency – as a visiting *Observer* journalist put it – to 'settle philosophical arguments by referring to his bank balance.' What is undoubtedly brashness could also be described as an unsettlingly honest frankness about money. When Colin Crompton claimed in 1976 that he earned £50,000 a year, Bernard commented: 'If anyone offered me £50,000 a year, I'd say, "Yes, that's all right for my manager, but what about me?" I've been paid £1500 for a night's work and I gave that to charity.'

Behind the bluster about being rich, and the jokes about his own parsimony, his generosity is in fact vast, although little known outside of his immediate circle in Manchester. But equally greater than he lets on is his wealth. Bernard claims emphatically to have no idea what he is worth, but amateur accountants who take vicarious pleasure in the affluence of others will enjoy doing their own sums. He was already a millionaire twenty-five years ago, with no mortgages, second properties, loans or onerous financial responsibilities. Currently, he has a regular £8000-a-week income, fifty-two weeks a year, from outside bookings, plus the profits from the Embassy Club, perhaps £5000 a week. On top of this income of approaching, perhaps, £700,000 a year, he has the fees and royalties from his several videos, newspaper columns in the *Sport* tabloid and other sundry fees. He has been earning at this level for at least the last decade, and at a similar level for the twenty years before that, while having very low personal expenses, thanks to his exceedingly modest lifestyle. He spends and loses a lot on gambling for amusement – especially since Vera's death. Bernard insists that he makes a net profit on the horses, regularly putting £5000 and more on a horse – 'I never gamble more than I can pick up by working the next week,' he said ten years ago. But Bernard also plays the stock market and other investments. It is probable that Bernard Manning's gift for telling a joke to perfection has netted him a personal fortune of £5m, and it may possibly be a lot more.

Bernard's fortune would certainly be greater had he not given such vast amounts of money away, both to charities and as gifts, over the entire period that he has been a wealthy man. He was, indeed, generous, even before he became rich. Barry Clark recalls instances of Bernard's munificence from over thirty years ago:

When Bernard first started travelling about, going from club to club, he was already friendly with Eddie Haughton. Now Eddie had been going on about this watch of his, and how it kept stopping. He would keep tapping it and messing about with it. Now, unbeknown to Eddie, Bernard had bought him a new watch. So there we were, travelling down the road, and Bernard said, 'Stop messing with that watch, let's have a look at it.' So Eddie handed him the watch and he looked at it and said, 'Huh, it's not worth having it,' and threw it out of the car window. Eddie's face fell, he came out with several expletives and was ranting and raving. Then Bernard pulled the new watch out of his pocket and gave it to him.

Another time, Eddie went away for a holiday. He lived on his own, he was an OAP and with there being no woman in Eddie's house, it wasn't in top form. So Bernard said, 'Right, when Eddie goes away, we'll do his garden, we'll paint his house, we'll get rid of that telly, we'll get him some new chairs and a bit of a carpet.' So that's what he did. Unfortunately, while we were moving the old suite out, I broke the front window. Now Eddie's front window had the figure of a little Dutch man in it and obviously we couldn't get another one, so we had to just put ordinary glass in it. So when Eddie comes back off his holidays, he walks up to this front door, looks at it, and he turns round and goes to walk away. But then he tries the key and walks in, and as he walks in we all follow him. It was all done secretly, so he didn't know that we were there. 'Oh, I'm in the wrong house,' he says, then when he turns round and spots us, he realised he wasn't and he burst into tears, and of course everyone else burst into tears.

The other occasion that stands out in Barry's memory of Bernard's largesse was the time he saved the day at a charity function. 'We were at a sportsmen's dinner in Manchester for the Variety Club of Great Britain and they were trying to raise – in those days it was £4000 – for a coach and they were shouting round the room auctioning things off like they do. Money was tight at the time, and they only managed to raise this certain figure. Bernard was doing the auctioning and he turned round at the end of the evening and said, "Right, I'll put the rest in," which was like three and a half grand. They named the coach after him.'

Today, Bernard does not make a great deal of his own benevolence (even if he is not exactly reticent about it, either) but stories of Bernard's open-handedness and generosity of spirit do emerge from everyone from his cleaning lady to strangers. A taxi driver who drove one reporter to Bernard's house said: 'Bernard Manning can do no wrong in our family. My daughter was ill in hospital and he went there and brought her presents and cheered her up. He didn't tell anyone. He just went to see her.' He has frequently bought football strips for boys' teams and twice rescued people from the threat of prison for non-payment of debts. Once, in the seventies, an elderly married couple were on the point of being imprisoned for failing to pay their rent, and Bernard sent his driver round with £200 to help them and instructions not to say who had paid the money. 'They were honest, hard-working people like myself. They weren't criminals,' he says. In the eighties, he similarly assisted a family in trouble for non-payment of the poll tax. At the same time, he heard about the terminally-ill child of Pakistan-born parents, who had said he wanted to go to Disneyland before he died. Bernard heard of the case and paid for the child's trip.

He has got a lovely disposition, he is really generous (says his sister Alma). The only wrong with Bernard is that he's too soft. He is a soft touch for anything and anybody. I remember once reading in the paper about him. There was some guy that had been conning celebrities, and he said the best touch he ever had was he went to Bernard Manning's club and he said to the doorman, 'I'd like to speak to Bernard.' He said he was in the Army with him, had hit hard times and could do with a hand-out. So the doorman rings Bernard up and says there is some guy here who was in the Army with you, and Bernard sent a guy out with £20 for him and he had never even clapped eyes on him. This was years and years ago when £20 was like £100. I thought, that's just typical of him.

'I do a fair amount of charity,' Bernard said in 1978, with some modesty. 'Every Thursday night is charity night in my club. I pay for the printing of raffle tickets and prizes and that sort of thing. The other night the proceeds went to help a family send their little girl to America for brain surgery. I like helping people. The wife always says that if a tramp came to the door I'd give him a couple of quid. Come to think of it, I've actually done it. I bought a colour TV for the local old-folks' home, too, but I don't go looking for publicity. I get nowt except knowing that I've helped somebody. Anyway, charity should be in our everyday lives.'

Bernard doesn't have a mean streak in his body (says his friend Melville Davies). A lot of people don't know this, but he is the most generous of men. When I came out of the air force, in my spare time I joined a charity committee to build a home for the handicapped in Manchester. Later on, I joined a group of businessmen who formed a charity organisation, known as the Charity Commandos. We were called upon to do shows, parties and dinners for various hospital charities, to pay for such things as transplants. I was the cabaret chairman because I knew a lot of people in show business, and they used to charge plenty. It was very difficult dealing with top theatricals, because they had other offers for the same nights so we used to have to pay them. But we found that of all the acts – and I have booked them all – the biggest drawing power from our sale of tickets for all our dinners was Bernard Manning. If you said Bernard will be on, tickets would be sold. We found this out very early on, forty years ago and, in that time, we did a very large number of these shows. A phenomenal amount of money was raised. To pay for one transplant cost £20,000, and I lost count of how many we sponsored.

On the first occasion that the committee said, 'Get Bernard Manning,' I went to Bernard and said, 'Now listen, Bernard, are you free on this date?' He looked it up, and said he was. 'Now, Bernard, be as lenient as you can and see what you can do.' 'Well I shall have to charge me usual fee to you,' he said – 'Not a penny.' That was his reply to me. That was the beginning. Now you ask a man once, you ask a man twice, that's not too bad, but this happened dozens and dozens of times and he keeps saying not a penny. I kept on ringing him saying, 'Bernard, you must help me out. We are doing one for this, we are doing one for that.' 'All right, then,' he would say. I'd say, 'Bernard, I know it's taking a liberty, and I have asked you a thousand times but how much is it this time?' He'd say something silly like, 'How about a percentage of the car park?' but he received not a shilling. Of all the theatricals, there are only two that have ever done that for me. The other was Alan King, an American comedian. He flew over from the States on a Sunday for a Sunday night show for the blind, and went straight back from Manchester for a matinee on Broadway the next day. The show was a sensation, and when I went backstage with a chequebook, he just said, 'No charge, down to me.' Some of the British performers would drop the price a little, but Bernard would never take a penny. On top of that, I would go and see him in the dressing room and he would say, 'How have you done with the show – stick that in,' and he'd always want to give a big donation, always a few hundred pounds.

There came a time when one of his dear friends, Larry Jason – Josser – was taken very ill, and was dying, and he told me he was in bad straits. He said he wasn't worried about dying, but that he owed a few quid here and there and he wanted to go out clean, not owing anything. I said, 'Leave it to me, Jos, I'll put a show on.' Now all the boys who are friends of mine knew him. I went to Bernard and told him that Josser was ill. Bernard said, 'What do you want? You can have anything.' I said, 'I want the Embassy Club, to put a quick show on and raise the money to make him comfortable for the rest of his life.' He said, 'Leave it to me, I'll put the show on. You've got the place free, I'll appear. Don't worry. Let's get it done.' So very quickly we got a show together. Bernard got tickets printed and everything, and it was an absolute sell-out. Nobody failed me. But the major part of it, Bernard did, because he was a lifelong friend. Josser sent a letter to thank everybody, and the compère read it out. It was a very pitiful letter, very touching, and in the dressing room, Bernard broke down. He was so upset and he said to me, 'Now have we straightened it all up? Has Josser got enough to keep him comfortable?' And he went in his pocket and said, 'Well, add this to it, and if you need any more, let me know and he threw over £500. Prior to doing that, before he was ill, Josser had once told Bernard that he wasn't doing well, and Bernard put £1000 in his pocket. That was when £1000 was equivalent to £10,000, and he thought nothing of it.

'Bernard did shows for me oblivious of race, or of creed,' Melville Davies insists. 'He has told me Jewish stories, and I have laughed. He has told coloured jokes to the coloured boys in show business and they have laughed, and I tell him stories about fat people, and he laughs at himself. Bernard is misunderstood. People don't realise that he is a great man, and a quietly good man, the opposite to this stage character. Other showbiz people do things when there are big plaudits and the Variety Club of Great Britain is involved, and it's in the public eye – sure, they'll do it. Bernard does it when nobody is looking, doesn't want them to know. If I went to Bernard with a hard-luck story about somebody, I wouldn't have to go any further. And it's not as though I would ask with trepidation. I know he will do it. He can't say no. Because of that, he is a very lovable guy.'

Bernard is still adept at playing the tight, canny northerner when it suits him. Young Bernard tells of the time recently when he tried to persuade his father to get an executive box at Manchester City's Maine Road ground.

There is a local businessman, who we'll not name, let's say Fred X, who was a friendly rival, and winding me up every time I saw him that he was going to get a box at Maine Road. Now I would love to have a box at City, but I've not got the time to go to matches. One night I saw him and he gave me a big kiss on the cheek, and said,

'Guess who's got a box?' I said, 'Congratulations', and went round to see me dad the next day. I said, 'Guess who's got a box ... Fred X.' I was winding me dad up about this box for a while, saying, 'Why can they have one and we can't?' I said, 'Just think of the benefits.' 'What benefits?' he said. I said, 'Well, we can all go out as a family on Saturday, our Ben can come, we can have a nice meal and watch the game. They've got tellies in the box, so you can watch the racing.' I was thinking of everything I could to try and turn him on to this box, and you could see him thinking. I said, 'Go on, let's get one.' He said, 'How much are they?' I said they were about £16,000 a season. He said, 'You what, sixteen grand a year? I can get you complimentary tickets any time you want,' which he can. I said, 'Yeah, dad, but it's the box, isn't it, it's the flash, and *he's* got one.' I had him right at it, so he says, 'Right, what's his number?' So I got Fred's number, and they know each other, because they are a similar age, and they've grown up together. 'Is that you, Fred?' me dad says. 'Oh, hiya Bernard.' 'I believe you've got a box at Maine Road?' So he says, 'Yeah, that's right, I was telling your Young Bernard.' And Dad said, 'I hope you'll be inviting me and our Young Bernard on a regular basis.' So I'm thinking, what's he doing here? 'Bernard, you're friends of mine, I've known you for years, you can come to every match.' Me dad said, 'I knew you wouldn't let me down, son, thanks very much.' He put the phone down, turned to me and said, 'There you are, son, you've got a box for fuck all.'

Another classic moment for Young Bernard involving his father and money – but in which, this time, Young Bernard got the upper hand – came three years ago.

We were on holiday in Portugal (he explains) in this beautiful apartment. It was a hot afternoon, so I thought I'd get away from the sun and sit in the cool apartment and put the TV on while the wife and kids were at the beach. At the time satellite TV was pretty new, and I found I was sitting watching the Haydock Park Races. It was throwing it down with rain back here, and I am sitting in Portugal watching *Grandstand*. I couldn't believe it. So me mind starts ticking over and I think, 'Just a minute, I can make use of this now.' I saw this horse come in and it's, say, Bernard's Boy, for

162

argument's sake, and so I get on the phone and I rang me dad. I said 'Dad, I'm sat round the pool here with a fella called Charlie MacAlister, a trainer.' 'Aye,' he said, 'I know Charlie MacAlister.' So I said, 'He's just given me a horse. It's going to be at Haydock this afternoon. It's called Bernard's Boy.' Me dad said, 'It's just come in that.' So I said, 'Oh, you're joking. Sorry.' So he says, 'Go down and see if he's got any more.' So I says, 'The pool is about a mile away, it's a massive hotel.' Me dad said, 'Just go and see if he has got any more.' So I gave it half an hour and watched the next winner come in – say, Bernard's Lad or whatever – and I rang me dad pretending to be out of breath and said, 'Right, dad, I've just got back and it's Bernard's Lad in the next race. He's going in this one.' 'You what?' me dad says, 'He's just come in at ten to one.' You could just hear the anxiety in his voice with all this money going to waste. Three times, he says, 'Go back and see if he has got any more.' I said, 'Oh dad, do me a favour, it's killing me, this is.' So I gave it another half an hour, and this time I rang just as the horse is romping home, and I gave him the name of the horse as it crossed the line. And suddenly, I'm not his wonderful son any more, and he shouts, 'YOU ARE RINGING ME TOO FUCKING LATE YOU CUNT.' When I told him, he said it was the greatest wind-up he'd ever heard. He went for it hook, line and sinker.

But it had not always been at all easy for Young Bernard being his father's son. It was not just the fact that he was so widely known to be the progeny of the great comedian, a fact only exacerbated by having the same name – Young Bernard was once sent off in a football match for having the temerity, after being booked, to tell the referee his name was Bernard Manning.

I just took it for granted that he knew me, and his next words were, 'Right, hit the showers, comedian.' But he went ahead and sent me off for being Bernard Manning. Things actually got quite bad towards my late teens. I was ready for the club scene, for going in pubs and clubs, and the area that we lived in was pretty hard. You could see people giving you the evil eye. There were some who genuinely were jealous, and I had to steer clear of those types.

My dad was always very much, 'don't you worry, son, your life is mapped out.' I had this horrible feeling that I was going to allow him to do that. He was quite happy for me to play golf all day and do nothing, and it was very tempting at that age, not having had much of an education. But I worked for several people before I went into business, I did my own thing. First, I sold cars, for a fella called Hymie Wernick and his son Robin. I worked for them for some time at their then British Leyland dealership in Prestwich. They used to sell Marinas and Triumph Dolomites – not the easiest of jobs. But it was an education for me, because Hymie really showed me how business worked. It was fascinating watching him actually. He was good, the best. You could just see how his mind was thinking all the time, and how he thought out every little way of selling something.

Young Bernard then set up in business on his own account, and a medium-scale conflict with his father developed.

I had my own valeting business, washing and cleaning cars. Me dad hated me cleaning cars for a living. He thought I was crazy. I wouldn't say we fell out about it, but I was trying to prove a point, that I didn't want to do nothing all day. That's the only time in my life when he got on my nerves a bit. But eventually, he started to come round and realised that perhaps I could look after myself and get on and do my own thing. It was interesting, because it gave me my own lease of life, my own business, although it was a relatively primitive sort of business. What me dad didn't understand was that we did professional jobs for people. We had a premises that they came to – it was only a bit of a shed of a place, but that's all that car-valeting places are, really. I did quite well, learned how to stand on my own two feet – and got £11.50 for playing football. (Young Bernard was good enough to have been signed for a season as a part time professional by Stockport County). I had a great time, but the penny dropped with me and I realised that I could only clean so many cars in a day. But it gave me an introduction into business, how to deal with people and how to handle money.

It was after these couple of quite tricky false starts that Young Bernard managed to impress his father sufficiently with a new

164

business idea for the old man to give it his approval and cash backing. As soon as Bernard Snr was convinced – just as John Manning had once been by his son, when he came up with the idea of selling the family greengrocery and buying a nightclub – the two men were set on level terms, and have stayed there.

At twenty-one, Young Bernard bought a snooker club in Rochdale, ten miles from Harpurhey. Then, two years later in 1983, Young Bernard, true to the Manning tradition of self-sufficiency and ingenuity, had the business idea which has made him independently a wealthy man. The story, as told by Young Bernard, has uncanny echoes of the founding of the Embassy Club.

It was a joint idea – I had a partner from the off (he says). I went to a roller-rink in Ashton, near Manchester, on a Tuesday evening in January, and it was heaving with people. The penny dropped. In the north, everything happens at the weekend, and after Sunday night, the money runs out, and that's it till Thursday. I thought, Tuesday night, I can't believe this, and, of course, you start doing the sums in your head, counting people and looking at the door charges and how many staff there are, and I reckoned this is not a bad little business this. I came on another night, and another, and it was packed nearly every evening. So we looked for premises somewhere that didn't have a roller-rink, and found the one in Rochdale, an old mill that needed a lot of money spending on it. I went to the bank and asked what they could do, and they said it was a new thing and they weren't over convinced, but they would go with it if I could match them pound for pound. Of course, I didn't have that sort of money so I went to me dad. At first he said, 'Rollerrink, what's one of them?' I tried to describe it, and I sold it as best I could. He backed me to the tune of the bank, and within three months it was paid back – it went that well. We had six hundred people in the place every night for four months. We just hit the jackpot. I just couldn't believe the success we had hit upon.

Bernard Snr's conversion to Young Bernard's idea had been complete. 'I'm proud of his business head and I admire the way he turned his leisure centre into a going concern,' he was soon telling the *Sun*. 'When he came to me with the idea for a roller-skating rink, I thought he was off his head. But he proved me wrong.'

By 1996, the roller-rink had expanded into a complete children's entertainment centre, called the Fun Factory, with roller skating, adventure play, ball pools and slides. Young Bernard also has a new nightclub, Mannings, in Middleton, close to Bernard's house. Young Bernard met his wife Julie when she worked for him; they lived together from 1988, had their eldest child, Ben, in 1989 and married in 1992. They now have a daughter, Hayley, and a baby girl, born in 1996, Chloe.

Today, Young Bernard feels free gently to criticise his father's business acumen.

Me dad mentions the Fun Factory every night on the stage because he's me dad, and that's the way he is. I have used him on certain nights, maybe a charity evening, where he'd come and present something, or I might use him for the odd photograph if we have got a bit of publicity going. Other than that I don't really involve dad in the business, because I think we are about forty years apart in ideas. He is very, very old school, and he doesn't understand why people need computers and cash-flow forecasts. He doesn't understand why you would want to do those things. We have got totally different ways of doing things in business to the point where, he'd admit it, we argue – only friendly – but we argue. We just don't see eye to eye when it comes to our ideas. We agree to disagree.

I don't know whether this will cause a bit of controversy, but I don't think my dad is a very good businessman. I think he is a very good comedian. When I say that, obviously he must be a good businessman, because he's had a club there for forty years. But people go to see Bernard Manning, don't they? They go there because he has created this niche, this image which makes people wonder what makes this fella tick – let's go and see him. But the clever bit about his own little way of doing things, his business acumen, is that he knows what he has got, and knows how to market it. If he is going quiet for a few weeks, he know how to stimulate it, perhaps by going on TV. But he will know the moment as only he knows it.

There's obviously a determination, a drive in the family. Every one of us has done well, his brothers, his sisters. His family have all said they would be nowhere without him, and he is a very domineering man. He started with his family around him, he was the entertainer of the family, and he was the motivator that got them all going, the one that had the talent, the one who could sing, the one that had the personality and the bottle to go up and do it.

Bernard Senior's other brothers, Jack, the eldest, and Frank, the baby of the family, and his sisters, Alma and Rene had, as Young Bernard said, done remarkably well, all declining a place in the shadow of their famous brother and making their own way in the world without any hint – yet – of a family fall-out.

There was some family tension in the early sixties, the time of Frank, Alma and Rene's virtual emigration to distant Newquay in Cornwall. Moving away from Manchester ran very much against the Manning grain. Frank was deeply involved in the Embassy's satellite clubs in Manchester, the Palladium and the Wilton. In 1963, he went on holiday to Newquay with his girlfriend of the day and another couple, and Frank twigged, in that typical Manning way, that there was something missing on the Newquay scene – there were no nightclubs, or anything very much to do in the evenings. He decided that he would remedy this lack, and, with his father standing guarantor for him, leased a property to turn it into a cabaret club overlooking the sea. When Alma and Rene and their respective husbands migrated south as well, Bernard and Jack were the only younger Mannings left in Manchester to keep an eye on the ageing parents. 'I'll never forget when Rene and I left,' recalls Alma. 'Bernard came on the phone one night and said me mother was very, very upset, because we all lived close to one another, and she was doing a lot of crying and saying she had lost us. Me dad said, they've not gone to Australia, they've only gone to Cornwall, but in those days, the journey took thirteen hours. Bernard said, "If anything happens to my mother because you two have gone down there and left her, I'll come down and kill the pair of you." He made us all upset.'

Of course, as upset as she was, Nellie survived, and Frank's club was a huge success. He ended up owning an amusement arcade, a casino and a hotel as well. Bernard, of course, was the star turn at the club whenever Frank could coax him down – it was, after all, one venue that was too far for Bernard to return home from every night. It was a matter of family satisfaction that Bernard was always a bigger draw than Jimmy Tarbuck among the holidaying crowds. Alma and Rene did well too in restaurants and various businesses and, both childless, retired in their forties to a life of endless holidays – until they got bored with that and started working on their second fortunes. Newquay became almost a Manning colony to rival Manchester. Frank was a polymath, into everything. 'When Frank was at the cabaret club, he compèred the show and got into telling the gags,' Rene says. 'He once started playing the xylophone on stage. We were in there and we nearly ran out. He'd have a go at anything. He could tell jokes, too. He knew that Bernard was better than him at it, but he used to pinch Bernard's jokes just to get the crowd going before Bernard got there, and when Bernard came on, he found Frank had done his favourite gags.'

Alma adds proudly: 'Frank liked to be in the limelight. He would always go to these big dos and functions and be up at the front. Frank was the pushy one. He was full of himself, even with a bald head. He had a Mercedes, a beautiful house overlooking the beach and wore beautiful Dunhill jackets, Boss suits, always the best. He had very good taste. Because me mother was thirty-nine when she had him, he got spoiled. When he died, he got buried in a Boss suit and Gucci shoes.'

In 1992, Frank stood as a councillor for the Liberal Democrats. 'After he sold the amusement arcade and he went into land development, he had an awful lot of spare time and he decided that Newquay had been very good to him and he thought he would put something back,' Alma explains. How Frank came to be a Liberal, and one apparently passionately interested in green issues, remains a matter of wonder within the family, which has a solid Tory tradition, with the curious exception of Bernard, a lifelong Labour voter until he stopped voting altogether. 'The Liberal Democrats approached him and asked him,' his sister says. 'He knew the fellow who was the MP for the area. Frank really got into it. He canvassed – him and his wife went round all the houses, knocking on all the doors. He said, "I didn't know there were so many dogs in Newquay." But unfortunately, he didn't get on the council.'

Frank died of a brain tumour in 1995, a few weeks before his mother's death. His son Billy, by his second wife Lynn (he has a daughter, Francesca in Manchester by a first marriage) is ten, and his mother was in 1996 thinking of putting him down for Eton. 'He is a very clever boy,' his Aunt Alma says. 'He goes to a private school in Truro and came fifth last year even after all the trauma with his dad being ill. He has always been clever. To hear him talk you'd think he was twenty-one – he's unbelievable.'

Bernard's elder brother, Jack, had a curious history. Seven years older than Bernard, Jack was always some way apart from the others. He married at twenty-one, when he came out of the Army, and had seven children. However, he divorced, and although Jack and Bernard remained extremely close, the children drifted out of the central core of the family almost entirely. As Rene recalls: 'Our Bernard used to laugh at Jack when he said he wasn't in love with his wife. "I don't know how you would go on if you were in love," our Bernard told him. "You've got seven kids – what would have happened if you'd have loved her?" '

After the divorce in 1978, Jack, who was, until he died of leukaemia in 1993, the director of a paint company in Liverpool, increasingly came back into the family fold. 'Our Jack used to come every day to see me mother,' Rene says. 'I can picture him about three months before he died. I was in the kitchen at home for a few weeks, ironing, and Jack said, "You know, when you think about it, it's marvellous. I'm sixty-nine and me mother is her age. How many people are still living and have a son of nearly seventy?" He used to say he was the oldest envoy in town, because she used to ring him up every morning and give him all these jobs – "Jack, go in Marks and Spencers and get me this and get me that." She used to treat us all like kids.' A measure of the estrangement of the core of the Manning family, which now included Jack, from Jack's seven children, came when Jack left his relatively modest estate of £80,000 to Bernard, having changed his will only a month before his death. Five of Jack's children tried, but failed, to contest the will. 'He left me the money and that was the end of that,' commented an angry Bernard to the *Sun*. 'It was his decision. If I leave all my money to the Salvation Army that's my business.'

Bernard's terseness over the will may well have had its roots in an unpleasant fall-out with one of Jack's children back in 1986.

169

It was then that Jack's son, Michael, who was then thirty-eight, spectacularly broke ranks, when he sold a wardrobe full of supposed family skeletons to Fleet Street after he had a dispute with Bernard over a piece of carpet. The story was a detailed account of an alleged infidelity of Bernard's with a sixteen-year-old girl, but lacked a certain credibility, partly because Bernard was a fat man of nearly sixty, but more because Michael Manning was a virtual outsider with very limited knowledge of Bernard's family. He had not met or spoken with any close family member for many years, and had only once been to the Manning home in Lewis Avenue to lay the length of hall carpet which led to the trouble. Crucially, the story in the *Sunday People* was never followed up by Fleet Street, which indicates that Michael's allegations did not quite ring true.

The thrust of his story was that the happy marriage and close family of Bernard and Vera was a façade, and that Vera had, in fact, thrown Bernard out of the house to live with his mother as far back as 1979. Young Bernard, Mike Manning asserted, stayed with his mother. Bernard Snr putting money into the roller-rink had been merely his ploy to get back in with Vera. 'It was all to win points with Vera – using the son as a pawn,' Manning said. His story was juicy stuff, even though, according to every conceivable witness to the events, it appears to have been a complete fantasy on the young man's part.

It remains, however, an interesting exercise in the art of putting two and two together to make several dozen – how a fact can look plausible if it is stated boldly, without qualification or explanation, and propelled forward with a mixture of guesswork and malice. One detail, of Bernard going to his mother's house for breakfast every morning, which he did with Jack, Mike Manning's father, was just such a fact, given an ominous spin by the disgruntled nephew. A man who in his fifties did not have breakfast at home, but at his mother's, was surely escaping from an unhappy marriage, the nephew's logic seemed to be.

Manning's timing for going to the *People* with the story coincided with Vera being in hospital with the heart problem that killed her shortly afterwards; it may be that Mike Manning thought the person who could most easily deny his story was on the way out, and would soon be dead. It may equally be that he believed, with such timing, he could hurt Bernard all the more deeply. And Bernard was genuinely distressed: 'She was in hospital at the time,' he says, still incredulous a decade after the story appeared.

> Vera and his mother don't get on at all (Mike Manning said). There has never been any love lost there since Bernard married her. His mother is very possessive towards him ... Even when Bernard and Vera were still together he never had breakfast at home. He went to his mother's every morning and she cooked him two breakfasts. While he was eating one plate of egg and bacon, she'd be cooking him another lot. Bernard adores his mother, but he's frightened of her. She treats him like a little boy. It's our Bernard this and our Bernard that, and 'Make sure you put your coat on, our Bernard.' It's pathetic really. I think he'd go to pieces if anything happened to his mother. She's been there to wipe his nose all his life.
>
> I used to go around with him a lot when he was working at different clubs and my wife Jane came too. But in all those years, he never took Vera. She was always at home, or working on the till at his Embassy Club. His mother was on the till alternate nights, so there was nothing to stop him taking Vera with him. I saw all his antics. One night, when my wife was with us, he brought another woman. My wife remembers her as being a very masculine type – butch, really. He told us not to say anything to Vera. I had no intention of telling Vera about his other women. It was nothing to do with me ... Bernard's not happy. All the success he's had and all the money he has made has all gone down the tube because he has lost Vera. My dad (Jack) went to Jersey on a job with him last year. They were there three days and Bernard never went out of his hotel room. He sat in all day watching telly.

The stitching began to show in Mike Manning's story when it was pointed out that Vera and Bernard seemed to be getting on perfectly together. They were, Manning explained, 'on speaking terms, but not sleeping terms'. He insisted that Vera was a conspirator in covering up the fact that Bernard and she had been living apart for seven years. 'He used to park his Cadillac, with the registration LAF 1, outside to fool everybody into thinking he still lived there. But he would have driven to his mother's in his Rolls-Royce. He couldn't

171

face the scandal of being kicked out – of being the butt of other comedians' jokes – and Vera said she would never show him up. She'd have people to the house for him and never let on he didn't live there, but she won't have him back. When people ring up, she says Bernard is out at his mother's and will call back.'

The unnamed girlfriend whose supposed existence caused all this disruption was said to live nearby in a luxury flat and own a sports car. After Bernard had a row with his driver, the driver had allegedly gone to Vera and told her what was going on. Mike Manning was quoted as saying:

> Bernard's always sending Vera flowers and presents trying to buy his way back in. But Vera has told me, there's no way I'll have that man back after what he's done. Vera is very stubborn. He'd do anything to get her back. I don't think he ever thought she would leave him. Bernard is having to pay a fortune maintaining her. Vera's got him by the short and curlies. She doesn't want for a thing. She goes on holidays – fabulous cruises – three or four times a year and has everything she wants. Bernard once told me, "I love that woman, I adore her." When she was in hospital the last time – a month ago – Bernard took, or had sent, a huge bunch of flowers every day. All the nurses thought how affectionate and lovely he was to her. He couldn't do enough. They never guessed the real story. It's a weird set-up.

Bernard's reply to questioning by the *Sunday People* was restrained. 'I'm a happily married man,' he was quoted as saying. 'My wife's in hospital. She nearly died last Friday with a heart attack. My son and I stayed up all night with her at the hospital. I've been visiting her every night. It's not the way you behave if your marriage is over. It's quite true that I spend some nights away from home, but that's not because I've got a fancy woman. It's because I've got an eighty-six-year-old mother whom I like to keep an eye on, partly because I worry about her health, and partly because I worry that she might be burgled.'

The circumstantial evidence for Mike Manning's story being invented is strong enough. Apart from the unlikelihood of the premise – Bernard Manning having a teenage girlfriend – the fact that Vera was terminally ill and unlikely to survive or answer back made it a perfect time to try to tell and sell such a tale. Another problem with it is that Manning had an axe to grind. Although Mike Manning was known in the family as a loser, Bernard had typically supported him with handouts and given him a job laying some carpet. His patience ran out when the carpet turned out to be faulty and Mike was unwilling to replace it. Bernard then attempted to bankrupt his nephew.

Among the rest of the family, bemusement rather than fury was the response to the Mike Manning 'revelations'.

Bernard was very good to that Michael (says Alma). He gave him money. I remember me mother saying over the phone that his sister and Michael's wife came to my mother to ask for a handout, and my mother said no because they had had money before, and she said you can't keep coming here. So what they did was go to Bernard at the Embassy Club, and he gave it to them. Every time Michael got into a bit of a scrape, it was Bernard he came to and Bernard always helped him out. Michael opened a club in Bacup and Bernard worked for him quite a lot and did him a lot of favours, but I think maybe he came once too often, and Bernard said no. I think that's when he decided that if he slagged him off in the papers, they would pay him.

Me mother was really upset about it because Michael had said awful things, like me mother treats him like a baby and she puts sweets in his pocket and all that sort of stuff, stupid things. He was me mother's blue-eyed boy and everybody knew it. So what? Vera hadn't thrown him out – he was still living there. As for the young girlfriend, none of us bothered about it because we all knew it was a load of tripe. It was untrue and Michael was just doing it to get money from the papers. You see, he was always in scrapes with money. But Bernard thought if he prolonged the issue, it would just add fuel to the fire, and, if he completely ignored it, it would just die a death, because today's news is tomorrow's chip paper. What gets me is that we hardly knew the man (Mike Manning), so how could he claim to know all this? We'd never bothered with the family for years – Bernard hadn't, except Jack, so how would Vera know them? As if Vera would go and tell Mike Manning anyway.

Mike Manning had had that many businesses and they had all gone. He wasn't prepared to go out and work. He thought the world owed him a living, not like us.

Bernard's belief that the story would blow over and be forgotten if he ignored it was proven by events. Because the 'girlfriend' never came forward with her story – which, the applecart having been upset, she might have been expected to do – the issue did indeed die the death. The Manchester press corps universally regarded the *People*'s story as a *flyer* and, in the mysterious way that Fleet Street has at times, newspapers seem to have decided as of one mind to ignore it. Mike Manning, who went to ground shortly afterwards and was last known to the family to be a publican, may have expected to become a celebrity for a while, but was left alone. Some tabloid stories smell of truth, and, sadly for him, this one did not. It still irritates Bernard a little, however.

> I rang the editor (Bernard says). I said, come down to my home and let's go and find this flat – I am supposed to have a bird in a flat – let's go to her flat and let's have a look at the car. I got on to my solicitor and he said, it's a nine-day wonder and, if I carried on with it, it would only blow it up every bloody week. Today I would have sued the bollocks off them – people do that sort of thing. In them days you didn't bother. You got slagged off in the paper and that was it. Vera saw it – I showed it to her. I said, 'Here, look at what Michael has said here.' I had no secrets from my Missus. She said, take no notice, because she was poorly. She didn't want to know. She said, 'You know what they are, don't mither.' I said, 'Well, it says I've got a bird here with a sports car and all this carry on.' She said, 'Well, I know that's not true.' Jack just said, 'I am sorry about this Bernard,' like a brother would do. 'There is nothing I can do about it.'

At the end of October 1986, Bernard's nephew's goading, mis-interpretation of fact, malice, or whatever it was, ceased to matter, when Vera suffered another heart attack while she was in Naples on a cruise with friends. Barry Clark, Bernard's best friend, and another close pal, Chris Graham, who is now Bernard's manager, were with him at the club when he got the phone call from Italy at 7.50 p.m., ten minutes before he was due on stage. 'They just kept quiet and carried on as normal to get me ready to go out on stage. To this day, I don't know how I went on and made people laugh, because I was feeling terrible. When I came off, the tears started. I cried and cried and cried. My eyes were like beetroots. It was murder. But Barry and Chris didn't leave my side for the next six months until I could cope.' (He had used the identical image of his eyes looking like beetroots fifteen years earlier, when his father died.)

Vera was rushed in an air ambulance back from Italy to Manchester, and it was obvious to all that she was unlikely to recover this time. The Saturday morning before Vera died, Bernard picked her up from the hospital in a wheelchair and took her for a drive around all their favourite places. At 4 a.m. on the following Tuesday, she died at home with a nurse in attendance. Bernard, on his way back from a job in an ex-servicemen's club in Nottingham, arrived home at 4.30. 'The nurse told me she'd gone about half an hour earlier. it was a bombshell. The awful thing was that I'd stopped for a meal at the service caff on the motorway. I never dreamed she'd go just like that,' he said in an emotional interview with the *Daily Mirror* two weeks after Vera's death.

Amazingly (although perhaps not to anyone who knows his ways) Bernard went on stage at a club in Coventry the night of the early morning Vera died. Bernard's way of coping, as ever, was to keep in control, and the only way he knows how to do this is by performing – a feat all the more astonishing in the circumstances, given the nature of his act. He was also granting press interviews only a day after Vera died. The date in Coventry, at the Lythalls Lane social club, had been a disaster, as it turned out. The club owner, Tony King, said Bernard insisted that no one should be told about his wife's death. 'When he arrived, I could tell he had been crying,' Mr King explained. According to press reports, Bernard was overcome by grief on stage, talked virtual gibberish for twenty-five minutes, used jokes which had just been told by another comedian, and finally rushed off stage and broke down as hecklers shouted him down. He insisted in the *Mirror* interview that he was not jeered off. 'I can't remember how I got through the act,' he said. 'Perhaps I wasn't up to handling the hecklers like I usually am.'

The following day, Bernard appeared again, this time even further from home, at the Festival Hall in Basildon, Essex, for 300 men at a boxing dinner and stag show. The customers had paid £19 each for the entertainment, and he refused to disappoint them, although he decided to go on before the strippers so he could get away early. Bernard, not the first bereaved person to find speaking to reporters therapeutic, told a *Today* writer: 'I've been crying all the way down here from Manchester. But you can't sit at home staring at the walls. The only time I can forget the pain is when I get out there in front of an audience ... It's a job of work, and you have got to do it. It takes you right out of it whenever you hear that applause – that's showbiz. That's my life.' Every few minutes throughout his act, *Today* reported, he stopped to sip orange juice. 'You can't stop us laughing. A good laugh is all we need,' he commented. He received a standing ovation at the end of his act.

His emotions, as expressed in the *Daily Mirror* interview, were tender and touching. 'Vera used to enjoy a good laugh,' he said. 'She'd look at me and say, "You're no oil painting – but you do make me laugh." Now she's gone. Born, married and buried ... all in the radius of two and a half miles. Everybody knows how much I loved her. And she knew too. I've done nowt but cry for a fortnight ... I don't know what I'm going to do without Vera. I loved that woman. She was just an ordinary housewife but she kept me in check. The thing that I miss most is not seeing her every day. Just sitting and talking things over. Having a good laugh.'

Vera was buried on 9 November in Blackley cemetery. Only the family attended, at Bernard's request. As Vera's coffin was lowered into the grave, the *Daily Star* reported, he stepped forward and burst into tears. Then, for more than a minute, he stood in silent, tearful prayer. 'I have lost the bedrock of my life,' he said afterwards.

From Blue to Black
and Blue

Let's have something nice now. None of that fucking nigger music.
What about something by the great Nat King Cole?

Favourite Bernard Manning introduction to song

From the late 1950s right through until the beginning of the
nineties, the foundation of Bernard Manning's notoriety was
his on-stage swearing and obscenity – the blueness factor. The
question of what were still termed his 'jokes about coloureds' – a
quaint description to the modern ear – was of secondary concern.
He was frequently attacked solely for swearing. His answers came
close to exasperation: 'I tell a joke as one working man would tell
it to another,' he would explain, clearly pained by the tediousness
of the issue. 'They're not going to speak in an Oxford accent. If
they drop a hammer on their toe, they won't just say, "Oh Dear."
The air turns blue, and that's the kind of language I use.'

Progressive thinkers in the 1970s – Esther Rantzen was one –
would pick him up publicly on the racial jokes, but she was years
ahead of her time. Although Britain's first Race Relations Act had
been in force since 1968, Charlie Williams on the first episode of
The Comedians in 1971, was still talking about a character in a joke
being a 'Jew boy', and even a young Lenny Henry was getting laughs
with jokes at the expense of black people. The concept of minding
your language – as well as being careful about racial content – in
jokes was a completely new development of the early eighties. And
even then, the fashion for what would be known (to the political
right, at least) as political correctness, in its full, semantics-obsessed
guise was still in the process of emerging from American university
campuses.

In comedy, we have, oddly enough, taken the PC ethic much
further than the Americans. Don Rickles, the nearest thing to
Bernard in the States, sounds off about Polaks, blacks, 'fat Mexicans'

and 'Chinamen' and gets rewarded by a starring voice-over part in the Disney movie, *Toy Story*. As an example of the tortured middle-class British attitude to dubious racial-based humour, an observer could do no better than to attend an event at the Edinburgh Festival three years ago, entitled 'Stand Up Black America'.

It was here that a black American comedian scandalised the audience when he started talking about Muslims. He had been scared of anybody middle-eastern-looking on the flight over, he explained, in case they were Muslim fundamentalists trying to blow the plane up. This sentiment alone caused prickles of concern; there again, the collective reasoning seemed to run, he's black, so he must know what he's doing, political correctness-wise. Then the comedian explained how he had seen a Sikh on his flight, and wanted to ask him to remove his turban in case there were any explosives hidden under its folds. The communal horror among the audience was now growing. Did this ignorant outsider not know that Muslims, Hindus and Sikhs are different? A full American Don Rickles rant ('In addition to immigration, our country also plays host to the United Nations, where the American taxpayer gladly foots the bill for the sons of foreign leaders to escape date-rape charges through diplomatic immunity.') would doubtless have caused all-round apoplexy, while if Bernard on full song had appeared at the Pleasance Theatre, a cardiac arrest unit might have been required as the (white) customers keeled over one by one.

It is, perhaps, no wonder, then, that Bernard and his close friends and family – people who know him to be a kind, generous man, a little stubborn, a lot outspoken, but a great benefactor of charity, especially Jewish charity, a man whose Indian GP neighbour thinks the world of him, who has put on benefit shows for black sportsmen, who used to test out 'coloured jokes' to make sure they were funny enough with the proprietor of his favourite curry restaurant, who stumped up to send a terminally ill Asian boy to Disneyland, and has frequently (he says) given money to anti-racist causes – are perplexed and frustrated by the extent of the loathing Bernard now engenders in many areas of society. A generation has grown up aware of Bernard Manning exclusively as a racist comedian; there is little doubt that when he dies the final word on Bernard will be a short and ugly one – 'racist'. Brief tribute will be paid by fellow comedians, through clenched teeth in most cases, to his comic genius, but every news item on the event will be dominated by a recap on the race controversy that has monopolised the latter part of his life.

Whether or not Bernard is a true racist – in the sense of believing in the innate inferiority of anyone not of his own narrow racial type – or whether he is merely a man who is honest enough to admit that he believes there are differences between racial groups – is probably immaterial. What he may think privately about people of different races is entirely overshadowed by what he says publicly, and a lot of that is pretty vile. It is arguable – a little tenuously, perhaps – that in the age of political correctness, Bernard is now a taboo-breaking underground comedian, a subversive, in that he says the disrespectful things other comedians dare not utter on stage. It is a valid argument, but does not, again, get away from the fact that comedian who talks about niggers, coons and Pakis, Japs and Chinks hurts them deeply, as well as cementing racial stereo-types.

Reinforcing stereotypes is one thing, but can Bernard Manning jokes actually cause people to harm those of a different race, as sociologists maintain? Do Bernard's race jokes inflame or, alter-natively, smother, the embers of racial prejudice among the alien-ated white working-class population? The latter suggestion is that, just as prostitutes help to prevent overwhelming sexual tensions becoming harmful, by airing unpleasant racist sentiment, Bernard acts as a lightning rod, articulating the petty, commonplace preju-dices that most members of his audiences feel, and conducting that sentiment down safely to ground.

Without Manning, the argument runs, racist jokes would be swapped secretly on street corners, as contraband, and as a result, valued and sought after ever more highly. Bernard, because he sees no need for racial jokes to be clandestine, does the bloodletting in public, and it is far better that verbal, mocking racism be isolated to the Embassy Club, like a bacillus in a bottle, then let secretly into the public water supply. It is a worthwhile theory, and one reporter, watching a Manning show in the Midlands, even found some evi-dence for it among the audience. 'He says things that people feel but have not got the guts to say themselves,' a panel beater who used to be a member of the National Front was quoted in the *Independent* as saying. Then, the man added, he discovered Bernard Manning video tapes: 'I laugh at them (the blacks) and then forget about them.'

A deeply fashionable hypothesis in the academic world currently holds that Bernard Manning is a prime example of the Soviet Russian literary critic Mikhail Bakhtin's Carnivalisation Theory. Bakhtin believed that pre-Lenten Saturnalia type festivities, in which poor people are given the temporary opportunity to laugh at the iniquities of their lives (in terms of Harpurhey this would mean at the foolishness of educated people, at the world going mad, at black people taking our jobs and running the country, etc.) act as a safety valve for society to maintain its status quo. While they're guffawing at the Embassy Club, in other words, they're not rioting on the streets and burning down black ghettoes, and society is free to continue undisturbed by the racist rumble from deepest Harpurhey.

Trendy speculation aside, the one certainty in the matter is that Bernard has, be it by malice or mere cussedness, brought the racist problem on himself. He is a man of his time, not of ours, a man to whom the Depression, the 'Japs', the Big Bands, Harold Wilson, Enoch Powell, and regarding black people as 'immigrants', are all vivid realities, not faded back numbers. He sees no reason to change anything he says – in fact, sees a positive advantage in remaining an anachronism. Bernard does not pretend to understand it, but neither does he claim for a minute that the controversy around him has been accidental, or something that just happened to him innocently as he was going about his business. While his old stock in trade, swearing and sexual obscenity, have become *de rigueur* among up-to-date comedians, even the most bland ethnic gag has been expunged from the contemporary culture; but this curious fact is not some elite secret that has been concealed from everyone bar Bernard Manning. Neither could it be difficult for him to notice that a large number of today's British heroes – from countless footballers to Trevor MacDonald to rock stars to actors – are black. He knows these things, but has made a conscious choice to ignore changes in society and carry on giving his audiences what he believes they want.

Racial jokes actually comprise a small part of Bernard's act, and frequently get quite a muted reaction, but, whatever their motivation, they are his thing. As he has said, when friends like Johnnie Hamp have urged him to drop this dated part of his act:

If I took race jokes out, I would be a run-of-the-mill comedian. I wouldn't stand out. You think of all the comedians over the years, and there is only one they have a go at, there is only one that gets the publicity, there is only one that packs the theatres. You put my name on a ticket at a sportsmen's dinner, you know the tickets are going to sell. The punters are going to see Bernard. I am a world famous comedian. I have played Las Vegas, and they talk about me in America. I did fourteen weeks, topped the bill at the London Palladium, and have done Royal Command performances. What more can I do? I told one gag at the Royal Command performance – it wasn't blue (heaven forbid), but I said, 'There's a Pakistani who wanted to be converted, so they took him to St Helens and kicked him over the goalposts.' I told that in front of the Queen, and she fell about laughing, shook me hands said, 'I enjoyed the performance immensely.' No doubt about it. I don't tell fucking lies.

It was in 1972, in the pages of the *Sun* (the corpse of the socialist *Daily Herald*, which had recently been bought by Rupert Murdoch but had yet to swing very far to the right), that Bernard was first taken to task over racial jokes. The newspaper was celebrating what it called 'Harmony Week in the *Sun*'. 'When I'm asked if I get my suits at rent-a-tent I laugh,' he explained to writer Ann Buchanan. 'I laugh at fat-man jokes, you see? Irishmen laugh at Irish jokes, Jews at Jewish ones, and the Paks love to laugh at coloured jokes ... People ask me how I get away with it. How I dare go into Moss Side, for instance, where there is a big coloured population, after all the Paki jokes I've cracked on telly and in my own Embassy Club. Well, there's only one answer – I'll show you, luv.' Bernard then took Ann Buchanan to some of the more run down districts of Manchester. 'We were instantly surrounded by coloured folk, teeth gleaming in smiles of recognition,' she wrote. ' "What did I tell you?" Bernard cracked. "Every time you dial 999 around here you get the Bengal Lancers." ' Manning granted the request of two Asian schoolboys to tell them a joke: "Well, there was this Pakistani boy kicking a football in the school grounds. A posh-looking fella watched his footwork for a while, then said, I'm Sir Matt Busby, son, how would you like to play for Manchester United? And the lad said, No thanks, it's bad enough being coloured around here."' Bernard claimed that he tested his jokes with restaurateur Shamsul Islam Choudhury, owner of the Shanaz restaurant in Stockport Road. One such, give the Choudhury seal of approval, might almost have been a anti-racist gag about the viciousness of British immigration officials: 'Hear the one about two Pakis on a day trip to Blackpool? One suggested going for a swim and the other said, "No, they might not let us in again."' 'Shamsul hears all Bernard's coloured stories,' Buchanan concluded reassuringly. 'If he thinks they could be hurtful, he has promised to tell Bernard, but so far they've all made him laugh.'

One of the earliest recorded instances of Bernard getting into trouble over racist gags came in 1980. It came about after his less than wholly wise admission in a *Sunday People* interview that he admired certain aspects of Hitler. It was the Jewish community that reacted; there was a move on to ban him from appearing at a Jewish charity do. Mr Leonard Cramer, son of the president of the Ladies' Aid Society said: 'There will be a number of Jewish ex-servicemen in the audience. They did not fight a war to be insulted by an Adolf Hitler lover.' Bernard reacted with uncharacteristic contrition: 'I know I have upset a lot of people – but no one is more upset than me. I do a lot of charity work in Jewish circles.' Melville Davies, one of Bernard's oldest Jewish friends, took it upon himself, not for the last time, to write to Jewish critics of Bernard to point out that in his experience Bernard was definitely not a racist, and was a great friend of the Jews in particular. He did not mention the fact that Bernard had Jewish ancestry – Bernard, probably with some wisdom, makes a point of never trying to capitalise on that.

When *The Times* interviewed Bernard in 1983, he was asked again about racial gags. 'Coloured jokes? I was the first to do a testimonial dinner for Clive Lloyd (the black Lancashire and West Indies cricket captain) – had him falling about – and in Birmingham last week I was having a go at them all and ended up singing "Me And My Shadow" with one on stage. It helps being older. An audience won't accept jokes about race, Jews, mothers-in-law from a young comedian who doesn't know what he's talking about.'

By the mid-1980s, of course, with the appearance of AIDS, homosexuality had become another subject about which it was wise for a comedian to watch his words. Although Bernard had experience of gay clubs going back decades, had worked at them without a qualm, and publicly said that he did not give a damn about people's private sexual habits, the raising of homosexuals to the status of an officially protected group (at least by the liberal establishment and, especially, by the luvvie show-business world) seems again to have sent Bernard into his most malevolent, subversive role. He expressed the view in a 1985 *People* article that camp showbiz personalities like John Inman and Kenny Everett should be banned, especially from children's shows such as pantomime. His views sparked a lot of letters to the paper, which were equally divided between being for and against Bernard. Mrs J. Lee from Burnley wrote: 'I have never been a fan of Bernard Manning. I always thought he was a big loudmouth. After your article, his mouth can't be big enough. Thanks for your voice, Bernard.' Mrs Joan Bruck from Hornchurch said: 'If Bernard Manning is supposed to be normal then heaven help us.' Mrs Gladys Saunders of Bournemouth tried to upbraid Bernard by invoking his oft-stated revulsion for joking about the afflicted: 'Has it occurred to him that these mostly decent people are victims of nature's imbalance of hormones?' she asked. Bernard still prefers there to be no blatantly camp punters at the Embassy Club. 'A feller came in here one night dressed as a woman,' he said to an *Observer* journalist in 1992. 'He had big hands, like a Manchester City goalkeeper. And I said, "Look pal, you'll have to leave. You can't go into them ladies' toilets." That's where he'd made a move for. Women are women and fellers are fellers. It says so in the Bible that that's not on.'

It was in 1990 that the anti-Bernard movement began to gather momentum. In May, Bernard played at Southampton Guildhall to an audience which included a 'race spy' who jotted down every gag with a racial theme. The jokes were duly typed out and distributed to the city councillors. The Labour-controlled council had threatened prosecution if the jokes were considered racist. However no one complained about the show, nor did the police, and so the matter was quietly dropped, but the principle was established for local authorities to ban Bernard, at least from their own premises. Dr Visveswara Rao Rudravajhala, a GP and Bernard's neighbour at his mother's house in Alkrington, where Bernard was now living, told reporters that Southampton Council had overreacted by sending a race-relations monitor. He described Bernard as 'a perfect gentleman, a good neighbour and definitely not a racist . . . We have been neighbours of Mr Manning for more than four years and there had never been an unkind word between us,' the doctor commented. Also in 1990 came a classic and instructive misunderstanding by Bernard over race. David Baddiel, the stand-up comedian, was in Manchester and had said he would love to go to the Embassy Club, but had heard a rumour that Asians were banned, and consequently would not attend. Bernard, assuming that Baddiel must be Asian (why, otherwise, would he care?) refuted any such ban. It seemed that Bernard could still not quite appreciate that a white person might be concerned about patronising an establishment where he could get in, but black people could not. And, anyway, Bernard insisted, despite having thrown out the transvestite, there truly was no bar on anyone at the Embassy Club.

In 1991, an Indian customer at a Stockport club, Quaffers, took issue in public with Bernard. The occasion was the recording of a twentieth-anniversary *Comedians* reunion, which Johnnie Hamp organised as a fund-raiser for Guide Dogs for the Blind. (Hamp's daughter, Merry, was blinded as a child in a school laboratory accident.)

> There were a crowd of Indians in the club (Hamp recalls) and a lot of the fourteen comedians had a little go at them. Bernard was last on, and he came up and said, 'Hello, my friends. Are you from Pakistan?' and they said, 'No, we are Indians.' Then this guy said, 'Mr Manning, could I tell you a joke?' So Bernard called him up on stage. The guy said, 'We are not Pakistani. We are Hindu, and we believe in reincarnation. And when I come back in my next life, I do not wish to come back as a fat ugly bastard like you.' Well, the rest of the comics and the crowd went 'Woooaaaahhh', because they all thought that Bernard was now going to tear him to shreds. But he didn't. He let this guy go on, he joined in the fun and let

him go on with his gag – a terrible joke, he told. At the end of it, Bernard said, 'Give him a big round of applause.' He could have slaughtered him.

Unfortunately, this scene did not make the final selection used in the video of *The Comedians'* reunion.

He doesn't need to swear and he doesn't need to use the racist stuff (Hamp reflects today). I am not black, nor am I Jewish, but I have seen them sitting through Bernard's shows, like those Indians. They seem to laugh along, but whether they should, or they're being Uncle Toms or whatever, is a very difficult question. Bernard does racist gags. There is no doubt about it, but I can't see any venom in it. I think it is the way it is delivered. If they're written down, they look racist; if they are told in fun, maybe it is not. I would personally never use any of that stuff because I don't like it. But he goes to a Jewish function and does Jewish gags, and they never get offended. Jewish people love it. My daughter is blind, and he does a gag about the guide dogs and she laughs like a drain. I really don't know the answer to it.

The Gulf War early in 1992 gave Bernard a new target – Iraqis. 'What is the difference between an Iraqi woman and a fish?' he asked Robert Chalmers of the *Observer.* One's oily and greasy with fucking bulgy eyes. The other's a fish.' When Chalmers suggested this was a foul joke, Bernard defended himself: 'It's a joke. We all know the difference between an Iraqi woman and a fish. It's a joke. Anyone with intelligence can see that. The Iraqis were our enemies, so you get a laugh. It's like the Japanese. Everybody's buttering them up now, but when they had our troops in their prisoner-of-war camps, they were starving them to death and humiliating them and giving them rats to eat and whipping them and cutting their hands off and cutting their heads off, these wonderful Japanese.' A favourite routine at the Embassy Club is for Bernard to pick any bespectacled customer and pretend to have mistaken him for Japanese. He then launches into a brief, if dated, rant about Pearl Harbor and the POW camps, ending on the line, 'Look at you. You can't wait to go home and make another fucking Datsun.' Given that the victim of this section of the act is blatantly not Japanese, the routine gives a curious effect because there is always an element of uncertainty for the audience; is Bernard really being this venomous about the Japanese, or could it all just be a joke *about* racism? It would not be hard to imagine an alternative comedian picking on a white member of the audience and abusing him for comic effect on the basis that he was black; the message would be that we are all the same under the skin. On the other hand, Bernard is probably just making a schoolboy-ish, out-of-date joke about somebody looking Japanese because they have glasses.

Later in 1992, Manchester's chief constable, David Wilmot, boycotted a police cabaret because Bernard was performing. In Southampton, the police were ignoring his performances; in Manchester, the police were hiring him, even though a newly introduced charter, posted at all the police stations in Greater Manchester and carried on laminated cards by the force's 7000 officers, said that they should be 'polite, sympathetic, tactful and understanding', and should 'treat everyone equally, irrespective of race or gender'. Wilmot was said to have issued an ultimatum to his force, saying 'it's Bernard or me', because his act was not in line with the force's philosophy. Fifty delegates decided that Bernard should stay, even if Wilmot would not attend. The council in Rochdale followed the new lead for public bodies to boycott Bernard. He was banned from a rugby league dinner, as the council believed he was too *risqué* to star in the clubhouse they owned. So the Rochdale Hornets Ex-Players Association switched the dinner to the privately owned Rugby Union club.

In 1993, Bernard turned up the mischief level a fraction higher. He told a reporter he was disappointed by Manchester's failure to win the nomination to hold the Olympic Games: 'We were all geared up here,' Bernard said. 'We were going to book international artistes and serve vintage champagne, go a little bit upmarket, if you like. We could have made that Linford Christie a waiter. It would've meant people got served quicker.'

The following year, Bernard appeared at a Round Table charity dinner for 500 men at the Pennine Hotel in Derby. It was increasingly evident as the nineties progressed that Bernard was abandoning all attempts at taste or restraint. He cracked racial jokes at the expense of two black waitresses, Freda Burton, then twenty-three, and Sonia Rhule, then thirty, who left their jobs after the incident. Of Freda Burton's hair braids, Bernard send, 'Lend us one. I need some new shoe laces.' There were also gags about the Ku-Klux-Klan and black men's sexual prowess – he said he wished he was hung like a black man, but hoped not to wake up in the middle of the night to find the KKK had granted his wish. The women said that Bernard had used the words 'wogs' and 'sambos', which seemed odd, as both are that rare thing among racially derogatory terms, in that they have never been used by Bernard Manning.

'It was like a National Front meeting, how I imagine them to be,' Sonia Rhule said. 'Nobody came to help us, nobody stopped it. Everybody was laughing. They could see we were distressed. The content of his jokes was degrading, disgusting and humiliating.' The Pennine Hotel wrote to the Round Table to complain, but a year later the now ex-waitresses lost their claim at an industrial tribunal against the Pennine's management for racial discrimination. 'I've no regrets,' Bernard insisted after the case. 'I said nothing to offend anyone, and that's why they lost. I never said a single word those girls claimed I did. I suppose I could be seen as a victim of my own success. People might see me as an easy target and think they can have a go at me, but I just want to forget the whole affair.' He added, 'I'll carry on joking about blacks, Scots, Welsh, Irish and Jews. Life was never meant to be taken too seriously. It's a good job I didn't come out with the joke about what do you say to a black man who has a job? Two big Macs, please.'

In April 1995, before the Derby tribunal had ruled, the *World in Action* film *Black and Blue* was shown on ITV. The film was about racism within the police, and was illustrated throughout by a secretly made tape of a show Bernard had done near Liverpool as a benefit for policemen injured in Northern Ireland. A large proportion of the men at the dinner were serving policemen, and £2500 was raised for disabled RUC officers. Bernard had been told that a black detective, DC David McIntosh, would be in the crowd, and proceeded to pick on him. The Granada film caused official and public outrage, although it was Bernard who seemed to catch more flak than the policemen who had hired him for the evening.

187

The performance at a 'gentlemen's evening' at the banqueting suite of Haydock Park racecourse was an exceptionally outrageous one. Knowing the kind of high-octane, full-fat entertainment men *en masse* like, Bernard bypassed his gentler material and got stuck into the hard stuff. 'They actually think they're English because they're born here,' Bernard said of black people. 'That means if a dog's born in a stable it's a fucking horse.' Then came a couple of jokes which appeared in a curious way to be anti-police, and, conceivably, even, anti-racist. There were local businessmen as well as police in the audience, and Bernard was presumably happy to take a crack at the constabulary.

When the police pull you up, you know they must caution you. Remember that, they've got to caution you. They say to you, 'You're not obliged to say anything, but anything you do say will be taken down and used in evidence.' Your next sentence must be, 'Please don't hit me again officer.' But if you're a nigger, 'again and again and again'. They knock the fuck out of them coons. Them Los Angeles police units kicking that fucking nigger on the floor (Rodney King, whose beating up had been filmed). I thought, fuck me, that's not on … not enough police there.

A Liverpool docker (he continued) went over to South Africa for a job. The boss there tells him: 'These credentials, we couldn't fault these. It's people like you we want over here. We have a lot of trouble with the blacks.' The docker says, 'We've got a few in Liverpool.' The boss tells him, 'It's not the same, we don't bother with them.' So the doctor asks, 'What do we do then?' The boss says, 'I'll give you a bit of a test. There's a revolver, go out and shoot six niggers and a rabbit.' The docker asks, 'What have I got to shoot the rabbit for?' He says, 'You've got the job.'

Even black slaves in the Deep South received the Manning treatment at the police dinner, again raising the question of whether Bernard was truly and unbelievably racist, or was in an arcane way (if highly unlikely for him), taking the mickey out of racism. 'They used to be happy people in the cotton fields,' he said. 'Singing their bollocks off day and night. Fucking happy it was. Give them a knife and fork and they're fucked. A fella used to go round with a whip.

"Oh, give us another crack of that whip, master, I love that whip . . . Overtime, lads, on my arse, on my arse." They fucking loved it. Six quid a week and all the cotton they could eat.' The routine seems so absurdly racist that it could be a parody from the mouth of an alternative comic; however, the extraordinary fact remains that it probably is not. 'Where's Mac?' Bernard asked towards the end of his act. When he alighted on McIntosh, Bernard started: 'How are you baby? How are you, son? Isn't this better than swinging through the trees? Having a night out with nice people. Lovely to see you, son, anyway. You're black, I'm white. Do you think it makes any difference what colour you are? You bet your fucking bollocks it does.' (The swinging-through-the-trees joke seemed to have a startlingly raw, new edge to it even for Bernard. Although it may be an academic point, he had in fact been quoted as using it in the *Sunday People* fifteen years earlier, when he said of Charlie Williams: 'I was pleased to see he did so well in *Planet of the Apes*. Show business has been very good to him. I'm sure he has come to realise it's far better than swinging on trees.')

The audio tape made at Haydock Park was broadcast with the film as the backdrop for a powerful documentary, the fallout from which catapulted Bernard back into the headlines. The affair was a blessing for Bernard's fellow guest at the dinner, the former Merseyside council leader, Derek Hatton. Hatton, whose socialist credentials were, for some people, in decline since he had become a public relations man and was also due in court on fraud charges (he was fully acquitted) had the opportunity to castigate Bernard in unambiguous terms.

> I've never heard such vile and evil racism in my life (he said). It had shades of Hitler's Nuremberg rallies. I was invited some weeks beforehand. It was rather amusing that it was three days before the trial that I was invited to speak to four hundred Greater Manchester policemen. (The police) have to accept some of the responsibility because, at the end of the day, they are the ones who were chanting and cheering, they were the ones standing on the chairs. I was very, very disappointed at what I saw that night on the basis of what the police are now saying about their policies as far as racism is concerned.

189

The master of ceremonies at the dinner, Peter Kerrone, tried to smooth over some of the embarrassment when the film was broad-cast. 'Within that audience you are going to find people from all walks of life. You will find homosexuals, coloured people, there'll be Irish people, foreigners, child abusers, paedophiles, wife beaters, and to take Bernard's act, he would at some stage attack every one of those minorities – if you call them minorities . . . I would be more worried if you were talking about a large group of policemen being at a National Front meeting.'

David Wilmot, the chief constable who had tried to face off the Manning problem three years earlier, but found that the ranks were intent on having Bernard in spite of their boss's opposition, was exasperated.

> I do not find sexist or racist jokes at all funny (he announced) and indeed, if we are to try and eliminate the problem of sexism and racism within our society, then one of the things we have got to do is stop abusing the humour. I can't control where my officers go when they are off duty. Yet I have clearly still a long way to go in terms of convincing people that sexist and racist jokes are not acceptable, and we have got to work harder at it. I would regard racism in society generally, and I have said so publicly, as being one of the most serious things we have to tackle over the next decade and beyond . . . I think the message is getting through, I think more people prefer to stand up and take action and again we have to keep pushing the boundaries forward, so that the dignity of our staff and the dignity of members of the community is not infringed upon.

The Bishop of Manchester said Bernard's material on *World in Action* was 'vile and offensive', while Geoffrey Bindman, the eminent race-relations solicitor, commented:

> It's quite extraordinary that this was essentially a police event, and that there were a large number of policemen present. This is what is so bizarre about it, because the natural action of anyone who was offended in such a situation would be to go to the police and report it. Here the police are already present, apparently enjoying it and doing nothing about it, and that absolutely appals me. I think that

it is very likely indeed that there would be a case which would have to brought by the Attorney General, or with his approval, under section 18 of the Public Order Act, which is the section that deals with incitement to racial hatred. I think there is a strong evidence – at least a likelihood of racial hatred being stirred up by many of the remarks and so-called jokes of Bernard Manning, and if an offence has been committed by Bernard Manning, there's a very good case for saying that the organisers are responsible for aiding and abetting.

Although Granada admitted that sixty per cent of the phone calls from the public had been supportive of Bernard and critical of the company for taping him covertly, the onslaught turned political. Lord Tebbit (the robust former Conservative Party chairman Norman Tebbit, known jocularly as the Chingford Skinhead since he was balding, right wing and had been the MP for Chingford) wrote in the *Sun*: 'I've often enjoyed a thoroughly tasteless Manning joke, but he went too far.' Clive Soley, the Labour MP, asked the Attorney General to consider charging Bernard with inciting racial hatred. The attacks on Bernard became almost ludicrously heavy when the Prime Minister weighed in. Ken Livingstone asked John Major in the House of Commons to condemn Bernard's use of the word 'nigger'. Major replied, 'I certainly think everybody should avoid expressions that give offence to those who are on the receiving end of those expressions . . . that is true of Mr Manning and every-one else.' The *World in Action* business may well have made John Major feel a little edgy; although Bernard has never played at one, it is not unknown for dodgy comedians to appear at Young Conservative conferences. Frank Carson played a date at their Eastbourne conference in 1993 at which he did blue and racist gags, albeit jokes which Bernard would not give houseroom – 'What do you call an Indian with no arms or legs? A conker,' was one such, recalls a journalist who attended.

Chris Graham, Bernard's friend and manager, put a bullish perspective on things, informing the *Independent* that Bernard had picked up eight new bookings the day after the *World in Action* programme was aired. As it went out, the documentary was apparently shown as a warm-up to Bernard's act at the Birmingham club where he was appearing. The reception was so good, Chris Graham said, that the club immediately rebooked Bernard. 'The phone hasn't stopped with offers from the Littlejohn and Esther Rantzen television programmes. The *World in Action* programme has helped a lot,' Graham was quoted as saying. He explained that he had talked to Bernard about it. 'He wasn't upset. He said he's paid to make people laugh and that's what he did. He wasn't selling people drugs or hitting them over the head. He certainly won't be changing his act.' At least two bookings had, however, been lost. The Comedy Empire in Willesden, north-west London, cancelled a Manning show. 'The directors feel Mr Manning's material is too offensive,' a statement said. Another club – the Island, in Ilford, Essex – also cancelled a Manning appearance, blaming 'disastrous ticket sales'.

Over the Pennines, in Leeds, Bernard encountered a serious problem in the form of the city's Labour council. The authority, seeing as it owned the Grand Theatre, decided it could exercise some control over performances on its premises. Bernard was described as an 'evil racist' by a black councillor, Alison Lowe, who had 'monitored' his performances. The leader of the Tory group on the council, Andrew Carter, duly accused the Labour group of being 'jumped-up, tin-pot councillors trying to impose their own brand of censorship', but the ban continues – leaving the Conservatives with the awkward question of whether they might have to revoke it should they return to power in Leeds. In 1996, Bernard announced in the *Sunday Times* that he was hoping to sue Leeds city council for restraint of trade, a matter as yet unresolved.

Chief Constable Wilmot in Manchester was faced, meanwhile, with the dilemma of whether to press for the prosecution of Bernard, and with him, the organisers of the police dinner. Detective Constable McIntosh, a thirty-four-year-old father of four, who had been the butt of Bernard's jokes, was later approached by the Greater Manchester Police internal inquiry branch, and asked if he wanted to make a complaint. He refused, saying he wasn't offended. *World in Action* had previously asked him to speak on the film, but he had also refused. 'They kept asking me if I had been offended or insulted, and I said no. They didn't seem to want to hear that,' McIntosh told Andrew Chapman of the *Mail on Sunday.*

'At the end of Mr Manning's act, he asked me if I was here, and I stood up and said, "Yes, Bernard, I'm here," and he made a joke. Everybody laughed, I laughed, I sat down again and that was it. I did not feel a victim of racist taunts or abuse. Everyone came under attack – Scousers, Jews, everyone.'

Despite the defiant front Chris Graham was showing on his friend's behalf, Bernard was a little shellshocked by the reaction to the *World in Action* exposé. Andrew Grimes of the Manchester *Evening News* went to the Embassy Club to see him in the wake of the affair. 'When I arrived he was in a Hawaiian shirt at the bar, poring over about sixty letters sent to him by his fans in the wake of the row over the coppers' benefit performance at Haydock Park,' Grimes wrote. 'One correspondent congratulated him on being a "true Englishman". But that was the only thing I read which smacked of racism. Most of his fans just wanted to tell him they loved him and to go on being outrageous and funny. In conversation, his voice is not at all like the ruffian bellow at the microphone. It is soft, quiet and measured, almost effeminate in its refinement.'

At the height of the *World in Action* affair, Bernard's life was even threatened by what the police seriously believed may have been an assassination attempt.

I got a phone call at home (Young Bernard recounts). It was about midnight, and the police said that there was a group of young black people from a particular area who had been seen around with guns. They had made a phone call to the police to say that they were going to shoot Bernard Manning. They were going to do it that night. The police asked if I could contact me dad and warn him.

I don't know how I did it but I found out he was in Bolton working at a club. So I rang his mobile, and it rang and rang but I couldn't get through. He was on stage, obviously, and I just kept ringing. The police surrounded me dad's house, and were hiding under cars, unmarked cars. They were in the garden, too, in bushes. Eventually I got through to me dad and he was on his way home. I thought, 'I have got fifteen minutes to put him in the picture.' So I told him the story, and his attitude was just unbelievable. 'Oh, right, OK then,' he said. I said, 'Dad, really, you've got to take this quite seriously. The police are taking it seriously. You'd best be a bit careful, maybe go round the street once or twice and make sure that there is nobody lurking.' But apparently, he just drove up to the front door, got out of the car and walked up to the front door, shouting, 'Right, you can come out.' I don't know if he fears for his life, but he certainly doesn't appear to.

The *World in Action* scandal, having gained such extraordinary momentum, eventually died away, as the threatened prosecutions failed to happen. As Chris Graham had suggested it might, the *World in Action* business even had a relatively beneficial effect on Bernard later that summer. The final observation made by Andrew Grimes was the beginning of a process of public reassessment of Bernard, out of which he did not come as badly as he might have feared. In June, Yomi Mambu, who had been Manchester's first black Lord Mayor five years previously, and was now the chairman of the council's equal-opportunities sub-committee, took along two fellow officers to the Embassy Club. Reports of her visit were contradictory. When Mambu walked into the club, according to the *Sunday Times*, Bernard greeted her with his standard joke that he hadn't seen her until she smiled: 'I found that remark offensive,' Mambu conceded. She also objected to jokes about Fatima Whitbread, and remarks aimed at a Chinese woman in the audience. She told the Manchester *Evening News* after the show, however: 'There was nothing I could really take exception to. He didn't use any black racist jokes.' He had obviously toned down a lot. Bernard was, unusually for him, in the process of moderating his act as a precaution against the possibility of losing his drinks licence. He successfully obtained the renewal, despite the objections of Hitesh Batt, a thirty-three-year-old Rusholme trader, who complained about Bernard's performance on the *World in Action* film.

Later in June, the *Evening News* took the chairman of Manchester council for community relations, Mr Kabir Ahmed, to watch the show and say what he thought of the material. Bernard – obviously not that nervous about losing his licence – cottoned on to who it was and said to Ahmed, 'You've got a fucking nerve coming in here,' but went on to say he hoped he enjoyed the show. Mr Ahmed's view was that some of Bernard's jokes were, as advertised, not acceptable in a multicultural society. He said: 'I was quite flabbergasted – it was quite horrible. It may be a private club, but it is still part of society.' Bernard's view of events was not quite the same as Ahmed's: 'He enjoyed the act, the same as everyone else. He was laughing his head off. I shook hands with him – he was a real gentleman.'

At the same time, Bernard was interviewed by Lesley White of the *Sunday Times Magazine*, complete with a startling photograph by Jillian Edelstein of Bernard in his living room, grinning and displaying his pot belly, while wearing little more than his boxer shorts. The resultant enormous and beautifully-written article, which appeared in August, was certainly critical but, by giving Bernard the full glossy-magazine treatment, its overall effect was almost to vindicate the dubious judgement Bernard showed by going in so hard at the police dinner. It also gave Bernard an upmarket platform to be serious for a moment on the whole question of racism. 'Racism is terrible,' he told White with apparent unambiguity, and no sucker punch jokes to follow. 'We've all got to learn to live together. It's our children's future, and we don't want racism or we won't get on. My little grandson doesn't even think about colour or people being different until some lunatic tells him it's the case. People come and see me because it's a laugh.'

Founded, perhaps, on some British sense of mischief, or on an abiding affection for outspokenness, or a dislike of authority, a mysterious process was underway by mid-1996. Bernard Manning, having come out of the storm largely of his own creation, was beginning to become a cult figure, an icon almost, for everything traditional and anachronistic. You didn't have to agree with him, it almost seemed, to admire his dogged stubbornness and refusal to acknowledge that the 1970s had been and gone, let alone that the late nineties had arrived.

He began to appear more in newspapers. For a sixty-six-year-old comedian who rarely appeared on television and was quite obviously a relic of another age, he was getting an enormous amount of publicity. Newspapers all over the country would phone him up to canvass his views on almost any subject. When the BBC *Watchdog* programme wanted in 1996 to arrange a stunt to prove how easy it is for anyone to set up in business as a 'counsellor', they asked Bernard to attempt to register as one. On the application form,

Bernard listed his occupation as 'a performer and performance counsellor' and in the space marked specialities, he put down 'sexual matters and racial awareness'. He also claimed to hold some sort of counselling diploma and sent off £50. He was accepted by one of the professional counselling organisations.

Bernard seemed at the same time to be making every possible effort to build bridges of some sort with the black population. In March 1996, Young Bernard hired a glamorous black DJ, Lainey D, for his new club, Mannings. The appointment was entirely at the instigation of Bernard Snr. Lainey was born Elaine Wilks, daughter of Jamaican immigrants to Britain, in the fifties. 'I respect people for what they are,' she told the *Mail on Sunday*. 'If people have a problem with Bernard Manning, then that's their problem. But I won't stand any nonsense. There's going to be no banter, and I'm not there as a send-up. I'm there to do my job.'

Lainey told how Bernard had approached her at a Manchester City function. 'He came across the room towards me and I instantly recognised him. I wondered with some trepidation, given his reputation, what was going to come of it, but he just said, "I think you're wonderful, brilliant." He told me his son was opening a new club and he thought I'd make a great DJ for them. I asked if he was serious, and he said, "Yes, absolutely," so I said I would be delighted to do the job. It's a professional arrangement. Bernard liked my style of music, which is American soul, and that was the sort of thing they want at the club.' Lainey said she had been criticised by black friends and family, but told them she took people as they come, and had no problem with either Bernard or Young Bernard. 'I am not naive,' she countered. 'I have been at the sharp end of racism, attacks and abuse in the past. I think Bernard is funny. Deep down, he has a heart,' she said. As it turned out, the plan for her to work at Mannings never quite came off. Lainey, who is qualified in telesales management, started her own business instead.

Another black personality in Manchester who became passingly associated with Bernard was Alex Williams, the former City goalkeeper, who appeared on the pitch with Bernard before a game at Maine Road as a kind of intercommunal morale-boosting gesture.

Bernard is very charismatic of course (Williams, who works as the club's community relations officer explains). When I finished playing in 1986, he very kindly put a couple of testimonial functions on for me free of charge to raise money. I wouldn't like to comment on Bernard as a gentleman, because I only know him for coming down to my two functions, and you don't get to see the full side of him, so the only things I can say about him are good things. He does a lot of good, and he did good things for me.

I have been to his club once. He obviously made jokes about me, but you have got to expect that with Bernard. He does go over the top, and I think if you find him offensive, the best thing you can do is not be there. But I don't think he does it with genuine intent. It's just the way he is. But then, I have played professional football, and you can't get more offensive than travelling away to the likes of Millwall, Chelsea and Leeds. When you've played there, then everything is an anti-climax.

An unexpected, although misleading, result of the process of Bernard becoming a born-again public figure in the late nineties was his appearance in a January 1996 Dutch advertising campaign for the Generale Bank. Advertising was not an entirely new venture for Bernard. In 1990, he had been paid £75,000 to feature in a TV campaign for mouthwash, speaking the lines, 'The boy stood on the burning deck, Eating red-hot scallops, White hot fat dropped from his chin, And burned him on the ... (he swills with mouthwash) ... ankle.' (The thinking behind the campaign was that if the mouthwash in question could sanitise Bernard's verbal halitosis, anything was possible for the more restrained consumer.) A foreign advertising campaign was entirely new ground for Bernard, however. His face, in its most lugubrious mode, in an unpublished frame from the Jillian Edelstein portrait series taken for the *Sunday Times*, appeared on bus shelters all over Holland with the copy underneath reading, 'How happy are you with your present bank?'

Had the impossible happened, and Bernard Manning's fame spread to Europe? Not exactly, explains Marje Alleman of the Amsterdam advertising agency Publicis. 'I talked to Bernard Manning's agent and he asked for a lot of money, so I had to explain that we are not after the artist, because nobody knows him, but it is just his face that we saw. It was very nice face. Bernard was looking very sceptical. It was a very nice expression. His mouth was down, he was very cynical. It is an English face in a way, and it is working-class. It was perfect for what we needed. So we came to an agreement.'

Another international accolade turned out not to be quite what it promised. It was discovered that a street in Duncraig, a smart suburb of Perth, Western Australia, had been named in Bernard's honour. Was this esoteric street-naming the work of homesick poms flying a flag for Harpurhey on the opposite side of the world? Not exactly, it seems. Bernard Manning Drive, which Bernard fondly believes was named after him, was actually a tribute to another Bernard Manning, who founded the Perth and District Gilbert and Sullivan Operatic Society. The discovery of the street made a nice story for the newspapers, all the same.

A third – but again misleading – sign of apparent foreign interest in Bernard cropped up at the same time in an American novel whose central character was named Bernard Manning by the author, Ronald Tierney. Any similarity between the Bernard Manning in *Eclipse of the Heart* and the one appearing three times a week at the Embassy Club in Manchester was coincidental, however; Tierney's Bernard Manning was an attractive young stranger who moves into the apartment of Zachary Grayson, a middle-aged San Francisco cookery writer, and spins him off to a romantic adventure in Mexico.

There may have been an intensification of interest in Bernard in 1995 – with all that publicity upsurge's concomitant benefits – but in most ways, it was the most disastrous year of his life, worse, perhaps, even than 1986, when Vera died within weeks of Mike Manning's debatable revelations of Bernard's personal life appearing in the *Sunday People*. Similarly in 1995 tragedy followed public embarrassment. Seven months before the *World in Action* programme went out, Frank, Bernard's youngest sibling, was taken ill.

He didn't know anything was wrong with him (Alma recounts). He kept on having double vision and headaches. He went to see a specialist and he gave him a CAT scan. They told him immediately that he had a tumour as big as a grapefruit in his head. He had asked before he went in that if there was anything serious he must be told, because he wanted to put his house in order. The specialist came straight out to him and said, 'You had better put your house in order.' Right away, Frank said, 'I want our Bernard.' Frank had always been the brains in our family, and made his own decisions in his life, but suddenly, all he wanted to see was Bernard.

Bernard chartered a plane immediately and came down. But when he finally got to Newquay he was only with Frank for twenty minutes, because they'd organised for Frank to see a professor in Bristol and hired a helicopter to take him there. The helicopter arrived just after Bernard, and Frank had to take off straight away. Bernard came round to see me, and I gave him something to eat. He did the same a few weeks after. They told us Frank might only live a few months, but we asked them to tell him it could be five years, and they did that. He lasted seven months. We took him to Florida for six weeks, but it was awful to go on holiday, all knowing what was coming. He died on 11 May. That really knocked our Bernard back, especially when two weeks later our mother died. She died from the shock of Frank dying. He was me mother's baby no matter how old he was.

Frank and Nellie's funerals both came during Bernard's aftershock period following *World in Action*. The same unfortunate few months also saw another funeral, of Bernard's girlfriend Lynn Hilton's mother. (Bernard has been close to Lynn, who is in her thirties, and the former wife of a footballer friend, since 1989.) Frank's funeral was a major public event in Newquay, reported on local television and with police brought in to control the traffic. Nellie's by contrast, was a quiet, family-only affair. For the first time in his life, Bernard was the only Manning within ten miles of Harpurhey.

A lonely figure suddenly, he started seeing more of Barry Clark, his plumber mate, and began to visit Young Bernard and his family up in Rochdale daily, rather than once a week as he had before. On his own in his mother's house in Alkrington, with the furore over *World in Action* still going on, and the first wave of big-name journalists already booking their tickets up from London to do the definitive Bernard Manning interview, he even made some tentative attempts to make his own hotpot: 'I can cook it myself – you have to remember to cook it slowly – but I usually send to the chippie. I can put eggs on toast as well,' he told one writer, Chrissy Iley.

Lynn Hilton, who is still Bernard's girlfriend, although both he and his friends point out that it is more of a companionship bond than a romance that is likely to lead anywhere, had been married to Mark Hilton, a former Oldham Athletic footballer. When the Hiltons were together, the couple had been close friends of Bernard. He had lent them his Rolls-Royce for their wedding, and employed them at one stage to help manage the Embassy Club. Bernard was godfather to the Hiltons' son, Mark. Vera's death coincided with Lynn and Mark's marriage breaking down, and Lynn found Bernard to be a fine, listening friend. The relationship has continued at this low-key, but affectionate, level. He does not tend to mention Lynn, however, either in interviews or in his stage act, in which it is understandably funnier to exploit a picture of himself as a pathetic and sex-starved creature – 'Every morning, I look down on the unemployed,' he says, with a melancholy, lingering glance groin-wards.

Bernard had been living at his mother's house since he was widowed. The house has one of those slice-of-tree nameplates over the glazed porch; its name is Shalom, Hebrew for 'peace', the legacy of a Jewish former occupant, that Bernard had no intention of removing. The home he had shared with Vera in Lewis Avenue, less than a mile away, was given to Young Bernard 'to put in the bank'. 'He went and emptied everything, I don't know how he did it. I couldn't have gone and put all these things together,' Bernard says. He has never been back to his marital home since he gave it to his son to sell. (In the summer of 1996, 34 Lewis Avenue came up for sale for £42,000, complete with all the improvements Bernard lavished on it – even the ornamental wall that cost, he insists, more than the £1400 he and Vera paid for the entire house in 1956 – and which took the builders longer than the Romans spent on Hadrian's Wall. 'Extensively improved semi-detached house,' the details from estate agents Ryder Dutton read, but stopped short of mentioning the house's famous former occupant.)

The nine years living with his mother after he left Lewis Avenue for good was a happy time in many ways. 'When Vera died, me mam said, you'd better come here, because I was in a right depression,'

Bernard explains, sitting in the vast, green leather armchair from which he holds court in what was his mother's sitting room. 'She said to Alma and Rene, they told me later, "Our Bernard has taken this very badly. We'll have to do something."' It didn't affect my stage work or anything like that, but I just wasn't the fella I was. So I came here and my mam started looking after me. I had my own bedroom. I could come and go as I pleased.'

His mother would implore visitors to keep an eye on Bernard, to make sure he didn't overdo things, even to try to ensure he wrapped up warmly in cold weather. Bernard used to talk about his old bachelor-like routine in his act: 'You don't want to get married, you barmy bastard,' he would jeer at stag nights to some young buck. 'Live at home with your mum. I do. I do as I please. I say, "I'll be home later, mother, unless I get a fuck," and she says, "Oh, good, then I'll see you later, son."'

His mother's death consequently affected him more deeply than it would have done had he been married at the time. 'It tears you apart, you never get over it,' he reflected when interviewed by Chrissy Iley, a perceptive writer, who concluded that he was a soft-hearted old man, whatever mayhem he had been stirring up in public. Bernard told Iley:

The pain destroys me. It's always in the back of your mind. You may think you've got over it, but then you will find yourself thinking. 'Would mother have liked that? Would she have thought this was the right thing?' It's the work that keeps me going, otherwise I get too sad. Work is my hobby, although I keep tropical fish in a tank above the fireplace. I watch them, it's therapeutic, better than TV, better than the O.J. Simpson trial, which I do like. I also had a budgie once called Beauty, good talker, came down one day, dead as a doornail. It broke me heart. I sobbed me heart out.

Prayer is all that keeps me going. I've never been a religious man, believe me. I do all the things you shouldn't do. But it's not until you lose someone close that you realise there is something there. (Every Sunday, Bernard puts flowers on Vera's grave and then sits and chats to her.) I tell her funny little stories about our grandson Ben and how our son Bernard is getting on. It's as if she is still with me.

The worry about the senior member of the family's solitude is shared by the whole inner-core Manning family. 'Bernard is lonely now,' Alma and Rene, down in Cornwall, say in perfect unison. 'He misses my mother terribly, because she was there all the time,' Rene continues. 'She idolised him. When he was going out at night in the winter, she made sure he had everything. She put his scarf on the radiator and his shoes by it to keep them warm. She was good to him. I said to him just recently, "It's a shame when you think of it. It's been nearly twelve months now since my mother died, but it's soon passed." He said, "It hasn't soon passed to me, Rene. It's been like a duration for me. It's been a long, long time." '

Having three grandchildren helps Bernard. He indulges them continuously with presents – there is usually something in his hall awaiting delivery to Young Bernard's house in Rochdale. Bernard has also developed a good relationship with his nephew in Newquay, Billy, whose mother is hoping he might go to Eton.

Billy gets on very well with Uncle Bernard (says Alma). When he was a baby and we used to take him up to our mother's, I think he was a bit overawed by Bernard being so big. But he loves him now – more so now his dad's gone. Billy fainted at Frank's funeral and Bernard laid him out on a bench and sat down stroking his head and saying, 'All right, son, all right.' I could see Bernard was as white as a ghost, it really frightened him. Bernard has said to Billy, 'If you ever need me at all, I am here for you all the time.' These days, Bernard will call up and Billy will answer the phone. He'll say, 'What are you doing, Bernard?' and Bernard will say, 'I'm watching the racing.' Then Billy will want to know what his uncle Bernard is backing.

Billy, who is already renowned for being exceptionally bright, is right to have noted that his uncle's racing tips are very nearly bankable currency. Bernard's invariable routine each morning involves swapping racing tips and gossip with trainer friends, whom he cultivates assiduously, with Melville Davies, who was once a successful bookie, with Richard Corgill, one of the BBC TV racing commentators, whose friendship he has also cherished over several decades, and even his old *Comedians* friend and sparring partner, George Roper.

In his career, Bernard continues to drive himself relentlessly. He barely needs the money, but still does as many as two gruelling dates around the country every night, even travelling on after his three-times-a-week shows at the Embassy Club. He seems to thrive on his notoriety, and to bask in press attention. He keeps the ornate stone mantelpiece, opposite which he sits all morning watching TV and receiving visitors in his underwear (vest, extra-gigantic Jockey Y-fronts, socks), as a shrine to the family and to his career. Guided tours to the mantelpiece are given to all callers.

All my life is on that mantelpiece (he rasps, hauling himself up from his chair). It'll show you how things have moved through the ages. There's me as a singer in a band. Then I went to the Oscar Rabin dance band in the West End of London, at the Lyceum on the Strand when I was twenty-one and I came out of the Army ... Oscar Rabin used to take me everywhere with him. We used to go to all the Jewish restaurants, have all the kreplach soup, salt beef sandwiches. Ooh, they know how to eat them Jews, good gear, they eat. That was the start of my ruination ... (Bernard slaps his stomach) ... Here's me and me mum when she was on the till at the Embassy Club. That's my wife Vera – she died seven years ago. That's Young Bernard, my son. That's me at nine years of age, just before the war, and that's my sister Alma and that's my brother who's just died, Frank. It was 1939.

That's my second grandchild, Hayley (he continues, moving along the crowded ledge). That's me with Harold Wilson, Don Revie and Jimmy Hill at a big function in London. Here's me and Mrs Thatcher at a football dinner. This statuette of me was presented to me by the Welsh centre-half – it's a one-off. They make them in Wales, and you have to be somebody to get one of them. That's me at fourteen, and that's me when I was in the theatres ... Here, read this, 'From the Variety Club of Great Britain Manchester Committee, to Bernard Manning on his 60th birthday, in appreciation of the valuable support he has given us over the years. August 1990' ... Now this is my prized possession. A photo of me shaking hands with the Queen at the London Palladium. The Osmonds were on that show, and Liza Minnelli. That's Roger Moore, the Bond fella, and Lou Grade and Des O'Connor ... Richard Attenborough. My whole life in front of me, to look at all day long. Unbelievable. *Un*beliveable.'